Town Without Pity

Town Without Pity

Don Hale

with

Marika Hūns and Hamish McGregor

C

Century · London

First published by Century in 2002

Copyright © Don Hale, Marika Hūns and Hamish McGregor 2002

The right of Don Hale, Marika Hūns and Hamish McGregor to be identified as
the authors of this work has been asserted by them in accordance with the
Copyright, Designs and Patents Act, 1988

First published in the United Kingdom in 2002 by
Century, 20 Vauxhall Bridge Road, London, SW1V 2SA

Random House Australia (Pty) Limited
20 Alfred Street, Milsons Point, Sydney, New South Wales 2061, Australia

Random House New Zealand Limited
18 Poland Road, Glenfield
Auckland 10, New Zealand

Random House South Africa (Pty) Limited
Endulini, 5a Jubilee Road, Parktown, 2193, South Africa

The Random House Group Limited Reg. No. 954009

www.randomhouse.co.uk

A CIP catalogue record for this book is available from the British Library

Papers used by Random House are natural, recyclable products made from wood
grown in sustainable forests. The manufacturing processes conform to the
environmental regulations of the country of origin

Typeset by SX Composing DTP, Rayleigh, Essex
Printed and bound in the United Kingdom by
Mackays of Chatham plc, Chatham, Kent

ISBN 0 7126 1530 X

It is important to note that, for legal reasons, several of the names have been
changed, and some identities disguised.

Acknowledgements

I WISH TO ACKNOWLEDGE the invaluable contributions made to my marathon campaign and this book.

In particular, I would like to thank Stephen's family, Ray, Nita and Christine Downing; West Derbyshire MP, Patrick McLoughlin; journalists Alan Taylor, Frank Curran and Rob Hollingworth; fellow campaigner Richard Brailsford and family and Stephen's hardworking lawyer, John Atkins, and his legal team including barrister Edward Fitzgerald, Paul Taylor and all at Doughty Street Chambers.

I also wish to thank all former journalistic colleagues at the *Matlock Mercury*, particularly Norman Taylor, Jackie Dunn, Phil Bramley and the late Sam Fay.

In addition, I would especially like to thank Nick Booth and Rachel Bowering from BBC Pebble Mill for their magnificent TV documentary and their hours of patience in understanding this complex case. I also wish to thank Channel 4 News, BBC News, ITN News, Carlton Television and BBC East Midlands Today for their continual support and encouragement.

Thanks to Nick Pryer, Bob Turner and John Carter for all their help during this long and complicated project. Thanks, too, to all national newspaper journalists and editors who ran supportive and investigative features, and for allowing me to reproduce extracts for this book.

My special thanks to all readers of the *Matlock Mercury* who eagerly followed my reports in the paper with the enthusiasm of true soap fans, together with numerous other supporters and fellow campaigners who shared my determination to seek justice for Stephen Downing.

Finally, to anyone that I may have inadvertently missed, my apologies, but thanks again for any help or advice received. Each have made their own contribution to my investigation into Stephen Downing's claims of innocence.

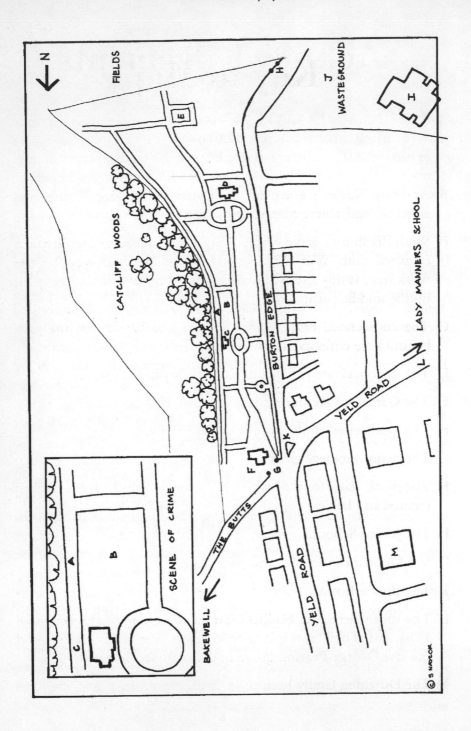

Key to Map

A Anthony Naylor's grave on the lower path where Wendy was attacked, and where Stephen found her.

B Sarah Bradbury's grave where Wendy had moved to after Stephen returned with Wilf Walker, and where she was seen by the workmen. Is this also where little Ian Beebe saw her as he cycled up the middle path?

C The consecrated chapel. Jayne Atkins saw Wendy on the path behind here embracing a man.

D The unconcecrated chapel used as the workmen's store.

E The Garden of Remembrance.

F The gatekeeper's lodge, home of Wilf Walker.

G The main cemetery gates.

H The back gate to the cemetery through which Jayne Atkins entered and left.

I The Junior School.

J Syd Oulsnam's van was seen parked here.

K The Phone Box.

L The spot where Mrs Hadfield saw the Running Man, going like a "bat out of hell" towards Lady Manners. Minutes before she said she saw George Pearson going in the opposite direction.

M The Downing family home.

This book is dedicated to my late parents, Charles and Doreen Hale, who provided continuous support and encouragement to the campaign throughout my darkest days, and especially to my wife, Kath, and family, who were always there when I needed them.

Prologue

I WAS TRAVELLING HIGH in the Derbyshire hills on the A515, which cuts through the lonely, barren landscape like a giant snake as it climbs and plunges through twenty-four miles of deserted moorland.

It was around 7.30p.m., a cloudy, drizzly evening, and the road was empty. For once I had broken my rule about not going to any isolated location, especially at night, and turned out for what I believed was a fire at a lonely farm on the Ashbourne-to-Buxton road. The tip-off had come to me, as editor of the local newspaper, over the phone, a young woman by the sound of her – and the location and details seemed genuine. But I wasn't totally alone, as behind me, on the back seat, was my collie, Jess.

Then suddenly it was right behind me, appearing as if from nowhere, from one of the notorious dips; a huge truck, either a dumper wagon or quarry tipper, with headlights blazing. It seemed unusual because, although the road was well used by quarry vehicles during the day, you rarely saw an HGV at night. I slowed to let it pass, but the driver also slackened his speed, and remained behind me.

Approaching the spot where the fire was supposed to be I realised I had been the victim of a hoax. There was no sign of any fire, not even a whiff of smoke, so I decided to head back home. The road, with a lay-by at the side, widened ahead of me and I opted to turn the car round there. I swung into the lay-by, steering in a wide arc, and almost clipped the huge vehicle as it clattered past. That's the last I'll see of him, I thought, as I changed up into third gear. But then, to my surprise and shock, I saw that the monster with its roaring engine, hissing air brakes and screeching tyres had performed a spectacular U-turn in my wake.

Again I looked back in my mirror and saw that the darkened cab was slightly illuminated. The driver was apparently speaking into some kind of walkie-talkie or CB radio. It was gaining speed. My dog was softly whimpering, so I reached back and patted her head.

The car almost took off on one of the major dips in the road. It took a second or two to adjust my vision as the headlight beams bounced back off the dark road surface. There was not another vehicle on the road, just me and my pursuer. I turned left off the 515 at Newhaven and on to the narrow road which would eventually lead to Cromford and Matlock. Still he followed.

I was sweating with fear. It was pitch black apart from the lights of a distant farmhouse, and I knew I must slow down soon. I had decided to cut off the main road to the left, which would take me back down the valley towards the villages of Winster and Elton on an even narrower road. I thought I'd be safe if I reached it.

The lorry was almost in the back seat again and its lights blazed into my mirrors. I jumped out of my skin as its horn, a deep and very loud siren, blared into my ears. Then the impact. A hard bump in the rear, which jolted the car forward.

The horn sounded again and there was another – and another – sickening bump. I tried to think quickly. In a minute or so the junction down to Elton would appear on my left.

Suddenly I had an idea. As the fork approached I thought I would try to confuse the lorry driver. I signalled right, then, at the very last moment, jerked the wheel and turned hard left. But I cursed as the lorry driver copied my actions. He clipped a signpost and ploughed over the triangular grass verge, but still followed.

I knew the road would come to another T-junction in less than two miles. My speed was constant, around the 55 mph mark. It was too dark and narrow to go any faster. The horn sounded again, then another bang. As I was pushed away from each shunt, I noticed the driver on the CB radio again. There was obviously someone else involved.

The road junction was fast approaching, less than half a mile away. I could see a signpost in the distance and noticed a large, dark shape in the middle of the road ahead, and it was growing rapidly.

'What the hell is it?' I asked Jess, peering into the blackness. Five hundred yards and closing, three hundred and fifty and closing.

Then the realisation hit me: 'Christ, it's another truck!' Two hundred and fifty yards and still travelling at around 55 mph. A tipper truck was parked sideways across the road, totally blocking it. I noticed a shadowy outline of someone standing near the front of the vehicle. He had something in his hand. A spanner? A monkey wrench? One hundred yards and my heart was racing. Where could I go?

As if by a miracle my headlights picked out a reflector on a small gatepost about fifty yards ahead. Maybe there was an open gateway into a field. It was too late for anything else. I touched the accelerator, then immediately hit the brake and yanked the wheel hard left, ramming the car through the open gateway into a rain-sodden field. There was a terrific bang as the lorry hurtled past. Its airbrakes hissed, screeched and locked, but it was too late for it to stop. It skidded on the wet surface and slid into the side of the other truck.

The field sloped crazily downwards from the gate. It was a sea of mud. I gripped the steering wheel with all my might in a desperate attempt to keep control and somehow managed to turn the car round in a large horseshoe to face the gate again. The rear wheels spun wildly, leaving deep ruts in the sodden grass. I kept up the revs, spun back up the field and drove out of the same gate.

I was so stunned by what had just happened to me that I didn't bother to look either way, and roared back down the road. I was saturated with sweat and through my rear-view mirror I could see white smoke and steam pouring from one of the lorries. Jess barked in defiance and, as I turned to offer a comforting hand, I noticed the driver's side mirror was hanging by a thread – as I realised my life had been.

All the way home I was still gasping for breath. One thing I did know for sure. *I knew they were trying to kill me, because they had tried to kill me before.*

Don Hale, March 1995

1994

1

September 1994

IT HAD BEEN one of those days. I had intended to be at work early, but we had forgotten to set the alarm and now the family was in total disarray. Andrew was rushing to catch his lift to Derby University. He was in his final year, reading computer studies, and should have been down at the bottom of Bank Road some ten minutes earlier. Rob, our youngest, at seventeen, was an ambitious youth, who was in his last year at Highfields School, studying for his A-levels. When I told him I would give him a lift to school he brightened up considerably.

Andrew slammed the front door and ran down the steep incline towards Matlock town centre, with a piece of toast in one hand and his jacket and a small case in the other. Kath had gone to unlock the tearooms she had been running in Crown Square for about four years. It was becoming a heavy commitment and she was in the process of trying to sell the business. She left with a list containing a thousand jobs that should have been done the night before. She knew the staff would be on the doorstep and the early morning regulars would not want to listen to any excuses about a cold boiler.

I ushered Rob out of the door and into my car as I straightened my tie. We lived in a Georgian property within a small cul-de-sac, just half a mile from the centre of town. It was a bright, sunny Monday morning and I thought how lucky we were to have a home in such a splendid location. It was a joy to look across the lush green valley first thing in the morning and admire the splendid autumn colours. But winter would soon be here and I was pleased I had bought a house below the snow line.

We had returned from Amsterdam the night before from a short break. In many ways I was delighted to be home. I didn't like being away from the *Matlock Mercury* for too long. After more than nine years as editor, I was still reluctant to leave anyone else in charge.

I dropped Rob off in a lay-by on Chesterfield Road several hundred yards from his school – so that his friends wouldn't see his dad giving him a lift – and drove back down the steep hill to the *Mercury* offices just off the main A6 on the road out of Matlock towards Bakewell. Situated a couple of hundred yards from the town centre, our office was a former print works sited in between the Trent bus depot and Twigg's engineering works. It had two large, old-fashioned, red-and-white painted shop windows.

As I turned into the car park, I noticed my own staff had already arrived and parked with care to make sure I didn't block anyone else in. Parking was limited at the *Mercury*, and places at the front of the building were usually snapped up by my advertising manager and his three reps. Editorial cars were parked around the side.

As you went in through the front door there was a reception counter and front office, with several smaller offices through the back. It was a ramshackle-looking place and reminded me of Dr Who's Tardis, appearing deceptively tiny from the outside but, once you entered, revealing itself to be much larger. The rooms were dark and dingy, cold in winter and hot and stuffy in summer. They always had a rather dank smell and, despite constant attention, the roof still leaked in numerous places. A line of pots and buckets stood ready for the next downpour. The only natural lighting in the main section came from a row of windows at the back of the building, but they looked out on to a jungle of overgrowth and were virtually useless and often, first thing in the morning, a large tabby cat would perch on the window ledge looking for field mice. The editorial department was in the former kitchen area and part of the old print production works. I had my own small office sandwiched some-where in between the two areas.

I could hear the typewriters clattering away as I opened the back door and saw the reporters going about their business. 'Morning, everyone,' I said as cheerfully as I could manage. I hoped they wouldn't notice that I was already more than ten minutes late.

'Anything special happened since I've been away?'

My trainee journalist, Jackie Dunn, a bright, bubbly Lancashire lass in her early twenties, called across and, with a grin on her face, asked me if the flight had been delayed. Cheeky so-and-so. She then gave me a brief summary of events from the previous week.

Norman Taylor, a retired train driver in his late fifties and now our sports editor, informed me Matlock Town had gained a corner in my absence – no goals, but a corner was better than nothing, wasn't it?

That earned a glare from the far corner of the room, courtesy of Sam Fay, my deputy editor. In his late sixties, he had served with the Grenadier Guards in some of the worst conflicts of the Second World War. Sam had retired, but returned on a part-time basis.

I settled down and began to plough my way through the paperwork, asking Sam for a meeting in half an hour or so to discuss stories for next week's edition. In the meantime there were freelance bills to sign, letters to the editor to check, rambling requests from a host of local organisations and a pile of photographs to consider.

I was just about to take off my jacket and was fishing for a pen in my top pocket when the small, sliding door in the frosted-glass partition dividing editorial from the advertising department, slid open.

'There's a man wanting to make an appointment, Don. Something about a murder,' said the receptionist. She cupped her hand over the receiver. 'Do you want to take the call?' she asked. 'He says it's something to do with his son, Stephen.' I beckoned to her to put the call through. Immediately the man at the other end of the line started talking nineteen to the dozen.

'Stephen who?' I asked, when I could finally get a word in.

'Downing,' replied the man at the other end of the line. Then, without further prompting, Ray Downing began to tell me about his son, apparently still in jail for a murder he claimed he didn't commit. He said the murder had taken place twenty-one years before in Bakewell, a town about eight miles from Matlock.

I let him have his say. At this point many a national news desk executive on a busy daily paper might have politely, or even brusquely, fobbed him off. 'Mr Downing,' I said.

'Ray,' he interrupted.

'OK – Ray then. Look, you don't need an appointment to see me. I'm usually here from dawn till dusk,' It was difficult to take in all the facts on a telephone. 'Yes, 2.30p.m. is fine, Mr Downing – sorry, Ray. Yes. Please bring the papers with you. I don't know what I can do but I'll have a look. Thank you, goodbye.'

I turned to look at my team. 'Something to do with a murder case from 1973. Ray Downing, a local taxi driver and his wife Juanita want to come and see me today. This afternoon, in fact.'

Sam pulled a cigarette from a new packet and lit it. He frowned. 'Don, I'll have to go out for a while this morning. I'll see you later, if that's OK? We'll have a chat about this Downing fellow.' With that he disappeared out the back way in a haze of smoke. I hoped he made it through the door before his fag ash spilled on to the carpet.

There was a knock on the glass-topped editorial door. It was exactly 2.30p.m. 'Mr and Mrs Downing to see you, Don,' said Susan, one of our advertising reps.

'Yes, of course, come through, please,' I said, showing the couple into my office at the rear of the building. I pulled out two chairs and sat opposite them, peering at them over a large wooden table. Ray carried a large pile of documents, which he placed on the table in front of him. I began to shift some papers and moved another of Sam's ashtrays out of the way, tipping its contents into a bin. Ray had a smooth rounded face which wore a worried expression. I thought he was probably in his late fifties or early sixties. His wife Juanita was about the same age. She had sharp features, seemed rather nervous and was extremely thin. Both were well dressed as if wearing their Sunday best. I had never met either of them before.

Ray immediately explained his reasons for contacting me. He claimed his son Stephen had been jailed in 1974 for the murder of a woman in the town's cemetery the previous year. Ray kept saying he was innocent and said everyone in Bakewell knew he was innocent. 'I can almost certainly tell you who was responsible,' he added. 'Nearly everyone in the area seems to know who did it.' I was staggered. At this point he did not mention any name.

The Downings alleged Stephen had been framed for the murder because the town wanted someone to blame. They claimed he had been forced into confessing to an assault on a young, married woman, which later landed him on a murder charge when the victim died. The woman, Wendy Sewell, was very promiscuous, according to Ray, and had taken several prominent local businessmen as lovers. He suggested a long list of individuals and said they were all well known in the Bakewell area. He believed the powers that be in the town had conspired to protect Wendy's secret life – and themselves, from scandal.

There were, he said, several other characters seen in or around the cemetery on the day of the attack. But potential witnesses had been ignored and some who had spoken out had been warned off. He strongly believed that one particular neighbourhood bobby who 'had it in' for Stephen had gone all out to get a quick confession out of him. His son had retracted this confession thirteen days later, some five months before the trial, but it had been the basis of the prosecution case on which he was convicted. There had been attempts at getting Stephen out on appeal – the first in October 1974, just months after the trial, the second some thirteen years ago in 1981. Both had failed. Ray said a private investigator had worked on the case for the first ten years, but had died some time back.

So far Juanita had let Ray do most of the talking. Now she began fumbling with their paperwork on the table and produced some old newspaper cuttings which outlined these previous attempts. She explained that the rest of the documents were a wad of court papers, copies of statements from years ago and various reports I might find interesting. Ray cut in and explained that the reason they were here today was because a woman had telephoned them anonymously saying she had sent both me and the editor of the *Star* some fresh evidence that could help clear their son's name.

'The *Star*?' I asked. 'Do you mean the *Sheffield Star*, or the *Daily Star*?'

'She just said the *Star*.'

'I've just come back from my holiday. I don't think anything's arrived here but I'll go and check,' I told them. I brushed past the couple and made my way back to the main office. 'Anyone know something about a letter concerning Stephen Downing? His parents think some fresh evidence may have been sent here while I was on holiday.' There was no reply. Jackie and Norman shook their heads. Phil was answering a phone call.

'Whatever came in that we couldn't deal with is on your desk now. I don't recall anything about a Stephen Downing,' said Jackie.

'What's it all about?' asked Phil, putting down the receiver. He was a young ambitious reporter and had his long hair tied back in a ponytail.

'Not quite sure, except he's been in jail for murder for over twenty years. The parents are desperate and looking for a lifeline. The murder doesn't ring a bell with me. I'll ask Sam when he comes back later,' I replied.

I returned to my office and told the Downings nothing had been received so far. I said I would call the *Daily* and *Sheffield Star*. I had contacts at both places and would let them know.

The Downings thanked me for my time and interest. They left some of their paperwork with me to study. I arranged to see them a day or two later at their own home. We shook hands and I escorted them to the front door. I promised I would read through their paperwork later.

I was intrigued by what I had just heard. The Downings were a likeable couple and, without doubt, genuinely believed in their son's innocence. Ray had been intense and full of conspiracy theories. Juanita had, throughout our meeting, said very little, maintaining a dignified, care-worn expression as she listened to Ray's conjectures. I was apprehensive about getting involved, and wanted to keep an open mind, but as a father of two boys who were just embarking on manhood and discovering their independence, I couldn't help but identify with the Downings' sorrow at the way things had turned out for their son. I realised with a jolt that my own teenager, Robert, was the same age Stephen Downing had been when sent down for murder.

Sam returned soon after they left. He still had a cigarette in his mouth. 'Did Downing come in, then?' he asked casually.

'Yes, Sam. What do you know about this case?' I enquired.

Sam grabbed my arm and led me back into my own office. 'He's well known in Bakewell,' he explained, once the door was closed. 'Drives people crazy with all this talk about his son's innocence. Runs a local taxi firm and has spent years trying to solve the crime and free his son. Poor sod, can't blame him, though. Stephen was only a kid. A bit simple too, from memory.'

We sat down opposite each other. Sam puffed on his cigarette. I looked for the ashtray I had just emptied. He still had his hat and coat on. He looked for a moment like a detective from a movie. Sam had been involved with the *Derbyshire Times* and *Matlock Mercury* as a journalist for more than forty years. He knew everyone and everything about this area. I explained to him about the family's claim of an anonymous caller and fresh evidence. I waved the bundle of paperwork at him. He didn't seem over-impressed. He had two or three drags on his cigarette. Then he started to talk about the case.

'It's a long time ago but I was on the story leading up to the trial. As far as I can recall, there *was* a slight feeling of surprise when he was convicted. He was only sixteen or seventeen, I think.'

'Seventeen, Sam,' I confirmed.

'Yes, whatever, I know other names were being bandied about and the murdered woman was well known in the area – if you see what I mean?'

'Not really, Sam.'

'She'd left her husband,' he continued, 'and I think there was some sort of scandal. You know what Bakewell's like. I probably have some old cuttings at home. I think Stephen Downing admitted something, then retracted it.'

I stared back at Sam. He was over six feet tall, slim, with a rather solemn face. He looked uncomfortable, hunched in the visitor's chair. It was often hard to tell his mood. 'I've agreed to go to their house on Thursday. They want to show me some things,' I explained.

'Be careful,' he warned, 'don't get sucked into all this.'

I called Jackie across and told her to bring her notebook. 'Jackie. Stephen Downing. Arrested for the murder of Mrs Wendy Sewell in Bakewell cemetery in September 1973 – some twenty-one years ago. I want you to go to Derbyshire County Council archives department. Get me everything you can on this case. The trial was in February 1974 and an appeal in November the same year. Then another review in the early Eighties. Look for cuttings around those dates, any editorial comment, even letters to the editor. Check our own files too. See if you can persuade the court clerk at Nottingham to send us a transcript of the trial. Anything else you can think of. Perhaps you can ask Phil to have a chat with the local bobbies?'

She nodded and dashed across to tell Phil.

I put calls through to Frank Curran, the Midlands reporter for the *Daily Star*, and Rob Hollingsworth on the *Sheffield Star*. Neither had seen any anonymous letters relating to the Downing case, but both told me to call if anything interesting turned up.

2

I WASN'T NATIVE to Derbyshire – I was born in the Glenside Nursing Home in Prestwich, north Manchester, on 31 July 1952, and spent my formative years in that area.

My father was an intelligence officer with Monty's Eighth Army in the Second World War who became an accountant on his return to civvy street. Charles Hale wanted his two sons to do well in life. When I left Whitefield County Secondary School in 1968 at the age of sixteen and announced I wanted to be a footballer, he was mortified. 'Get yourself a proper job, son,' he told me in no uncertain terms.

But his advice fell on deaf ears. I had signed for Bury's Youth, Junior and Reserve sides two years previously. At that time Bury were in the Second Division of the Football League, and I worked as an apprentice cleaning boots, mending nets and turning out for the reserves on the wing. I was noted for my speed, having won medals for running, and become Lancashire sprint champion.

Sadly, though, my early footballing days were blighted by injury. I soon realised I might have to look for a career outside my chosen sport. I had always enjoyed writing stories and, when at school, had edited the school magazine for two years. I always thought then that a reporter's life might be a fairly pleasant and exciting one. To that end, while earning the princely sum of £7 a week from Bury FC, I began filing several sports reports to the *Manchester Evening News*, as well as scoring forty-two goals for Bury's Youth, Junior and Reserve sides in the Floodlit League.

In my early twenties my persistent injury problems eventually forced me to abandon any ideas of full-time professional football. I concentrated my energies on journalism, firstly as the Salford and then North Manchester reporter for the *Manchester Evening News*, and subsequently as a full-time reporter in local radio. At Radio Manchester I became showbiz reporter, then I was recruited by Eddie Shah to become sport and then news editor of the *Bury Messenger*.

When the Johnston group took over I moved to the *Matlock Mercury* as editor: a quiet little paper in a quiet little town. My wife Kath, and our sons Andrew and Robert, immediately took a shine to the Peak District. I accepted the appointment immediately – this was my chance to be part of a small rural community, to influence its decision-making and campaign for its residents.

As I walked through the door of the dilapidated building in Dimple Road on 23 September 1985, to be greeted by a small, enthusiastic but apprehensive staff, I had no idea what the future held for me.

I settled down at my desk with one drawer stuck half in and half out, and a folded-up beermat under one of the legs to keep it steady, unpacked my contacts books and was about to store them away safely when my phone rang. I picked it up and the girl who manned the tiny switchboard put through the first call of my editorship. 'It's the local Women's Institute, Mr Hale,' she said. 'They're not at all happy with last week's report on their whist drive. I'm sure you can sort it out.'

'I'm sure I can,' I said.

Jackie spent every spare moment of the two days following the Downings' visit trawling through old newspaper cuttings from the early 1970s, building up a picture of the Wendy Sewell case. It was to become a familiar pattern in the months ahead . . . hours were spent rummaging through micro-discs at the Derbyshire County Council archives department in Matlock, phoning round several other newspapers and doing background research. She contacted the Home Office to get papers relating to the case or subsequent appeals. I tried to track down relevant forensic or medical reports.

Jackie's initial file of newspaper cuttings was impressive. They gave quite a bit of detail about the victim and her husband, and would provide me with a good foundation before I set aside more time to read the official papers. They related to the original arrest, to the development of the case, the trial itself, the early appeal and further attempts to seek justice over many years.

My other reporters were also eager to join in the investigation. Murder inquiries made only rare appearances in the columns of the *Matlock Mercury*, and this one had already grabbed everyone's imagination. I still remember one Friday evening as I was leaving the office for the weekend I had to smile as I passed Phil, my junior reporter, busily photocopying clippings handed over to him by Jackie. It occurred to me that the young lad was not even born when Wendy Sewell met her death, and that Stephen Downing had been in prison for the whole of Phil's lifetime. 'Couldn't it wait till Monday morning, Phil?' I asked. 'Why not get yourself out and enjoy the weekend?'

'Stephen Downing's waited twenty-one years, Don,' he reprimanded me. 'How many weekends has he enjoyed?'

Over the following days I read and reread the old cuttings. The attack in the rural cemetery had not made much impact on the nationals. But the reports and headlines from the county and regional newspapers were fairly consistent.

On Friday 14 September 1973 one said:

MURDER BID CHARGE

'Critically ill in Chesterfield Royal Hospital with serious head injuries is an attractive 32-year-old housewife, who was found unconscious in a Bakewell cemetery just after lunchtime on Wednesday.

Yesterday morning, Derbyshire police said that a young man had been charged with attempted murder and would appear at a special court in Bakewell later that day. The accused is understood to be 17-year-old Stephen Downing, a gardener from a Bakewell council estate.

The woman, Mrs Wendy Sewell of Middleton-by-Youlgreave, was discovered just after 1.15p.m. She was rushed to Chesterfield Royal Hospital but early yesterday morning had still not regained consciousness. Police are waiting at her bedside.

She was discovered lying face downwards between grave-stones in an old part of the churchyard, close to dense woodland. The cemetery was sealed off as police began their investigations.

Fifty CID and uniformed officers were drafted into the quiet market town and the area surrounding the cemetery was combed by tracker-dogs. Det. Supt Peter Bayliss announced that a 17-year-old youth had been formally charged with attempted murder.

Mrs Sewell worked for the Forestry Commission. She left the office just after midday and was seen walking along the 'Butts' in the direction of the cemetery shortly after 12.30p.m. Neighbours said on Wednesday night that Mrs Sewell often visited her mother at Haddon Road, Bakewell, after finishing work.

Before her marriage, Mrs Sewell was a student and lived in Sheffield. She married her husband, David, a physicist with British Rail at Derby, nine years ago. Mrs Sewell is known locally as a pet lover and keeps nine cats in the farmhouse.

A slightly later cutting, dated Friday 21 September, said:

Woman dies after attack in cemetery. Stephen Downing (17), a gardener, is due to appear in court following an eight-day remand in custody. The papers for the case have been forwarded to the Director of Public Prosecutions, but no information was available this week as to whether the charge would be increased to one of murder. Downing made a two-minute appearance before a special court in Bakewell last Thursday and was charged that he did attempt to murder Mrs Wendy Sewell.

Mrs Sewell was born in Sheffield and studied music at a college in the city. Her family lived there at one time and it was there she met her husband David, who lived in the same district. The couple were married at Grenoside Parish Church in 1964 and moved shortly after to set up home in a bungalow in Wyedale Crescent, Bakewell.

When she first arrived in the town, Mrs Sewell worked at

the magistrates' clerks office. She later joined the Forestry Commission as a secretary working at Catcliff House, King Street, Bakewell.

Mr and Mrs Sewell moved to Green Farm, an 18th-century country house in Middleton-by-Youlgreave in 1971. The couple have no children. Mrs Sewell shared her husband's interest in vintage cars, and was a keen collector of antiques. She also loved walking and often walked the mile and a half from the bus stop in Youlgreave to her home.

Mr Sewell is employed as a principal scientific officer by British Rail in Derby. Mrs Sewell's mother, Mrs Margery Crawshaw, also lives in Bakewell.

On 22 February 1974, following the trial at Nottingham Crown Court, the *Derbyshire Times* claimed:

YOUTH ON MURDER CHARGE IS FOUND GUILTY
Stephen Downing, aged 17, was found guilty of murdering 32-year-old typist Mrs Wendy Sewell in a cemetery in Bakewell, Derbyshire, by a unanimous verdict.

Downing, who was alleged to have bludgeoned his victim with a pickaxe shaft and sexually assaulted her before leaving the body among the tombstones, was ordered to be detained at the Queen's Pleasure. They took only an hour to reach their unanimous verdict last Friday.

Passing sentence Mr Justice Nield told Downing, who worked in the cemetery as a gardener, you have been convicted on the clearest evidence of this very serious offence.

Mr Patrick Bennett QC, prosecuting, had described how Downing had followed Mrs Sewell in the cemetery before carrying out the savage attack with a pickaxe handle. Downing claimed that he had found Mrs Sewell's half-naked body and then sexually assaulted her.

Mrs Sewell, who lived at Green Farm, Middleton-by-Youlgreave, died in hospital two days after the attack from skull and brain injuries. Downing was alleged to have admitted the assault late at night after spending several hours in the police

15

station. He was alleged to have described how he struck Mrs Sewell with the pick shaft on the back of the head and undressed her.

Police officers denied that Downing had been shaken to keep him awake after spending hours at Bakewell police station. His mother, Mrs Juanita Downing, told the jury that her son had never gone out with girls and only had one good friend.

Downing said that blood spots on his clothing got there when Mrs Sewell raised herself on the ground and shook her head violently. He had told the jury that he found the victim lying semi-conscious in the graveyard after going home during his lunch hour, but the prosecution said that his lunchtime walk was only an alibi after he had carried out the attack. Downing had pleaded not guilty to the murder.

Other regional papers carried similar headlines. They also gave similar descriptions of the court proceedings, stating, 'A savage assault by a teenager with a pickaxe handle. She had sustained repeated blows – as many as seven or eight to the head – and had then fallen against tombstones.'

Most papers also made particular reference to Judge Nield, who had kept referring to Downing's statement which was 'signed over and over again and formed the main plank of evidence for the prosecution'.

To all intents and purposes, it read like a straightforward conviction. A confession had been obtained on the same day the attack took place, although Downing retracted this confession five months before the trial. Yet the prosecution case relied heavily on this confession. The trial lasted three days. The jury heard just one day of evidence, and took less than an hour to reach its unanimous verdict of 'guilty'.

I wrote to Derbyshire police headquarters at Ripley, asking if they could release the paperwork, and make available the murder weapon and other trial exhibits for forensic testing. I knew if I was even going to attempt to understand this case fully I would have to look at the scene of crime and try to clarify in my mind the various allegations being made by the Downings. So, on the Thursday, three days after

Ray and Juanita first approached me, I set out on the drive along the A6 to Bakewell.

Although Matlock and Bakewell are near neighbours, they are worlds apart. Bakewell is a traditional market town of just under 4,000 inhabitants, where the farmers of the area gather each Monday to buy and sell cattle and keep up with the news in its six old, hospitable oak-beamed pubs, or the bars of the British Legion, Conservative Club and Working Men's Club. It is a community of limestone and gritstone houses, traditional homes of generations of families and traders tied to the working of the land, built on the banks of the River Wye in the heart of the rugged, rolling landscape of the Peak District.

Matlock is a more sprawling conurbation with a population of nearly 10,000, more than twice the size of Bakewell. It is the home of Derbyshire County Council and the Derbyshire Dales District Council, and host to several large factories, garages and offices, although the local mill has long since shut its doors. It is a place where the youth of the area, and in truth the not so youthful, meet up every Friday and Saturday night at the 'Pav', the Victorian pavilion where gentlefolk once came to take the healing Matlock Bath waters. Nowadays refreshment of a different kind is taken at the packed and lively weekend discos.

Although Bakewell remains an altogether more sedate place, many changes have come to it in the last few years. The cattle market has moved from the centre of town to the outskirts, a supermarket is built on its former market square site and new 'executive' homes, out of the reach of the locals' purses, spread along the banks of the Wye where generations of Bakewell children had traditionally come to feed the ducks. New shops now sell hiking gear and designer clothes, and the numerous little cafés serving the famous Bakewell puddings seem to multiply every year. The peaceful little valleys of the town and its environs, previously known as West Derbyshire, have been trendily renamed the Derbyshire Dales. The population, like that of many of the Peak District villages, is shifting from native to incomer. The town, with the blessing of the Peak District National Park Authority, has given itself over to tourism. It is difficult to find anywhere to park on weekends or market days. Yet old habits die hard. Bakewell still retains its snobbish character. A walk down its small streets bears testimony to its old-established family businesses – butchers, solicitors, estate agents, surveyors, grocers, clothiers, the list goes on – which all bear name plaques over their small front door-ways that have not changed in generations.

One source of bitter rivalry between established tradesmen is the Bakewell Pudding. Bloomers, the bakers, and the Original Bakewell Pudding Shop, each lay claim to the true recipe for the sweet, some would say rather sickly, invention. The legend surrounding its origin goes back two centuries when a chef at the town-centre Rutland Arms Hotel was preparing a dessert for a special guest one evening and accidently mixed the wrong ingredients together. The resulting disaster turned into a great success when the VIP declared the botch-up to be delicious. The chef made a note of his mistake, wrote down the recipe and it was passed down through generations of town chefs. But who has it now? One thing everyone agrees on is that its name is the Bakewell Pudding, *not* the Bakewell Tart.

Bakewell even has its own hunt, surely the ultimate countryside institution. What's more, Prince Charles has been known to ride out with the Bakewell Hunt during his visits to Chatsworth House, the stately home of the Dukes of Devonshire some three miles away. Matlock can't match that.

The hunt kennels are right next door to Lady Manners School, itself something of an institution, built at the very top of the town in open fields beyond the cemetery and the council estate where the Downings live. Lady Manners was bequeathed to the town in 1636 by Grace, Lady Manners, of the Vernon family of nearby Haddon Hall, to 'provide good learning and Christian religion for the children of Bakewell and Great Rowsley'. It is a state school, which has always liked to consider itself run along public-school lines. House buyers with children ensure that their potential purchase falls within the 'Lady Manners catchment area'. It has become a selling point with estate agents. It is considered a 'nice' school, with history, founded by a titled family. Matlock, which also has a perfectly good secondary school, can't boast that.

Within three short miles of Bakewell are as many families of the landed gentry. As well as the Devonshires at Chatsworth and the Duke of Rutland at romantic, medieval Haddon Hall, formerly the home of the Vernon family, there are the Davy-Thornhills at Stanton Estates. This family's wealth is founded on an ancestor's invention in the early 19th century, the Davy safety lamp once used down every coal mine in Britain. The family own vast acres of land to the south-east of Bakewell. As recently as thirty years ago they also owned almost every home, pub, barn and outside toilet in the village of Stanton-in-Peak.

In the 'old' Bakewell of the Sixties and Seventies, where Stephen Downing grew up, there remained an almost feudal class system, a tiered structure of society, which people raised in urban conurbations would find almost impossible to comprehend. Beneath the land-owning families were the professional classes and gentlemen farmers, the stalwarts of the Bakewell Rotary Club and the magistrates' bench, solicitors and owners of established businesses or small factories in the surrounding areas. Many lived in the town itself, some in the 'posher' outlying villages like Ashford-in-the-Water, barely a mile from the town centre. Beneath them were the village bobbies and farmers, shopkeepers and garage owners, employers of a dozen or so men in one trade or another, a type of man who kept the local Masonic lodge going. At the bottom of the pile were the 20th-century equivalent of the feudal 'serfs', farm labourers, factory hands, estate workers, quarrymen hewing the Derbyshire stone from the surrounding hills. They lived in the pebble-dash council estates tagged, as if in embarrassment, on to the end of each small village street and, in the case of Bakewell, out of sight at the top of a steep hill on the outskirts of the town opposite the municipal cemetery.

In such a house lived Stephen Downing, in a loving family home and simply unaware of the formidable social barrier separating the haves from the have-nots. When they had come to see me, Ray and Nita had brought a photograph of their son, aged seventeen, shortly before his arrest. It showed a smiling, slightly chubby youth, his face topped by a mop of unruly hair, wearing flared loon pants and platform shoes. I wondered how he'd appeared to the older, more conservative inhabitants of a place still clinging to its image of old market town respectability in the face of the swinging Sixties and liberated Seventies.

In the relatively short time I had been at the *Mercury*, too short to be accepted as a real 'local', I had nevertheless spoken to enough people to get a picture of what the town must have been like at that time. In old archive photographs from the *Mercury* library, the new streamlined Capris and Triumph Stags from Ford and British Leyland appear on the streets but, despite these big-city trappings, the world of the young and old began and ended in the peaceful little valleys of Bakewell and its environs. The car had then not completely taken over and people had a greater reliance on public transport in their everyday lives. During the week the local buses, run by Hulley's of Baslow and the Silver Service line from Darley Dale, had busy timetables. Every seat was taken to ferry the workers from villages and hamlets over the hills – scarred only by the quarries, whose stone had built their homes and guaranteed local employment.

While husbands remained the main breadwinners, the wives – like Nita Downing – earned extra money doing part-time jobs. They fitted them in between seeing the children off to the village school in the mornings and rushing to catch the bus back from Bakewell Square in the late afternoon in time to get the tea ready for when everyone got home. Most people knew each other, and a stranger in town stood out like a sore thumb.

The 'townies' came from Sheffield or Chesterfield which, for generations, had been distant glittering metropolises in the minds of the youth of Bakewell and its surrounding villages. At weekends and Bank Holidays there would be an invasion of the city 'yobbos' in their late teens and early twenties with drunkenness, rowdiness and fighting with the local lads the inevitable outcome. The same would happen on Mondays, Bakewell market day, when opening hours were extended and all-day drinking ensued. The old farmers who had come in from a radius of thirty miles to sell their cattle could hold their ale, not so some of the younger farm hands or the 'townies'. Bakewell magistrates' court was always full at its weekly Friday session, most addresses of defendants given as somewhere in Sheffield. 'These townies are a bad influence on our kids,' said the locals.

No one notorious was born in Bakewell and the resources of its little constabulary had seldom been stretched beyond its limits, at least not by the activities of the townspeople. It had never featured high in the league of crime statistics of Derbyshire police and, before the autumn of 1973, no one could remember any of its inhabitants ever being charged with murder. Yet, as things were to turn out in the last quarter of the twentieth century, Agatha Christie might have been inspired to dispatch Miss Marple or Hercule Poirot to this particular part of the English countryside. Stephen Downing became the first of the townsfolk to feature in national-newspaper headlines for alleged serious wrongdoing, a young man accused of the most serious offence ever committed in that beautiful spot on the map.

That day in September 1994, as I drove to see Nita and Ray, it struck me how incongruous a brutal murder must have seemed in this town of picture-postcard prettiness. I imagined the shock waves reverberating through this tight little community, followed quickly by shame that something like this could happen in this town of solid respectability. Bakewell must have felt its rural idyll had been shattered. Was it still hiding more secrets than the ingredients of a pudding recipe?

I turned sharp left up the hill from the Square, up King Street and then left into Yeld Road, leading to the town's cemetery and the adjacent council estate where the Downing family still lived after all these years. The semi-detached house on Stanton View was just a few minutes' drive from the centre of town. It was a large and well-maintained corner site some couple of hundred yards from the cemetery gates. To reach it you had to turn right off Yeld Road into a cul-de-sac, down a small lane just wide enough for one car to pass along, until it opened out into a parking area. From the Downings' house the cemetery was out of view.

I met Ray outside his home. He had just returned from a taxi job and I declined his offer of a cup of tea to go with him straight to the cemetery and have a look around.

This was the scene of crime. I was surprised at just how close it was to the Downing home and how it was situated next to a very busy estate. It was hard to imagine that such a gruesome murder had been committed in broad daylight so close to dozens of houses – and in such a public place. I mentioned this to Ray. He agreed. He said that

when I had time to read all his paperwork thoroughly I would see that children had been seen playing in and around the cemetery during their lunchtime break from school. There was also, he said, a window cleaner nearby, neighbours talking by the main gates and outside their homes adjoining the top side of the cemetery, and people on their way to and from town.

I explained that at this stage I needed to keep an open mind and just wanted to check out the scene of crime for myself before studying his paperwork in depth, and talking through his evidence and allegations.

The cemetery was built on a steep hill overlooking the town. It was entered by main gates at the end nearest the council estate. Immediately on the left was the gatekeeper's lodge and to the right of the gates a telephone box. On entering, the panorama to the left over Bakewell was obscured by woodland adjoining the bottom side known as Catcliff Woods, a dark and secluded area popular with courting couples. From here, the hill sloped away in the direction of the town. On the top side, to the right, was a high hedge separating the cemetery from a row of houses known as Burton Edge. Their bedrooms overlooked the cemetery, which was sunk into a bowl beneath the level of the hedge and the houses.

The cemetery was about 450 yards long, with two main drives running parallel along its length. One went straight down the centre, while the other ran along by Catcliff Woods and was known as the lower path. Both were straight and tarmacked. The old, weathered gravestones hewn out of local gritstone, now blackened and moss-covered, were at the end nearest the gates. Some of these old edifices had been vandalised and a few headstones were toppled or leaning at acute angles. About two-thirds of the way along were the more recent graves, with a Garden of Remembrance containing cremation urns at the farthest end some several hundred yards away and surrounded by a hedge.

Ray led me down to the left and along the lower path to where Wendy Sewell had been attacked. He showed me where Stephen had said he found her, lying on the path next to an old grave. The headstone bore the inscription 'In the Midst of Life We Are in Death'. It was the grave of Anthony Naylor who had died in 1872.

It was extremely close to Catcliff Woods, the grave backing on to a very low old drystone wall which marked the cemetery boundary, and I realised how easy it would have been for someone to have just disappeared into the thick undergrowth beyond. As I peered into the dense foliage I noticed a secluded pathway heading back slightly to the left in the direction of town. Alternatively, if the attacker had hopped over the wall and headed right, he or she would have come out the other side of the woods into open, hilly farmland with little chance of being seen.

I tried to picture the scene twenty-odd years or so before and wondered if much had changed. There were several large bushes interspersed among the gravestones and very close by between the two paths was an old church-like building. We had passed it on our right as we approached the grave. It was rather dilapidated and had obviously seen better days. Ray told me it was known as the consecrated chapel to distinguish it from a similar building some 150 yards further along which was an unconsecrated chapel used as a workmen's store.

We continued our walk along the lower path where Ray pointed across the old gravestones towards the centre path. 'Now here,' he announced, 'is where Wendy moved to.'

'Moved?' I asked, puzzled.

'Yes,' he continued, picking his way through the imposing stones. 'After Stephen found her, he went to get help. When he returned, she'd moved.' He stopped between the two paths by the grave of Sarah Bradbury. Amazingly I noticed it, too, bore the inscription 'In the Midst of Life We Are in Death' and, like Anthony Naylor, its occupant had died in 1872. I was pondering these coincidences when Ray interjected, 'She was just here.'

'But how?' I asked, wondering if a battered, dying woman could drag herself the twenty or so yards between the two tombstones.

'Well, there's a question!' said Ray. 'No one's ever really answered that one. It never came up at the trial and the police never seemed to query it.'

He then indicated in the distance the unconsecrated chapel, the store where Stephen and others had worked as council employees. We crossed over more graves to the centre path and walked towards the second chapel. It, too, was a run-down building, at the far end of the centre drive. The Garden of Remembrance lay some eighty yards behind it. Between the store and the far boundary of the cemetery were many interconnecting pathways offering quiet areas of reflection. We walked to the far perimeter. There was a gate and beyond it an area of rough wasteland. A junior school was in the same direction and could be clearly seen from the gate. Beyond that, slightly to the right, were dozens of other semi-detached homes and, to the far left, just open fields and countryside sweeping down to the Wye valley below.

We turned back and headed towards the main gates. On the way I was drawn again to the scene of the attack. I kept looking across at the spot some twenty yards away to which Wendy was said to have moved. I tried to put the case into some sort of perspective as I half listened to Ray. He was mentioning names I had never heard of, people who were meant to have been seen in the area. I made a promise to myself to start delving into the paperwork he had left me.

After we left the cemetery, we made an immediate turn right into the Butts, the main steep walkway which ran adjacent to the cemetery for about thirty yards with a beech hedge separating the two, and then continued down into the centre of town. It was the route taken by the victim as she approached the cemetery during her lunch hour. It was also, Ray explained, the same section used by a number of key witnesses. Again he started talking animatedly and yet more names tumbled out. I began to get the impression that the cemetery had been as crowded as Piccadilly Circus on the day in question. But I knew I could not get too sucked in to Ray's version of events until I had had a chance to clarify my own thoughts.

We made our way back to the Downings' home. En route Ray insisted on showing me the local shop, which he said played an important part in the reconstruction of the story. He said Stephen had made a detour there first, after leaving the cemetery on his way home that lunchtime.

I had made a rough diagram highlighting all the landmarks Ray had pointed out, although their full significance was not yet obvious to me.

The kettle was whistling on the stove as we climbed the three stone steps and entered the Downings' home via the back door into the kitchen. Juanita was preparing a cup of tea. She had been looking out of the kitchen window and had seen us coming. 'Thought you'd have been back before now,' she exclaimed.

'There's a lot to see,' Ray replied. 'Mr Hale wanted to see everything.'

'It's Don, Ray. Call me Don. This Mr Hale sounds like a bailiff.'

Ray laughed. 'Don't mention bailiffs. There's one around here that we don't care for – isn't that right, Nita?'

She laughed. It was obviously some in-joke.

'And I'm Nita to you.' His wife smiled, handing me a mug of tea. We sat down round the kitchen table. It was a true family home full of mementoes and photographs. One familiar face, though, was constantly missing from meals around the kitchen table. Their only contact now with their son Stephen was on infrequent visits to a distant jail somewhere down south.

I asked Nita where she had got her exotic name, as Juanita did not sound like your average Derbyshire lass. She laughed and explained that she had been adopted at the age of three and had hardly any memories of her natural parents. Her adoptive parents had decided not to change the unusual name given to her by her birth mother. She had been brought up in the Bowring Park district of Huyton-with-Robey in Liverpool. Many years later she had attempted to discover her roots, but by the time she managed to trace her mother the woman had died. So the origin of her Latin-sounding name remained a mystery. In any case, she said, she had her own family now. A good husband – the young RAF man she married in 1954 – and a boy and girl. She was proud of them all.

'So is Stephen your eldest?' I asked.

'He's our only son,' Ray told me, 'born on 4 March 1956, at our family home. Exactly three years later to the day, when we moved to Holywell Flats, Nita gave birth to our daughter Christine.'

Nita asked if anyone wanted another cup of tea, but I declined. Talk of Stephen had obviously reminded Ray of something. He disappeared for a second or two, then emerged with a large basket. 'This is Stephen's clothing from the day of the attack,' he said, tipping out a bundle on to the table.

It took me by surprise as Stephen's old jeans, his T-shirt and working boots, together with rings, a watch, and a leather wrist strap almost landed on my mug of tea. I instinctively pushed my chair back a few inches.

Ray began to flatten and straighten out the items of clothing. Nita abstractedly stroked the T-shirt as if trying to connect with her estranged son and make sense of what she saw before her. I was astonished that they had still kept his clothes after so long and realised that time had stood still for this middle-aged couple. I was also struggling to understand why these items had been returned to them. What were the police thinking of? Incredibly, as I looked closer, I noticed tiny spots of blood on the T-shirt, highlighted by small squares drawn by a yellow-coloured forensic marker. Ray pointed out a dark stain on the left knee of his grubby jeans, which he said was congealed blood. No other stains were obvious to the naked eye on any of the other items of clothing or jewellery.

'Look at these clothes,' said Ray. 'You can hardly say they're drenched in blood. But our Stephen was meant to have battered this poor woman to death. If he had, he would have been covered in blood from head to toe. The only blood he's got on his clothes is from kneeling next to her when he first found her. What's more,' he continued, 'I know the ambulanceman who took Wendy to hospital that day. He carried her into the ambulance. He said he was covered in blood she was bleeding so much. He had to burn all his clothes afterwards, they were ruined. Absolutely soaked in blood. You can talk to him yourself. His name's Clyde Bateman. I used to work with him at Bakewell ambulance station for four and a half years. I was a senior ambulance driver and he was my boss. He was summoned to attend an appeal eight months after the trial, but was never called as a witness. He was most put out by that because he wanted to talk about the blood-staining. He's retired now, but every time I bump into him he maintains that Stephen didn't have enough blood-staining on him to have committed the attack.'

Ray paused for breath and I interjected, 'How come you have Stephen's clothes here?'

'They told me to take him down a change of clothes to the police station,' Ray explained, 'and then they sent these off for testing. They gave us back the watch and the jewellery the same night as the attack.

The clothes came back later. It's obvious there's not enough blood on them, though.'

By now, it was beginning to get dark. I had spent several hours with Ray and decided to make a move, but he motioned me to sit down. 'Wait a minute,' he said. 'I've more to show you. I've got more files and notes this thick.' He spread his arms apart like a boastful fisherman. 'You'll need to see them.'

I felt I had to take a step back at this point. It had been quite an afternoon, culminating in the extraordinary sight of Stephen's clothing and personal effects. The Downing family had obviously made this a very personal crusade for the past twenty-odd years, and I was not keen to be drawn in too far before I'd got my bearings. I politely declined Ray's offer. I told them I had to get back to work, although I was anxious to see them again. I also wanted to spend some time going through some of the paperwork they had given me so that I could examine their claims in more detail. I thought of their papers still piled high on the floor next to my desk where they had left them. For a split second I felt panic. What if the cleaner had arrived and dumped them, not realising their importance? My head was throbbing. There were so many unanswered questions. I felt I needed to make an early start the next day and had already decided to cancel my weekend engagements.

When I got back to the office I discovered to my relief the papers next to my desk were still there. I phoned Ray to arrange another meeting. He suggested I might like to go the next afternoon, as Stephen was due to ring. He thought I should talk to him directly.

By now everyone else had left the office for the day. I put my coat on ready to follow them. My hand was on the door handle when the phone started to ring. 'Blast,' I said out loud, but made the decision to answer it.

'Evening, *Matlock Mercury*.'

Silence.

'Hello, *Matlock Mercury*.'

'Keep your fucking nose out of the Downing case, if you know what's good for you!' a man's voice barked at me. 'Get my drift?' he added.

Before I had the chance to answer, the phone went dead.

3

WHEN I WENT back the following day at about half past one, Nita had a piping-hot mug of tea ready. I decided not to mention my anonymous caller from the night before. He had sounded quite young, with a slight local accent. I had been surprised more than anything. How many people knew I was talking to the Downings?

The couple explained that Stephen's calls from prison were monitored and restricted to a few minutes' use of a prison-issue phone card during his breaks from work. They were expecting Stephen's call some time around 2p.m.

I realised I knew hardly anything about their son, other than what I had read in the old newspaper cuttings and from listening to Ray's descriptions of his arrest and trial. 'Had Stephen been working long as a gardener for the council?' I asked.

'No, no.' Nita smiled. 'He'd only been there seven weeks. He was based at the cemetery; he worked from the old unconsecrated chapel. He liked it, though. They'd shown him how to keep the hedges tidy, prune the trees, mow the lawns and keep the graves tidy, that kind of thing. Although he was left to his own devices for much of the time, other workmen regularly visited to work on the buildings in the cemetery and Stephen would help them out. To be honest, though,' she continued, 'he was a bit of a come-day go-day kind of boy. He didn't seem to stay in any kind of work very long.'

Both his father and mother had to admit that their first-born had a tendency towards laziness and bad time-keeping, a trait that had lost him three other jobs in the short time since he had left school.

I asked them to tell me more and, as I listened, I started to get a picture in my mind of the teenage Stephen Downing, the boy who was meant to have brutally attacked a married woman nearly twice his age . . .

Stephen was not as bright as he might have been. He lagged behind most of the other children at Bakewell Infants, the Methodist Juniors and the Church of England Boys' School which he had left at sixteen with the reading age of an eleven-year-old.

He did, however, find employment in a job he really liked after he left school, perhaps his true vocation, his parents felt. He was taken on by Bloomers the bakers, who had a shop and restaurant in the town centre. It did indeed seem to be his true niche, and one of his proudest moments was when a bread wheatsheaf he had designed and baked was chosen as the centrepiece of the harvest festival in the parish church.

Despite his poor learning ability at school he had developed a mischievous sense of humour and one example of his handiwork had many people in Bakewell chuckling, though some tut-tutted, when the gingerbread men he and some of his workmates had made went on display in Bloomers shop window. For the little confections wore currants not only as eyes, nose and buttons, but as naughty appendages indicating their gender. The prank had brought a stern rebuke from their superior. But that was not the reason why, after a year, Bloomers decided to dispense with his services. Much as they liked the agreeable, simple lad from the council estate, he was late for work once too often.

Next he worked as a plasterer. For just five days. His new employer swiftly decided that he was not cut out for this work.

Stephen then worked at the Cintride's engineering works for five months. Again he was sacked for bad time-keeping.

If he was interested in something he shone. He could strip a car to bits and put it together again perfectly. He loved model-making, even needlework and especially cooking. He would take over the kitchen many a time and make a meal, and was really good at baking.

Most people liked Stephen Downing. The neighbours on the council estate knew him as a gentle and caring lad with a ready smile, who would never see a woman struggling with heavy shopping without offering to carry it home for her. If his mother felt ill he would fuss over her by filling a hot-water bottle or bringing her aspirin and a drink.

For his latest job as a gardener in the cemetery, he was paid £9.75 a week before stoppages by Bakewell Urban District Council.

Stephen Downing had little in common with many of the other teenage lads of the town, now savouring new-found pleasures like alcohol and the pursuit of girls. He talked to girls but, as far as anyone knew, had never been on intimate terms with them. Some people thought him odd and a loner. But others, with maybe more insight into his character, could say nothing worse about him than that he was 'as daft as a brush'.

'We used to tease him something rotten,' a woman who worked at Granby Garments, a small underwear factory in the town centre, later told me. Herself a teenager at the time, she remembers, 'Stephen used to hang around and sit on the wall with us during our dinner breaks in the summer. We regarded him as a bit of a joke, he was just daft. We used to make him fetch ice creams for us. He seemed happy enough to do it. I feel a bit guilty now, looking back, after everything that's happened to him. He was a lovely little lad, really.'

Though a trendy dresser in his flared trousers and big-collared shirts, and knowing all the latest hits of the pop stars, he disliked discos, preferring to spend his time doing things like tending two baby hedgehogs he had found near the cemetery and kept in a cardboard box in the kitchen, feeding them with warm milk through an eye-dropper. He loved animals but had a dread of spiders and, as a young child, had been found sleeping on the stairs by his mother because he had seen one of the dreaded creatures in his bedroom. He would never, however, cause any harm to them. If he found one in the bath he would call his mother to remove it, rather than take the simple option of turning on the tap and dispatching it down the plughole. His mother even remembered him bursting out crying once when she cut a bar of Fairy soap in half, because the knife had gone right through the 'baby' emblem embossed in the middle of the bar.

As I listened to the Downings talking about their son, I could not equate him with the supposed cold-blooded killer who had spent over twenty years in prison.

I was startled out of my thoughts by the ringing of the telephone in the adjoining lounge. Nita rushed through from the kitchen to pick up the receiver. Ray and I followed her. The phone was sitting on top of the sideboard in what was obviously kept as the Downings' 'best' room. Stephen was on the other end of the phone. I felt embarrassed, as if I were intruding on a very intimate moment between mother and son. But she quickly passed the phone to Ray, who explained to Stephen that I was there and wanted to talk to him. Ray eagerly thrust the receiver into my hand.

I cannot remember our exact words. The voice on the other end of the phone seemed slightly nervous. He was quietly spoken, but was relatively jovial, thanking me for my interest and offering to help in any way. I knew we did not have much time so I told him that I had agreed to look into his case and would appreciate as much help from him as possible. I had already decided I needed to get Stephen's own account of the day. I asked if he could write to me with a description of what happened, with as much detail as he could remember. He promised he would do everything he could and thanked me for getting involved. By then it was time for him to hang up. He did not even have time to say goodbye to his parents.

Ray and Nita were elated. After all these years they were extremely grateful that someone had agreed to take up the case. Another mug of tea. Ray said he was sure Stephen would begin work on his account that very day and that I would have it on my desk the following week. He was eager to talk about what he remembered of 12 September 1973. It was obviously a story retold many times, but he seemed to enjoy the opportunity to go over things once again in front of his local newspaper editor. We settled down around the kitchen table once more . . .

'It was bitter cold that morning, that I do remember. I had wakened early – about 5.30a.m. I was a bus driver in those days for Hulley's at Baslow. I had the early morning route that day. I recall pulling open the curtains to see a very heavy frost.

'I had a wash and went down to the kitchen for some breakfast. Nita had come down by then.'

Nita was now fumbling to light a cigarette. She spluttered a little, perhaps in anticipation, even before the match lit the end of her filtertip. Her hands shook slightly. She was hanging on Ray's every word, even though she must have heard the story many times before.

Ray smiled at his wife and indicated he wanted another brew. 'You asked Stephen if he was going in, didn't you, Nita?'

'Yes, there was a sleepy reply, if I remember rightly,' Nita said.

He turned back to me. 'Stephen just couldn't seem to get up in the morning. He had been off work on Monday and Tuesday with a heavy cold. I doubted whether he would make it to work that day. I knew Nita would wake him early enough but she couldn't be behind him all the time. She also had to look after Christine. She was about fourteen then, and had to get to school. That day was especially important, because it was her first day back after the summer term. Christine wanted to be early so Stephen would have to fend for himself. He'd seemed OK the night before and had said he wanted to go in. Something about wanting to work on an old mowing machine. I asked Nita before I left if she thought he'd be fit for work. She wasn't sure, but said she already had his lunchtime sandwiches ready if he decided to go.'

'So did Stephen get off to work on time?' I asked, amazed at Ray's detailed recollections.

Nita grinned. 'He was on the last minute as usual. I called him at twenty past seven and said Ray had been gone ages, and Christine was already down in the kitchen checking all her school stuff. Even though we only lived a few minutes' walk away from his work, he was often late. In fact, he was in such a rush he put on the wrong boots. They were probably the first pair he could find in the half-light, but were in fact his best blue dress boots. He probably only realised on his way to work, and panicked, thinking his dad would shout at him. In any case, he changed them when he came home at dinner time.'

'Anyway,' Ray butted in, keen to carry on with his own account, 'by that time I'd reached the depot. I was pleased to see the coaches weren't frosted over. Several were revving and belching smoke into the air.

'I'd not driven the early morning bus for some time and fumbled in my pockets for a cash float. A few coppers, just enough to get by. The relief man poked his head inside the bus again and said she wasn't so keen first thing. I replied who is, when it was this cold? But she started first time and I drove out of the main yard just ahead of the Buxton link. At the gates I took it very steady in case there was still ice about. I knew that it was unlikely I'd see anyone until the Middleton-by-Youlgreave terminus. Out of Baslow, I passed the main bus stop – clear. Then I went down several heavily frosted country lanes, past the cuttings at Pilsley, Ashford and into Rutland Square in Bakewell, and finally on to Haddon and Youlgreave. As I approached each stop, I slowed and peered both sides for any signs of passengers. It was looking like a typical day on this route.

'When I approached Middleton village, which was up a slight gradient from the Monyash Road junction, I noticed two, maybe three people huddled in a small group, waiting north-bound by the bus stop under the school warning sign. One woman was stamping her feet to keep warm and all seemed well wrapped against the chill wind.

'"All aboard the skylark!" I shouted as the door swung open, and a cold breeze came in with the first passenger, a tall woman, in her late fifties, wearing a dark coat and a navy blue shawl. She made hard work of stepping on to the rubber running board and climbing the two steps into the bus. The woman put her change on the counter, took her ticket and found a seat without saying a word. The others then followed her on.

'I checked the change and adjusted my ticket machine ready for the next stop. The clock on the front dashboard was visible to all the passengers and the minute hand clicked and showed 8.05a.m. I had arrived on time just before 8a.m. but couldn't leave until the scheduled time of 8.10a.m.

'The bus seemed to shiver against the cold as I checked my watch and waited for the clock to move on to the appointed time. I felt everyone else was also watching and waiting for that very moment. Several eyes seemed to burn into the back of my head. The sun was just coming out and dazzled on to the road surface. Ahead, the fingers of the three-way road sign began to drip. I knew this route like the back of my hand. There was an old water trough, a Georgian post box, plus a red telephone box next to the Memorial Gardens. I had often gone to this village as a lad just after the war. It was a picturesque tourist site in the summer – but those days had gone again for another year – the frost was a sharp reminder.

'The clock suddenly clicked again. It was 8.10a.m. precisely. I asked, "Is everyone on?" not really expecting a reply! "Yes, go on," came a muffled response from one of the passengers, as if she had been nominated to speak. I glanced in the rear-view mirror, released the handbrake and engaged first gear. The front of the bus lifted slightly and the engine roared with relief after all that standing. Suddenly, though, I had to stand back hard on my brakes. The bus came to an abrupt halt. The passengers were immediately shaken from their slumbers and tipped forward in their seats. Someone had appeared directly in front of my bus at the very moment of lift-off.'

Ray spluttered and seemed to shake, as if trying to recall his precise feelings. 'I pulled on the handbrake and fell back into my seat. I opened the door again and this time it brought a welcome gust of cool air. I recognised the dark-haired young woman, Wendy Sewell. She lived just up the road from the bus stop at Green Farm. She was now inside the bus and skipped up the steps in one. She had been completely oblivious to any danger and was fiddling for change inside her purse. She had actually brushed against the front radiator of the bus as it was setting off and was now offering me a £5 note. I automatically held out my hand and, still breathless with shock, said to her, "You were lucky!"

'She replied, "Yes! I'd laddered my tights and had to look for another pair. I thought I'd miss the bus."

'"No! I don't mean that," I said indignantly – then it dawned on me she hadn't even realised her lucky escape. My heart was still thumping and I explained, "I nearly knocked you over!" She seemed unconcerned. Flustered, I said, "You're not usually on this bus," and she replied, "Yes, but I've some business to attend to in Bakewell."

'Wendy sat on the front passenger seat by the door. She looked straight ahead and didn't acknowledge anyone. I glanced at her again as she sat down. She had long, dark-brown hair, which curled just above her shoulders. She was wearing a beige trouser suit with a dark jumper. As she crossed her legs, the left trouser leg ran up slightly and I noticed that she was wearing tights underneath with small white ankle socks and rather dingy-looking white plimsolls. I thought she had probably put the tights on to guard against the cold. She carried a light-brown wicker-type shopping basket over one arm, and put her purse into a small handbag, which she placed under a cloth in her basket. I shook my head slightly and thought, What a pity! A pretty young woman – shame about the shoes.

'We were approaching the next village, Youlgreave. The sun was now bright. It was going to turn into a beautiful, crisp, clear day. We'd just gone round the bend where the church spire comes into view over beyond the allotments, when I remember telling her that I was running a trip to Cliftonville in the near future. I said I was trying to get a party together for next year. I asked if she would be interested. I often organised special excursions and had, in fact, only just returned from Cliftonville about four weeks earlier, and was planning ahead for 1974. "No! Not Cliftonville," I remember her saying. Then she added, "If you ever run one to Edinburgh, to the Tattoo, I might be interested. My mother and I like antiques."

'I was still trying to work out the significance of Edinburgh and antiques, when I had to stop for a small group of new passengers waiting by the Farmyard pub. I exchanged a few more pleasantries with Wendy before we reached Haddon Hall, and then we were fast approaching Bakewell town centre. She seemed more intense as we came into Rutland Square. She seemed to have things on her mind. As soon as we stopped, she was up and out in one, and ran down the street without a word. I shouted, "Cheerio then," half expecting her to wave back but she didn't. I licked the point of my pencil and scribbled down, "Edinburgh Tattoo, Wendy Sewell and her mum."

'I never saw her again.'

Ray seemed emotional as he went through these final details, but he soon regained his composure. He dipped his biscuit into his second mug of tea and grinned without any trace of irony. 'I had a funny feeling that it would be a memorable day. The strange thing is that I could have killed Wendy Sewell myself that very morning, quite by accident, and then we wouldn't have had twenty-odd years of all this bloody nonsense.'

Nita then explained that she had arrived home from work that day on the bus just after 1p.m. She said the kettle had only been on a few minutes when she heard Stephen's key in the back door and shouted to him that it wasn't locked. 'Stephen said the shop up the road had already closed for lunch and he asked me if I could get him another bottle of pop and take it across to him later at the cemetery. He had an empty bottle with him to collect the refund and he put it on the kitchen table with some money. I asked him if he was staying for a cuppa as I was making one for myself. He said no, he had just come back to change his boots and feed the hedgehogs. I explained that I had already fed them. I told him I would get him another bottle of pop when the shop opened and would take it down to him in the cemetery. He stayed for another minute or so but said he had to get back to his work and would see me later.

'He never returned home.'

4

I DON'T KNOW WHAT made me do it. I saw this woman walking in the cemetery. I went into the chapel to get the pickaxe handle that I knew was there. I followed her but I hadn't talked to her and she hadn't talked to me, but I think she knew I was there. I came right up to her near enough. I hit her twice on the head, on the back of the neck. I just hit her at the back of the head to knock her out. She fell to the ground and she was on her side, and then she was face down. I rolled her over and started to undress her. I pulled her bra off first. I had to pull her jumper up and I just got hold of it until it broke, and then I pulled her pants and her knickers off. I started to play with her breasts and then her vagina. I put my middle finger up her vagina. I don't know why I hit her but it might have been to do with what I have just told you. But I knew I had to knock her out first before I did anything to her. It was only a couple of minutes. I was playing with her and there was just a bit of blood at the back of her neck. So I left her, went back to the chapel, got my pop bottle and went to the shop, and then went home to see my mother and asked her to get a bottle of pop for me because the shop was closed. I suppose I did that so that no one would find out I'd hit the woman.

I went back to the cemetery about fifteen minutes later and went back to see the woman. She was lying on the ground the same way as I'd left her but she was covered in blood on her face and on her back. I bent down to see how she was and she was semi-conscious, just. She put her hands up to her face and just kept wiping her face with her hand. She had been doing that when I first knocked her down.

I went back to the telephone kiosk to ring for the police and ambulance so that they would think someone else had done it and I'd just found her. I hadn't any money so I went to the Lodge and asked Wilf Walker if he was on the telephone, but he said he wasn't. So I told him what I'd supposed to have found. He came to have a look and then he went to ask these other blokes in a white van outside the cemetery if they had seen her, but they said they hadn't, so one of them went to phone for the police. I just stayed because there was no place to go.

Jackie had received a massive new bundle of paperwork from the courts and other sources. Among it was the Home Office summary of the case from which the above confession made by Stephen Downing is taken.

So far I had only heard the Downing family's version of events, which, understandably, was all very cosy and supportive. I had to look at the official papers to get a really objective perspective on this. If I was ever going to find out the truth and put this case to rest once and for all, I had to know as much as possible. I was determined not to come down on the Downings' side through sentiment alone. Stephen Downing, if innocent, could only be helped if I thoroughly understood his best lines of defence.

I noticed the inconsistency with what Ray had told me over the question of whether Wendy Sewell had moved when Stephen returned to the cemetery. There was no mention in this confession statement of her having done so.

In stark contrast to his confession, a report from one of Stephen's prison officers had also arrived via a contact of mine at the Home Office. It related to a home visit Stephen had made to Bakewell six months previously, in March 1994 – the first time he had set foot in the town since his trial almost exactly twenty years before. He had been accompanied by prison officer Clive Tanner who had commented, 'He coped very well. There were a lot of people there who knew him before and were coming up to him and greeting him. It came across as very strange to me how in a small community, where I assume a murder only takes place possibly once every hundred years, when the offender returns he is warmly welcomed by a great deal of the local people. Maybe there is something in the point he is trying to make about *not* being guilty.'

A copy of the trial judge's summary had also arrived from Nottingham Crown Court. I had told Jackie to ask for a full transcript, but she had been informed that there wasn't one. I found this strange. The Sheffield firm of court shorthand writers, who had taken down every word that had been said, had told me all their records would be at court. They had nothing going back to the early Seventies in their own archives. A check with the court clerk confirmed however that no full record of the trial had been found. As a result, all I could do was work from the judge's summing up.

The Honourable Mr Justice Nield, whose job it was to guide the jury in their deliberations having heard one day of evidence, began his summing up on 15 February 1974, reminding them of their duty, and pointing out that Downing, soon to have his eighteenth birthday, had a 'perfectly clean record'. They were told that 'manslaughter does not arise, because it is agreed that this unfortunate woman was murdered. The issue is whether the Crown has proved it was this man who committed that murder.'

Turning to Stephen's confession he continued, 'One of the main planks of the prosecution case is the statement made by the accused and signed over and over again.' He stressed that the Prosecution had to establish that the statement had been 'voluntarily made' and 'accurately recorded', and went on to explain, 'If the jury thought there had been oppression, any improper conduct by the police to induce this young man to make a statement, or to threaten him if he did not that such and such things would happen, then the statement is valueless.'

Mr Justice Nield then began to turn his attention to the various accounts of what had happened on 12 September 1973. I turned the page and read on with increasing interest as the judge began his narrative. Employing a quaint blend of austerity and chattiness, he described how several witnesses for the Prosecution had claimed to see Wendy take the last walk of her life . . .

This grim story begins thus, does it not. Wendy Sewell, a young married woman, worked for the Forestry Commission at Bakewell, and that Commission had an office in Catcliff House in

Church Street, and the District Officer was Mr Osmaston . . .

At about twenty past noon Mr Osmaston was speaking on the telephone, and in came Mrs Sewell and handed him a note to say she was going out for a breath of fresh air.

Now that woman's movements are followed meticulously, until she reaches the cemetery – you may say, perhaps, it is a tribute to the thoroughness of the investigations.

We learn from Mr Read of the Department of Employment in the same building that he saw this woman leave at about 12.40.

It is clear that she made her way along Butts Road. Two joiners, Mr Lomas and Mr Bradwell, who were working in that road and were having lunch at that time, saw her . . . three, four or five minutes after she left the building . . . and they exchanged greetings.

At about 12.45 Mrs Hill, in a Land Rover, came up to the cemetery gates where she always turned her vehicle, and saw Mrs Sewell walking into the cemetery, and there was no one else about.

At about 12.50 Mr Pearson saw Mrs Sewell walking on Butts Road *towards* the cemetery, and they exchanged greetings.

And about the same time Mr Carman, who was near the telephone kiosk just outside the cemetery gates, said *he* saw Mrs Sewell through the fence walking along the back path *in* the cemetery, the path along Burton Edge.

At this point Mr Justice Nield stressed that the timings given by witnesses had to be viewed as approximate.

He then turned to the movements of the defendant, Stephen Downing:

About 1.08 Mr Wilfred Walker, who was the cemetery attendant and lived in the Lodge by the main gates, saw the accused who walked out of the main gates with a pop bottle under his arm. He appeared to be perfectly normal . . . this young man was not hurrying. Mr Walker did not notice anything about his clothing.

Mr Justice Nield pointed out that the jury had later heard from Stephen Downing that he had greeted Mr Walker and his wife, who were at the door of the Lodge. Mr Walker denied any such exchange had taken place. He continued,

At about 1.15 Mr Walker saw the accused again. This time he was coming back to the main gates and there was no pop bottle with him.

Just before that time Mr Fox and Mr Hawksworth, workmen employed by the Urban District Council, had come into the cemetery in order to go to the store.

At 1.20 or thereabouts the accused came to Mr Walker's Lodge. He seemed very calm. Mr Walker said, 'He asked if I was on the telephone. I said no, what is the matter? He said there was a woman who had been attacked in the cemetery. I asked where she was. I went with him and he kept pointing down there.'

At this point Mr Justice Nield drew the jury's attention to a further discrepancy in the accounts given by Wilf Walker and Stephen. According to Mr Walker, as they approached the injured woman, Stephen told him, 'I don't want to lose my job. I like it.' When questioned, Stephen denied saying this. The judge told the jury, 'Make up your minds, having seen Mr Walker, whether it is true.' He went on with his summary,

And so these two reached the spot where this woman was lying. Mr Walker said the accused told him, 'There was a pick shaft handle covered with blood, and then I saw there was a van parked by the store.' Mr Walker told you, 'I noticed this unfortunate woman trying to get up. She fell back on the gravestone, and never moved after that.'

Well, after some minutes Mr Walker and the defendant called over the two workmen, Mr Fox and Mr Hawksworth, to come and see what there was to be seen.

You were told by Mr Hawksworth, who arrived at the scene, that they saw this body half naked, naked up to the thighs, and

Mr Hawksworth went to telephone for the police.

Now at some time about this point two other people arrived, also employed by the Urban District Council, Mr Dawson and Mr Watts, and you have important evidence from them.

Mr Dawson told you, 'I went across and saw a person lying on the graves. The person was trying to wipe blood from the eyes with the back of his or her hand.'

Here the judge noted that Herbert Dawson had been unable to say if the victim was a man or a woman. He told how the witness had said he shouted for someone to fetch an ambulance, and that nothing struck him about Stephen's manner as he stood there with the rest of the group. The judge then repeated the rest of Dawson's evidence, in which he had told the court:

'I said "What the hell is going on?" I turned to the accused and I said, "Where are you working?" He said, "Just across here." I said, "Was it here this morning?" meaning the body, and he said, "No!" And then I saw that the woman moved again, and was trying to stand up.'

Mr Justice Nield continued,

Mr Dawson went forward to try to save her from falling, but was too late. Then the police arrived and the officer, Police Constable Ball, obviously rightly said to those assembled, 'Don't anybody touch anything,' and at that the accused said, 'I did turn her over, but I had my gloves on.'

Mr Watts, one of the Urban District Council plumbers, told you he ran for the ambulance, having seen this body, and then 'I went back' he said, and 'I saw the defendant'. He heard the defendant say to Mr Dawson that he touched the body, but he had his gloves on. 'Then I saw,' said Mr Watts, 'blood on the defendant's knees as if he had been kneeling down, and I saw a pick handle on the path.' He said when he first saw this woman there was blood on her face and body.

It was here that the judge highlighted a major difference between the Prosecution and Defence accounts. Stephen Downing, he said, had denied saying he made the remark about his gloves. 'Make up your minds about that,' instructed Mr Justice Nield, before turning to the evidence of the next witness.

> There came then Mr Fox, another of these workmen. He went to the scene, and saw the body lying there partly clothed. The accused told him he thought someone must have been in the chapel and taken the pick shaft out. The accused added that he had gone home at dinner time, and also that the woman had moved. The accused then said, 'There looks like being an identification parade.'

The judge pointed out a further 'sharp conflict' between the Crown and Defence cases. Stephen Downing denied making any remark about an identity parade. He continued,

> Well, from that aspect of the evidence, one turns to consider the weapon, the pick shaft handle.
> Mr Hawksworth, the council workman who'd telephoned the police, told you about this. He said, 'I had been in the cemetery about eleven o'clock that morning, and I saw the accused coming away from the store with a pair of shears which he would want for his work. I went into the store to check some asbestos sheets and found something else we wanted, which was a chimney cowl placed on top of the lectern. I noticed a pick shaft nearby. I picked it up to have a look at it, then I put it back.'

At this point Mr Justice Nield reminded the jury that Fred Hawksworth had identified the pickaxe handle he had seen in the chapel store as 'Exhibit 1', the handle shown to him in court, which the Crown claimed was the murder weapon. Hawksworth had agreed, 'This is it.' He had then gone on to say, 'Later on I saw the pick shaft on the pathway.'

'Continuing with the narrative,' said Mr Justice Nield,

the ambulance was sent for and Mr Bateman, a senior ambulanceman, arrived on the scene. At that time Mrs Sewell was still alive and she tried to put away those who were trying to look after her. On the journey, according to Mr Batemen, she became very restless, moving about a lot, throwing out her right arm all over the place, and his uniform was covered in blood but, according to that witness, she was not shaking her head.

PC Ball told the court that she resisted violently with her arm. This is all important in the light of the submissions which have been made to you by Counsel for the Defence.

I was unsure what the judge was referring to here. I was to find out later in his summing up.

After summarising the evidence given by the lodge keeper, workmen, and the ambulanceman, who were all present in the cemetery at some point, Mr Justice Nield told the jury, 'I think I am right in saying that, within the cemetery at the relevant time, no one else was seen,' although he went on to remind them that 'there are holes in the hedge, and another gate, where anybody could come in or out'.

He drew their attention to the evidence given by two Defence witnesses, both of whom had claimed to see 'a person, or two persons, coming away from the direction of the cemetery'.

The judge placed emphasis on only one of these witnesses, Mrs Louisa Hadfield, whose evidence was, he said, 'greatly relied on by the defence'. He reminded the jury, 'She told you she was walking in Upper Yeld Road with her dog at about 1.15 and saw a man running ever so fast towards her . . . that means *away from* the direction in which the cemetery lay. She described his dress. She was very frightened. The dog snarled at him.' She was so concerned that she had reported the matter to the police.

The judge then described the evidence of George Paling, which had been read out in court. 'Mr Paling, upon whom reliance is not so strongly placed, was a long way down on the left of the plan. He was in Upper Yeld Road and saw a chap coming up on the other side. He was dressed respectably and was in a terrific hurry. This is all about 350 yards off the plan. He was asked if he noticed any blood on the man. He did not notice any. You may wonder if that witness really helps you.'

He then spoke of the evidence given by Stephen's next-door neighbour, Peter Moran, who said he saw Stephen coming from the direction of the cemetery towards the shop at around 1.15. Mr Moran had left his house and was on his way back to work in Bakewell at this time. Stephen had told the court he saw Mr Moran outside the cemetery gates.

Mr Justice Nield then moved on to medical and scientific evidence presented by the prosecution.

At 2.40 Mrs Sewell reached Chesterfield Royal Hospital. Mr Stillman, the surgeon, found multiple lacerations of the skull, and an X-ray confirmed there were fractures. Doctor Usher, the pathologist, performed a post-mortem examination on 15 September, the day after this woman died, and he found ten lacerations to the skull as if she had been violently assaulted by someone using the pickaxe handle. He took the view there must have been at least seven or eight or more violent blows and, whoever did it, would seem to have been in a frenzied state.

The judge pointed out that several witnesses had described Stephen Downing as 'calm and cool, certainly not frenzied' just moments after he was supposed to have carried out the attack. One witness, PC Ball, had not regarded him as cool. He had said: 'He was very excited. I told him to calm down.' This contradicted the evidence of other witnesses, who had seen nothing abnormal in Stephen's demeanour.

He then turned to the scientific evidence, and a report which the Prosecution case had relied upon heavily. It was written by Mr Norman Lee, a Home Office forensics expert. Mr Lee's evidence concerned the blood-staining on Stephen's clothing and on the pickaxe handle, the murder weapon. He said there were stains on his trousers on the knees where he might have kneeled, and on the front of the trousers mainly on the lower legs. There were also a large number of splashes and heavy smears. There was some blood on the right leg as high as the thighs. He said these stains would have been visible to the people in the cemetery. In addition there were small spots of blood on his T-shirt and his gloves.

An examination of Stephen's boots showed a lot of smears and small spots of blood, mainly at the front.

Stephen Downing claimed at trial that, after finding Mrs Sewell, he had knelt down and turned her over, whereupon she had raised herself up and begun to shake her head violently. That was the explanation, he said, for the blood on his clothes. Mr Lee conceded that the blood on the boots 'might arise from somebody getting up from his knees and pressing on his toes on the ground'. He also went on to say that 'the blood-staining on the clothes, some of it, *is* consistent with someone turning over the body'. However, the very *small* spots and splashes found on the clothes, boots and gloves were *not* consistent with turning someone over. And he did *not* accept Stephen's explanation that the small spots of blood flew on to his clothing from her head and long hair, as she violently shook her head about. He said, 'I cannot imagine how you could get splashings as small as those in the way Downing is suggesting.' He added, '*If* she had flung herself about, then for such tiny spots a lot of energy must have been applied.' His preferred explanation was that the spots came from Mrs Sewell being beaten 'and the harder you hit, the smaller the spot of blood'.

This was a complicated, but vital, point. I read and reread it to make sure I understood the argument. Norman Lee seemed to be saying that violent force produces a spray of blood, which would appear as tiny, almost microscopic spots, on any surface hit by this spray — such as clothing. Only violent force could produce these kinds of *tiny* blood spots. He did not believe Wendy Sewell could have shaken her head so violently as to produce those minute spots found on Stephen's clothing. They must have come from the violent blows of the pick shaft.

I could not see why Norman Lee was so sure. When cross-examined, Lee repeated that she could *not* have shaken her head so violently as to produce that result. And yet it was not only Stephen who described her thrashing around in an aggressive manner. PC Ball had given a similar account, as had the ambulanceman Clyde Bateman when describing the journey to hospital . . . although Mr

Bateman had not noticed her moving her head. I wondered if this could be explained by her worsening condition. Stephen must have found her just after the attack, whereas she was in the ambulance almost an hour later. She was soon to fall into a coma due to horrific head injuries, from which she never recovered. Could this be why her head was relatively still at this point?

Turning to the murder weapon, Mr Lee said the stains on the boots and lower legs of Downing's trousers were similar in size and proportion to the stains on the pickaxe handle. He went on to conclude, 'There was very probably a close relationship between the handle and this man's trousers and boots, and I do not think this would come from offering succour. The boots and trousers were in close proximity when the deceased was battered.'

My search through Ray Downing's files had brought to light a document, which showed that doubt had been cast on Lee's conclusions even before the trial. I had been rummaging through Ray's paperwork a few days previously and had come across a forensic report written in January 1974. I had not realised its significance at the time. Its contents had seemed dry and technical. Now I retrieved it, as there were things I wanted to check.

The report, by Mr G. E. Moss of Commercial and Forensic Laboratories in Reading, had been written at the request of Stephen's Defence team. Mr Moss visited the Nottingham Forensic Lab to examine the murder weapon and various other exhibits. Norman Lee and police officers were present. He found the pickaxe handle heavily blood-stained at the thick end, the end used to hit the victim, while the handle end was smeared with blood. He agreed with the pathologist, Mr Usher, that 'at least seven or eight violent blows' had been struck. He pointed out that, therefore, this was inconsistent with Stephen's confession.

I grabbed the Home Office summary of the case and turned again to the confession to double check. There it was in back and white: 'I hit her twice on the head, on the back of the neck. I just hit her at the back of the head to knock her out.' *Two* blows! The confession, relied on as the main plank of the Prosecution case, contradicted the pathologist's evidence – also used by the Prosecution – on this vital detail.

I turned to it again. The blood, he continued, on the back of the gloves could only be seen through a microscope and was not visible to the naked eye. I recalled the disputed evidence about the gloves. PC Ball and the workman Herbert Dawson maintained Stephen had said he was wearing gloves when he turned Wendy over. He was adamant he had never said this and claimed he had said his gloves were in his back pocket all along. It was one of the apparent inconsistencies which may have made the jury doubt his account. It seemed to me that if he *had* been wearing his gloves, they would have been soaked in blood considering the extent of Wendy's injuries.

Mr Moss went on, 'The pattern of staining on the front legs of the jeans is consistent with kneeling in blood. This would be consistent with Downing kneeling beside the body some time after the attack.' Mr Moss seemed to be saying that the blood was congealed and not fresh when it reached Downing's jeans. He went on, 'I assumed the linear markings on the inside right leg were probably caused by rubbing against a bloodied surface, possibly a boot while in the act of getting up from a kneeling position. The smears above knee level would also have been made by rubbing against a bloodied surface. Downing said he had turned the body over. If he did, the smearings might well have occurred at this time.'

Then I saw what I had really been looking for. It was in the matter of how the tiny spots and splashes of blood occurred that Mr Moss and Mr Lee differed most. Unlike Lee, Moss said, 'The blood splashing on the clothes *could* have resulted from head shaking, as Downing got up from a kneeling position.' He concluded that the blood-staining overall was consistent with Downing's version of events, including his assertion that there was a lot of blood about Wendy's face and on the path. Again, he insisted the forensic evidence was *not* consistent with the version of events in Downing's confession.

But there was no reference to Mr Moss's report in the judge's summing up. I found it incredible that his evidence would not have been presented to the jury. Once again I regretted the fact that a full trial transcript was not available. It was so important to know whether Stephen's Defence team had used this vital forensic evidence. From the papers available to me it suggested they had not, but I could not be sure.

Mr Justice Nield then reached the police's account of Stephen's interrogation and confession, and the case presented by the Defence.

I put the papers aside for a while. Before moving on to these other matters, I wanted to thoroughly examine the movements of people in and around the cemetery that day, and check the timings they had given.

Some of the accounts contradicted each other. I supposed that it would have been difficult to remember what you were doing on a particular day minute by minute.

Wendy's workplace, Catcliff House, was less than a minute's walk from the entrance to Butts Road, which then became the pedestrianised path known simply as The Butts. But where was Wendy between 12.20p.m. – the time she passed Mr Osmaston a note saying she was going out and 12.40p.m. when she was seen leaving the building?

And could Stephen really have only been away from the cemetery between 1.08p.m. and 1.15p.m., the times given for his departure and return by the gatekeeper? He seemed to have done a fair amount in seven minutes – walked to the shop, then to his house where he stayed chatting to his mother, and then back to the cemetery.

In addition to this, one of his neighbours, Peter Moran, claimed to have seen him at 1.15p.m. walking *towards* the shop – the same time the gatekeeper says he saw him re-entering the cemetery.

There were many similar examples. The timings given were certainly not accurate in every case. It would mean trying to find the trial witnesses.

I noticed the trial summary had not mentioned the fact that Wendy had moved across gravestones from the place where she was attacked, to the place where the workmen first saw her. So far I only had Ray's word for this. I wanted to get to the bottom of these inconsistencies.

Disappointingly, around this time I received a reply from Derbyshire police headquarters saying that all their paperwork and exhibits relating to the case had been destroyed, along with the murder weapon which had been burned. I was furious. How dare they destroy all the evidence before the man had even served his time!

5

BEFORE I had a chance to visit witnesses, Stephen's own written description of the day arrived. Enclosed was a diagram of the cemetery which he had drawn himself. For a man who was supposed to be simple, the prose was graphic and descriptive. Even today it brings a lump to my throat when I read it.

> The cemetery always seemed empty even when there were other people milling about – although I felt particularly isolated when I was alone.
>
> The creaking of the huge timbers in the roof structure of the unconsecrated chapel gave the place an eerie feeling, as if you were never quite alone. It was never what you would call warm in there, even at the height of summer, so it was not uncommon for a fire to be burning in the pot-bellied stove which stood in one corner. It was September, and while the day was warm enough to work without a jacket, the chapel had a chilliness that cut to the bone. I wasted no time in getting a fire going with the hope I could push back the blanket of cold – at least enough to be able to enjoy my break.
>
> I then collected the tools I needed. Long-handled shears, rake, wheelbarrow and fork. The previous week I had spent every morning mowing the grass, which just left the edges to be tidied up.
>
> I don't have any recollection of any unusual visitors to the cemetery during the morning before my break, although I do recall one lady who regularly walked her dog in there. More often than not I would see her in the afternoon, but on that day she came in the morning. I never got to know her name but, as

was customary, she stopped by me and we chatted briefly.

She asked me where I had been for the past two days as she had not seen me, and I told her that I'd been off with a cold. She told me to keep warm and I informed her that I had a fire going in the unconsecrated chapel. I heard the clock strike and stopped clipping grass and took out the pocket watch I had borrowed from my father. It was 12 noon.

I gathered my tools and returned to the unconsecrated chapel where I had my lunch and a cup of coffee. I followed this with a cigarette and reluctantly pulled myself away from the fire's inviting warmth to tinker with an old Allan mower. I felt like being a little lazy, so I took all of my break time smoking a few cigarettes. I took out my father's pocket watch again and saw that it was about 12.55.

I then lit another cigarette and went to smoke it standing by the steps to the right of the unconsecrated Chapel. I noticed a woman walking up the path towards the Junior School. I had never seen her before so I continued to watch her until she went behind the hedge surrounding the Garden of Remembrance.

There had been some damage caused to some of the graves, nothing too serious, just childish vandalism, so I was asked to look out for such behaviour. By the time she had passed behind the hedge I had finished my cigarette, and realising she would not be the kind of person to do any damage, I went back inside the chapel where I stoked up the fire. I then put on my jacket and picked up my lemonade bottle with the hope of getting to the shops before they closed for lunch.

By the time I left the unconsecrated chapel it would be about 1.05p.m. The shop I was heading for normally closed at 1p.m. but had on occasions been known to stay open for a few minutes longer if they had customers in already being served.

As I walked along the main drive I soon noticed that the woman, who I later learnt was Wendy Sewell, was walking along the bottom footpath that runs alongside Catcliff Woods. She was a little way ahead of me and seemed to be in no rush. She appeared to be looking from side to side at the inscriptions on the headstones. I estimate that it would have taken around

2–3 minutes to cover the length of the path with the woman disappearing behind the consecrated chapel moments before I drew level with the building.

As I went past she did not continue on her journey and I naturally assumed that she had turned around to retrace her steps. I didn't turn around to look.

When I came level with the Lodge, I saw Wilf Walker and his wife at the door. I don't think his wife acknowledged me but Wilf and I nodded to each other. I turned left outside the gates and passed Peter Moran crossing the road on his way back to work. We both said hello to each other without stopping. As I got nearer to the shop, I passed Charlie Carman also on his way back to work. We both greeted each other and again neither of us stopped. Moments later, I realised the shop had already closed so I went home.

Something struck me as odd. Trial witness Charlie Carman could have helped Stephen establish his alibi, but Carman was only called as a Prosecution witness due to his sighting of Wendy Sewell. It was only ever said in court that Stephen saw Moran, *not* Carman. I found it strange that Carman had not been called by Stephen's Defence team. He only gave written evidence for the Prosecution.

I continued reading:

Upon arrival I went to unlock the door and my mother called to me to say the door wasn't locked. I went in via the back door where my mother greeted me. She was in the process of making herself a cup of coffee and explained that she had not long arrived home.

I asked if she would buy me a bottle of lemonade when the shop reopened. My mother said she would. I then counted out the money – minus the allowance on the returned bottle. She asked if I would like the bottle of lemonade bringing down to the churchyard and I said something along the lines that it would be all right either way as I could always take it with me the next day. I then asked her if she had fed my baby hedgehogs as that was one of the main reasons I had gone back home. She said she had.

A couple more minutes passed and then I said I had better be getting back. My mother offered to make a cup of coffee but I refused. I never liked to be away for too long in case anyone checked up on me and I had to explain the reason for my absence. I had perhaps spent about five minutes or so with my mother before leaving and making my way back to the cemetery by the same route.

As I entered the main gates of the cemetery, I noticed that Wilf and his wife had gone into the Lodge and closed the door. After going a little farther I took my jacket off and carried it over my shoulder. It wasn't until I was passing some of the first graves that something caught my eye, so I looked to my left. It took a few seconds to realise that it was someone lying on the bottom path, so I walked over. It was impossible to see the blood from the main drive or any of the external signs of injury.

I threw my jacket down at the victim's feet and then I knelt at her side. It was not possible to check for any signs of life while she was lying on her front so I rolled her over towards me. There was quite a lot of blood on the path and her hair was heavily soaked in it. I don't recall seeing any facial injuries.

I felt for a pulse at the neck but found none. It came as a shock when she raised herself up, and I too reacted by getting to my feet.

It was at this point that I had something sharp pressed into the small of my back and I began to turn to try to see who was behind me. I was ordered not to turn around and was told if I was to say anything my sister would get the same. The man said something along the lines of 'Have you found it?' as if to address another person. No reply came and then the next thing I knew was that the person had left me and I turned at the sound of rustling foliage as they made their escape down into the woodland area.

I gave him and his companion no more attention but picked up my jacket and ran over to the Lodge, whereupon I asked Wilf Walker if he was on the phone. He said he wasn't and asked me why I should enquire. I informed him that a woman had been attacked. He asked me to show him where and followed me to the corner of the Lodge. I pointed in the direction of where she lay. He said that some of my work colleagues had come into the cemetery and we should check first to see if they had already called the emergency services.

As we got to within a few yards of the chapel we were met by other workers carrying out sheets of asbestos and leaning them against the outside of the building ready for loading on to a Land Rover. They had arrived in Watts's white van. Wilf asked them if they had seen anything or called the police or an ambulance. They said they hadn't and one of them went off to make the call.

Shortly afterwards Dawson arrived in the Land Rover. As I recall, Dawson made to go over to where she was and at the same time shouted she was getting up.

I had my back to her and turned to look. She was already on her feet and managed to take a few steps, perhaps two or three, before losing her balance and falling forwards banging the left side of her forehead on the corner of a headstone. Dawson was slow to react and had taken only a couple of steps by the time she was falling over. Watts shouted to Dawson that he should just leave her alone and not touch anything.

We then stood outside the unconsecrated chapel near to the steps leading to the bottom footpath. It must have been about 10–15 minutes before a police officer, PC Ball, arrived on the scene and came over to where we were standing. He asked a few questions as to who had found her, what we were doing there, then asked where she was.

We indicated, and he went over to her and had a look and then walked part of the way back before calling me over to where he waited. He asked if I had been the one who found her and I said I was. He then went on to ask me to say where, and I told him, and even pointed out the place from where we stood.

Finally he asked if I had touched anything. I said I hadn't except for turning her over and I showed him my blood-stained hands. I asked if I could wash the blood off my hands, but he said no, it would be needed for forensics. We then went over to where the rest of the group stood. I seem to recall him asking a couple of questions – if any of them had seen or touched anything. They all answered no.

I think it was Dawson who asked if it was all right for me to help them load the Land Rover and the policeman said it was. The policeman then went back and placed his tunic over the body before going to his car and making a call on the radio. It would be a good 15–20 minutes at a guess before anyone else arrived and maybe as much as another 5–10 minutes before a Detective Inspector Younger came to ask me the same questions that PC Ball had just asked. I gave him the same answers.

He went back to the others for a brief moment and then came back with someone else in a suit. I was asked if I would be willing to go with them to the station for further questioning which I agreed to do. I was led over to a blue and white police car where I sat in the back with one of the policemen, while the other got in the front with the driver.

As we were about to go through the cemetery gates the ambulance arrived.

I already had many queries and misgivings about the case. This latest account from Stephen threw me into even greater turmoil.

The thing that immediately stood out was his description of someone assaulting *him* and threatening his sister, as he knelt by the injured woman. If this were true, and this unidentified person had a companion as suggested, then who were these two people? And why had no mention of them been made at trial? Could one of them be the man whom trial witnesses Louisa Hadfield and George Paling saw running away from the direction of the cemetery? I wondered why more effort had not been made on the part of the police to establish who the running man was.

Of course, this latest account was also at odds with Stephen's original confession, which he had retracted after thirteen days. Apart from the omission of seeing someone in the cemetery who threatened him, the story he was now telling me was the same story he had told the police at the scene, the same story he had told them during the first nine hours in the police station, the same story he had told at the trial and the same story he had been telling in the twenty years ever since. I needed to know why Stephen had briefly deviated from this version, and had admitted attacking and sexually assaulting Wendy Sewell.

Ray had made mention of him having a reading age of only eleven when he left school just a year before the murder, and the fact that many in Bakewell had considered him 'backward'. He had told me that among the bundle of paperwork he had left at my office was a psychiatric report on Stephen attesting to his limited intelligence, which had formed the basis of a failed appeal in the 1980s. He had also described how he and Nita had been denied access to their son throughout his hours of interrogation, at which a solicitor had not been present. Equally worrying was a mention in one of the news-paper reports of his trial – that Stephen alleged police officers had shaken him during the hours of relentless questioning, in order to prevent him falling asleep. Even without further investigation, I felt there might be several grounds on which the confession could be challenged.

This confession statement had been used by the Prosecution to gain a conviction. When I re-read it there were bits which did not seem to match the facts. Stephen had said that he hit Wendy twice on the back of the head to knock her out. The Home Office summary revealed she had been hit 'seven or eight times' with repeated, savage blows to the head. It quoted the forensic and autopsy reports to back this up.

I also questioned how, after such an attack, any jury could have imagined Stephen Downing walking out of the cemetery appearing 'calm' and 'normal', with no apparent blood-staining. Yet this is how several witnesses had described his demeanour and appearance. I compared this with the ambulanceman, Clyde Bateman, who had told the court that he had been 'covered in blood' after attending to Wendy.

After finding Wendy, and calling others to the scene, Stephen had some blood-staining to clothes and hands. Yet the police allowed him to continue working. Surely he could have contaminated other possible pieces of evidence with the blood of the victim? This seemed like bad procedure on the part of the police.

There was no mention in his confession of Wendy having moved from the path to the graves. He said, 'She was lying on the ground the same way I had left her.'

One of the workmen, Hawksworth, said he had picked up the murder weapon earlier in the day. In which case *his* fingerprints would have been on it, as well as those of the murderer. Were any fingerprints taken from the murder weapon? Or from the workmen, who were allowed to carry on working in and around the chapel even though the supposed murderer had gone back there after committing such a violent attack? If the pickaxe handle had come from the council store, any of the workmen's fingerprints could have appeared on it quite innocently – even Stephen Downing's. Once again I cursed the police for having burnt the murder weapon, thereby destroying such potentially vital evidence. If it had still existed, it may have been possible to bring into play DNA testing, something unheard of back in 1973.

More telling, in Stephen's own recent account of the day he described how, on his way home from the cemetery at 1.08, he had spoken words of greeting to one of the Prosecution witnesses, Charlie Carman. Charlie, he said, was between the shop and the cemetery walking in the direction of town on his way to work. Unfortunately, Carman was now dead. I found out he had been employed, like Stephen, as a gardener with the council. That day he was on his way to work in Bath Gardens, a pretty walled square in the centre of Bakewell. I again checked his evidence, read out to the jury. It confirmed he was heading back to town that lunchtime, but made no mention of seeing Stephen Downing. Carman said he had looked over the hedge of the cemetery somewhere near the phone box and had seen Wendy walking along a path. At this point on his route he would already have passed Stephen who was on his way to the shop. So Wendy must have been uninjured *after* Stephen left the cemetery. Why had Charlie Carman not been called as a Defence witness? Had Stephen ever told the police he had seen and spoken to Carman? I noticed a major time discrepancy. Carman said he had spotted Wendy at 12.50, but everyone agreed that Stephen Downing had not left the cemetery till around 1.08. If Stephen really *had* seen

Carman, then Charlie's timing was about twenty minutes out.

Yes, there were many things which did not make sense.

But I also needed some answers from Stephen. Why did he change his story at the police station and admit attacking and, moreover, sexually assaulting Wendy? Why did he wait thirteen days before retracting his confession? I was also interested to know more about Nita's assertion that he had changed his boots when he came home at lunchtime. She had claimed it was because he had put on the wrong ones in the morning. Above all, I needed to clear up the puzzle of the mystery person in the cemetery who had poked him in the back and threatened him. Why on earth had that allegation not formed part of his defence? I knew I would have to ask some difficult questions, which the Downings, too, might not like.

I wrote to him again and asked him if he could answer some of these questions. In particular, I wanted to hear his version of the interrogation at the police station. Ray had told me his confession was forced out of him. I needed to hear it from Stephen.

6

IT DIDN'T TAKE me long to realise my face was becoming familiar in Bakewell and especially on the council estate. I was still apprehensive about involving myself in such a delicate and potentially controversial project. I knew the case was likely to make enemies in this small rural community, and was certain to reawaken thoughts and emotions which had been repressed for many years.

One morning as I breezed into work Elsie, the receptionist, who was on the telephone, began frantically beckoning to me with her free arm. I was about to ask her what the matter was when she put a finger to her lips. I hurried through the door and round the back of the reception counter to where she was sitting. 'Really, young man,' she announced in her best telephone voice, 'do go away and stop being so silly!' With that she slammed the receiver down.

'Who was that?' I asked.

'I don't know, Don. But he said he was going to kick your head in,' she replied, raising her eyebrows quizzically. Elsie had been with the *Mercury* for years and was used to dealing with irate callers. She was not easily fazed.

'Did he say why?' I ventured.

'He said you would know why.'

'Well, I might.'

She peered at me over her glasses. She was a tall, sharp-featured woman with a quick temper, in her late forties and always impeccably dressed. She did not suffer fools gladly and had a bee in her bonnet about 'time wasters' interrupting her regimented routine, whether on the telephone or at *her* counter.

'To be quite honest, it's the second time he's rung,' she confided.

'When was the last?'

'A couple of days ago. I wasn't going to mention it. He was more abusive the first time . . . not really threatening. But if he's starting to talk about beating you up, well, you should know. It was definitely the same chap. Didn't sound particularly old.' She paused, obviously waiting for me to explain.

'I'm really sorry, Elsie. If you get any more, don't even try to talk to him. Just put him straight through to me. Or if I'm out, hang up.' I walked through to my office, leaving the receptionist burning with curiosity. If they thought they could put me off that easily, they had another thing coming.

Even at this early stage, I had a gut feeling about the case, for lots of people kept singing the same tune – Downing was serving time for someone else. I recall an overwhelming desire on my part to seek out the truth once and for all. If Stephen Downing was guilty and I could prove it, then it would at least end the mystery. But what if he was innocent?

Certain prominent local characters and traders were showing a peculiar interest in my preliminary enquiries and displaying a curious nervousness about the victim's past. Calls came to me at the *Mercury* from a publican and several shop owners in Bakewell, asking me why I was suddenly making enquiries into this old case. Surely he was guilty, wasn't he? A number of local councillors contacted me on the same matter. All said they had been under the impression that the case had been cut and dried. Some of these callers implied that Stephen Downing had been well-known as an oddball, even a 'pervert', whose actions had upset the town all those years ago. Why drag it up again?

Feedback about my investigation also came from my advertising reps. They felt that pressure was mounting on them to persuade me to drop the case. Advertisers in the town were becoming nervous that it could have an adverse effect on the place – after all, Bakewell was not that sort of town! An employee at the district council's tourism department told me that the publicity could put people off visiting the area.

More interesting to me was what the reps reported, that the place was buzzing with gossip about the victim's love life. It was being said that she had had several boyfriends, echoing what Ray and Sam Fay, my deputy editor, had told me the first time the Downings came to my office, and there was even mention of a love child. It had been said at the trial and in the Home Office report that the Sewells had *no* children. I decided I must look more closely at the life and times of Mrs Wendy Sewell.

All this, and I had not yet published one word in the *Mercury*.

My reporters told me the local police weren't happy either about my kicking up dust over an old case like this, which was already long gone and forgotten. Reputations were on the line. Phil and Jackie had made preliminary approaches to the local duty inspector but he seemed to be advising us to leave well alone. I asked her if he had given a precise reason. She shrugged her shoulders. 'All he said was that Downing was guilty. A right little pervert,' she explained. That phrase again!

I told her, 'It's strange, but that's what other contacts have said. All very interesting, but I can't find anything so far to substantiate their claims.'

I did, however, begin to gain a lot of support in the area. It was as if people had been waiting all these years to voice their doubts. I was particularly drawn to Burton Edge and Yeld Road overlooking the cemetery. Many residents were still living in the same houses after twenty-one years, and complained to me that no routine house-to-house enquiries had been carried out at the time.

Mrs Marie Bright, an elderly lady who still lived near the cemetery, finally agreed to talk to me although she was worried even now about possible repercussions. She told me she had seen a 'pasty-faced' man with a bright orange T-shirt hanging around the main entrance gates about an hour before the attack. She claimed the man got off the bus from Bakewell about 12 noon. 'This man was aged about forty to forty-five and was acting rather queer. I hadn't seen him around before and I think he was a stranger because he kept looking around and at his watch. He looked suspicious, as though he was waiting for someone,' she said.

I asked her whether she had actually seen him get off the bus. She couldn't remember for certain, and I wondered if he might have just walked past it as it was parked. She also said she 'saw this man coming over the top of the wall' out of the cemetery about an hour later. Mrs

Bright added that she had seen another man parked up in a dark-coloured van near the phone box by the cemetery gates some time that lunchtime. She described him as a fat, bulky figure.

Another elderly woman who lived close by, Mrs Margaret Richards, told me she had seen a man standing close to the beech hedge by the cemetery gates. Her description of him was almost identical to that given by Mrs Bright of the man in the orange T-shirt. Her timings indicated he was there a little later – perhaps about 12.30p.m. She too explained that he appeared to be 'acting suspiciously'. She added, 'He was looking at his watch and was very nervous.'

Both Mrs Bright and Mrs Richards said they had been to Bakewell police station to report their sightings. They had seen PC Ernie Charlesworth, who had not seemed interested and told them they had someone in custody charged with the crime. Charlesworth was a uniformed constable on the beat who, I was told by one publican, boasted for years afterwards in the bars in town that he had been the one who got the confession out of Downing. I wondered why he had apparently not referred these witnesses to a more senior investigating officer?

I wondered, too, whether the noon bus driver had been questioned about his passengers, or any suspicious characters running around. In those days everyone seemed to know everyone else and a stranger would certainly be noticed.

I was then contacted by another witness, a Mrs Gibson from a neighbouring road, who said police did call at her home on the Saturday night after the attack, and actually took a statement. She claimed she was told not to tell anyone, or say anything to anyone else. But she agreed that the police did not make general house-to-house calls.

This was confirmed by housewife Pat Shimwell, who explained to me that she had been chatting with a friend at the door of her house on Burton Edge overlooking the cemetery, and noticed Stephen Downing leaving by the main gate at about 1.10p.m. with his pop bottle. Mrs Shimwell stood at her garden gate with her arms folded as we spoke, relating her story in a matter-of-fact manner. Now in her mid-fifties, like many of the women who were eager to talk to me, Pat Shimwell had been at her home near the cemetery all day on 12 September. I realised that the police would have had a ready-made set of witnesses in these plain-speaking women who noticed everything. If only they had bothered to talk to them. Mrs Shimwell told me that later she was in her bedroom tidying up, when she saw a 'commotion' in the cemetery with several workmen yelling to each other. She remembered someone shouting out something like 'Leave her!'. At about 1.30 she saw the police in the cemetery. She told me that a policeman asked if she had seen anything. She claimed, remarkably, that she was then told, 'If anyone asks, I haven't been here.' She said no other officers called and added that the police did not call at any of the other houses along the row directly overlooking the cemetery on the day of the attack.

I asked her if she could be sure that Stephen had left the cemetery at around 1.10p.m. She said she could be because she had seen the bus at its scheduled stop at the same time. Once again I had reason to thank Hulley's buses for helping to plot the course of the day's events. Back in the early Seventies, before the days of the two-car family and the regular school run by 'mum', most people in Bakewell knew the bus timetables like the back of their hands. But again I wondered why the bus driver and passengers had not been interviewed. After all, a woman was meant to have been battered to within an inch of her life minutes before, just over the hedge in the cemetery.

Finally Mrs Shimwell asked me if I'd spoken to any of the youngsters who were playing around the area that lunchtime. I recalled Ray mentioning something about children when we walked around the cemetery. Mrs Shimwell informed me that I should track down Ian and Lucy Beebe. The story going around at the time was that something had frightened them. They were only very young then. She told me they used to live along Burton Edge, but had moved away.

In fact, I discovered that the Beebe family had played a crucial, but often ignored, role in this murder inquiry. The eldest daughter was Jayne Atkins, a fifteen-year-old at the time who was half-sister to little Ian and Lucy, then aged four and seven. Jayne had appeared as the main witness at the Court of Appeal in London to give evidence in support of Stephen in October 1974. Ray and Nita's original bundle of paperwork contained documents relating to this appeal, which had been prepared just a few months after Stephen's conviction. I had had a cursory glance at them before and now looked in more detail.

The case was considered by the full Court of Appeal on 25 October 1974, when Jayne's new evidence was heard by Lord Justice Orr, sitting with Mr Justice Boreham and Mr Justice Shaw. Jayne told the three appeal court judges she had seen 'a man and a woman with their arms round each other' in the cemetery on the day Wendy Sewell was attacked. The man was *not* Stephen Downing. Minutes before, Jayne had seen Stephen Downing *leaving* the cemetery. She said the embracing couple were standing on the lower path, behind one of the chapels, not far from the spot where Wendy was later found bleeding to death. Jayne told the Court of Appeal that she had been afraid at first to tell the police what she had seen, for fear the man had recognised her – and that she might become a victim as well.

At a pre-trial hearing, the three law lords decided she could not be believed. They maintained that, had she been a credible witness, she would have come forward much earlier with such vital information. They therefore said her evidence was 'not credible' and rejected it. Downing's appeal against conviction was dismissed.

I decided to try to meet Jayne Atkins to see if her story had changed over the years. I was also keen to see the younger children, to find out what had frightened them. This proved no easy feat. Former neighbours told me the Beebes had moved house because they had been so terrified of reprisals after Jayne gave evidence to the Court of Appeal. They said the family had received several anonymous threats.

Back at the office, having spent the whole morning on the estate, I received a telephone call on my direct line. 'Been snooping around again, then?' a man's voice sneered.

'Who is this?' I enquired. It was not the same voice as before. This man sounded older.

'Never you mind. I tell you, Hale, that little sod got what he deserved.'

'OK, let's discuss it, then. How can you be so sure?'

'Discuss!' He almost spat out the word. 'You want to discuss? I'll discuss. I see your car on that estate again, you're dead.' He replaced the receiver.

This was getting more serious. I would not have liked Elsie to take *that* call. My heart was pounding and my thoughts immediately turned to Kath and the lads. What if this person knew where I lived? Not for the first time, I wondered what I was getting myself into.

Later that week I tracked down the Beebes. They were living on the outskirts of Chesterfield, a solidly working-class market town in north-east Derbyshire fringed on the west by the Peak District and surrounded on the other sides by industrial estates and former mining districts. If the town is famous for anything it is its church with the crooked spire. The Beebes had a council house in Renishaw, on the road out towards Sheffield. It was on a neat estate with well-tended gardens and several plots of allotments scattered between the blocks of houses. I guessed that many of its inhabitants had moved there from surrounding rural areas, priced out by the middle-class incomers who wanted a home in the countryside, but who were still clinging to a lifetime's habit of growing things.

Margaret Beebe opened the door to me. She was a heavy-set woman in her fifties, who greeted me with a friendly smile. When I told her the purpose of my visit she appeared enthusiastic and ushered me inside. She told me that the children, by now in their twenties and thirties, had all left home. She and her husband Ken were on their own.

Once she started talking about past events, her mood changed. She told me that she and her family had left Bakewell in 1977, moving first to Lichfield in Staffordshire before ending up here, about fifteen miles from Bakewell. She confirmed what I had been told – that they were forced to move because they believed their lives were in danger after Jayne gave evidence at the Court of Appeal. They had received anonymous threats for more than two years, and could take no more.

'The worst thing was, no one believed us,' she said. 'No one took us seriously, except for our immediate neighbours. We were just left to get on with it and deal with all this bother on our own. It was very upsetting. And terrible for the little ones.'

'So what happened that day, Margaret?' I asked.

'The children, that's my Ian and Lucy and their little friend Pam Sheldon, were out playing on waste ground, then in the cemetery, when something frightened them,' she told me. 'I think they told me at the time that somebody with blood on them jumped over the wall out of the cemetery and frightened the life out of them. They wouldn't go into the cemetery for a long while after that.'

'What time of day was this?'

'Ian and Lucy had come home at lunchtime from the Infants' School and were out playing on their bikes,' she continued. 'Then Ian came in as white as a sheet. He'd left his bike somewhere. He couldn't say anything at first. I sat him down on the couch. He was very scared and talked about a man with blood on him. He had nightmares for a long time afterwards. He couldn't go back to school and had to stay at home.' Margaret, sitting on the sofa next to me, was talking nineteen to the dozen, flailing her arms around like a windmill as she became more and more engrossed in her story. I had to duck several times. 'I put my little one, Adrian, in the buggy and took Lucy back to school,' she continued. 'As I passed the cemetery there were police and an ambulance. I remember looking, and saw them putting a body into the ambulance. When I went back home, Ian had messed himself with fright. I thought I'd fetch a doctor, then he calmed down a bit and said, "Mummy, that man got blood all over him!"'

'Were the police told about all this?' I asked.

'They came round on the Friday night, two days after the attack, but they didn't take any statements. Ian was in bed asleep, so they said they'd come back to talk to him. They never did, though.'

'And this was the first time the police came to your house? They didn't come on the day itself?'

'No, Friday was the first time. They didn't go to any of the houses on Burton Edge on the day it happened.' Margaret added that at one point that lunchtime, some time after ten past one, she had popped her head round the perimeter hedge of the cemetery to look for the family's pet dog. Her daughter Jayne had already gone out to look for it. Margaret had seen no one at all. A few minutes later, though, she remembers hearing a shout, something like 'Hey!' or 'Help!'.

'So it must have been a shocking experience for your whole family?' I continued.

'Well, later that day when I went to work at Cintride at six o'clock, I heard all about the woman battered in the cemetery. I kept Ian off school till the following Monday. But he continued to suffer with his nerves until 1977. Four years of misery until we moved to Lichfield. I had a breakdown after all this. Our family was called a pack of liars by the police. We only said what we saw. I used to work at Cintride on the 6–10p.m. shift. One night, when I was walking there on my own up Bagshawe Hill, a car came alongside me and slowed down. There were people in the front and back, and someone wound down the window and shouted, "You had better keep your mouth shut or else things will happen to you and your girl." I think this was after the trial but before the appeal. When Jayne gave her evidence the judges called her a liar.'

Mrs Beebe added one other interesting fact to my ever increasing portfolio of information – her husband Ken, a quarry worker, had been approached by a workmate during one of his breaks, some two or three years after the murder, who told him, 'It's a shame that Stephen Downing is doing time for someone else. I know who did it.'

This latter gem of information was typical of many statements I was to encounter over the next few years. If all were true, then the identity of the murderer of Wendy Sewell had been one of the worst-kept secrets in the Derbyshire Dales. The more I talked to people, the more it appeared that half the population of the town and its surrounding villages knew what had 'really happened' and were 'certain' who the murderer was. About half a dozen names regularly cropped up. I came to realise that in a small community back in the late Sixties and early Seventies, gossip and rumour spread like wildfire. Yet if you attempted to trace the rumour or gossip back to its source, a wall of silence would come down, the usual responses being that it was just 'something everyone's always known' or the more sinister 'I don't want to get involved'. Amazingly, I was to encounter tales of drunken boasting in the town's numerous pubs of men claiming to have been 'involved' in the killing. Many of these claims were contradictory. Yet one remark was uttered consistently: 'Stephen Downing didn't do it.'

I thanked Mrs Beebe for her help and asked if she could put me in touch with her three children, Ian, Lucy and Jayne. Ian and Lucy, she said, were a possibility, although how accurate their memories would be after twenty-one years was debatable considering their tender years at the time. She took my telephone number and said she would pass it on to them. She added that they both lived nearby. Jayne was another matter. Now a woman of thirty-seven, she had lived in fear for her life since she was a teenager. She was sure the person or people responsible for Wendy Sewell's death still meant her harm after all these years, because she had dared to speak out about what she saw. Mrs Beebe said she could not reveal Jayne's whereabouts.

Lucy Beebe, or Lucy Wood to use her married name, telephoned me a few days later. She was helpful and described the events as she recalled them: 'I went into the cemetery looking for my brother Ian and friend Pamela at lunchtime on the day of the murder. We used to play there all the time. We were little devils. We used to play with the flowers on the graves. Ian and I were playing hide-and-seek that day.'

'So did you see anything unusual on that particular day?'

'I saw Ian. He was pale and shocked, and I helped him back home. He didn't or couldn't say anything. I remember that it took him a while to recover. He even left his bike in the road. He'd obviously seen something that frightened him.'

'Did he say what had scared him so much?'

'He spoke later of a blood-stained man on the graves.'

I did not press Lucy further, or ask her any leading questions, as I wanted her memories to be untainted by suggestion as far as possible. So many rumours had flown around Bakewell for the past twenty years or more and I was acutely aware that someone who had been a child at the time could have come to believe half-overheard adult gossip or often repeated theories. I asked Lucy to get in touch with me if she remembered anything else.

I remained determined to speak to Jayne Atkins, and had been making strenuous efforts to discover her whereabouts, pressing her sister and mother to tell me where she was. The girl who claimed to have seen Wendy in the cemetery embracing a man after Stephen

Downing had left was a vital witness, whatever the appeal court judges thought.

Jackie Dunn, who had been eavesdropping on my call, obviously felt as I did. Once I had put down the receiver, she said, 'Don, we really must talk about Jayne Atkins.'

For the past week Jackie had immersed herself in the details of the failed 1974 appeal. Mrs Beebe had agreed to talk to her on the telephone. Jackie had spent hours questioning her about Jayne, and talking to the Downings about the case that had been prepared for the Court of Appeal. She had pored over newspaper reports and court papers from the time, as well as old police notes provided by my friendly informants in the force. They all confirmed that Jayne's evidence was rejected mainly on the grounds that several months had passed before she came forward.

I was delighted at my young trainee's enthusiasm. 'We'll arrange a proper meeting, Jackie,' I replied. 'We need to go through everything with the whole team.'

A few days later I met up with Alan Taylor, a presenter on Central Television, in a local pub, which had plenty of large tables and secluded nooks and crannies. He was a tall, wiry character – I always thought he looked in need of a good feed – who spoke in a slow and deep Scottish drawl. I had known Alan for five years and, during my time at the *Mercury*, we had co-operated on many stories. I outlined the case and my findings to date. Alan was particularly concerned about Stephen Downing's original statement and the amount of time he was detained without support. Over the next few days he began making some enquiries of his own and went to see the Downings. On his way back to Nottingham one day, he called in at the *Mercury* offices. Jackie got her chance to tell us about her research on Jayne Atkins. She filled Alan in with the background, explaining how Jayne was a fifteen-year-old girl at the time, living in a house on Burton Edge, the row along the top side of the cemetery.

'She had come home during her school lunch break from Lady Manners,' said Jackie, 'and was out looking for her pet dog. She remembered she had left the house after listening to the one o'clock news headlines on the radio. She had turned right along the path by the top of the cemetery towards the Junior School. Halfway from her home to the end of the cemetery there's a bit where the hedge stops and there's a wall. Just there, she looked into the graveyard and saw a woman near the Garden of Remembrance. In her statement she told police the woman was young and slim with dark hair and wearing a beige-coloured trouser suit with dark brown matching jumper. She didn't know her.'

She went on, 'Jayne continued walking along the path by the cemetery. By the beech hedge at the far end, she looked into the open fields beyond. Still no sign of her pet. The dog often went into the cemetery, so she decided to have a look in there. As she walked along to the side gate at the Junior School end, she remembers seeing a dark-coloured van, she thought it was brown, parked on waste ground close to the school. There was a man sat inside, a biggish bloke. Then she went into the cemetery and walked along the top path towards the workmen's store.

'When she reached the main drive, she saw Stephen Downing walking a good way in front of her towards the main gate. She knew Stephen by sight, as he lived on the same estate. He didn't see her. She passed the store at the unconsecrated chapel and, as she got about level with the little grass island near it, some movement to her right caught her attention. She glanced across and noticed the woman she had seen a few minutes earlier standing behind the consecrated chapel on the bottom path with her arms round a man. Later, when she saw newspaper photographs, she was able to identify this woman as Wendy Sewell. She told police she didn't know the man, but said he had sandy-coloured shoulder-length hair, was about five feet eight inches tall, wearing denim jeans and jacket.

'She couldn't see her dog, so she turned round and retraced her steps along the middle path. She then spotted the dog at the end of the cemetery near the far wall which bounded the fields and, after a few minutes, managed to catch him near the bottom gate. Whilst putting on his lead she heard the sound of a motor and, on looking round, saw that a white van had come into the cemetery. She left by the side gate near the school, and turned right towards her home. As she walked along the path she heard a shout. She couldn't see who it was because the boundary hedge at this point was about six feet high. She didn't think much of it.

'As she continued back to her house on Burton Edge, she saw Stephen again, this time walking back across the road and heading towards the main cemetery gates. She thought it must have been about twenty-five past one when she got home. She went back to school, and was late.'

Alan was fascinated by this witness. He had been scribbling down notes the whole time Jackie and I were speaking.

'She confirms Downing's own timings!' he exclaimed. 'Her account of seeing this woman in the Garden of Remembrance coincides exactly with what Stephen wrote to you, Don. And the time he left the cemetery, Stephen returning . . . it all fits. And the description of Wendy Sewell's clothing was accurate, although she could have got that from newspaper reports afterwards, I suppose. But why didn't she say all this at first?'

Jackie held the 'Jayne Atkins' file aloft. 'Plenty of reasons!' She was impatient to continue. 'In the Court of Appeal Lord Justice Orr made the point that she didn't come forward with her story for months after the murder, even though the police visited her house and asked if anyone had seen anything. She said . . .' Jackie paused and studied the paperwork more closely, searching for Jayne's exact words. 'She said . . . "I was afraid the man in the cemetery might have recognised me and I might be the next one!" Now we know the judges didn't accept this as a good enough reason for her keeping quiet for several months, but there were things they were never told about Jayne Atkins.

'For a start, she was only fifteen when all this happened, and a very vulnerable fifteen at that. I don't know the exact details, but she had quite a troubled home life. Soon after the murder, around early November, Jayne ran away from home. She was eventually placed with foster parents in Buxton. I know it's only ten miles away, but it would be like another world away from the estate and all the neighbours gossiping about the murder and Stephen Downing. She simply lost touch with developments on the Wendy Sewell murder case.

'That is, until she saw an article in the newspaper. She had a Saturday job at the Barbecue Café in Buxton, and *this* had been left lying on a table by a customer.' With a flourish, Jackie produced a copy of the *Derbyshire Times* from 23 February 1974. She turned to page six. There was the headline, YOUTH ON MURDER CHARGE FOUND GUILTY. The article began, 'Stephen Downing, aged 17, was found guilty of murdering 32-year-old typist Mrs Wendy Sewell in a cemetery at Bakewell, Derbyshire, by a unanimous verdict at Nottingham Crown Court last Friday.'

'Look at the last paragraph!' Jackie insisted.

We read on, passing the article among us. It ended, 'He had told the jury that he found the victim lying semi-conscious in the grave-yard after going home during his lunch hour, but the Prosecution said that his lunchtime walk was only an alibi after he had carried out the attack. Downing pleaded not guilty to the murder.'

'When Jayne read that,' exclaimed Jackie excitedly, 'she *knew* that Stephen Downing had told the truth at his trial. That phrase – "the Prosecution said that his lunchtime walk was only an alibi *after* he had carried out the attack" – she knew it wasn't like that. She had *seen* Stephen leaving the cemetery on his lunchtime walk. Wendy Sewell had been very much alive at that point. She had been in the arms of another man!

'It dawned on Jayne that there were probably only four people who knew that Stephen had told the truth – herself, Stephen, the victim who was dead and the man she had been embracing some time before she was attacked. The mystery sandy-haired man had not come forward, for whatever reason.'

'So is that when she went to the police?' asked Alan.

'Not straight away. It was in March. It kept playing on her mind, though. You see she'd always assumed that Stephen must have attacked Wendy later in the afternoon, after she saw him going back to the cemetery. I mean, the police were so confident they'd got the right man, that's what they kept telling everyone on the estate – "he's confessed, he did it" – so why should Jayne really query it? She'd only heard about the attack when she got back from school late that afternoon. No one had told her the exact time it was meant to have happened. And of course she was now terrified. This mystery man was out there somewhere. But who could she tell? Remember, she was fifteen, cut off from her family, and maybe she knew she wouldn't be believed. Eventually she told her foster-parents what she knew. Ironically, the foster-father was a Buxton policeman. He told her she should go home and tell her family and the police in Bakewell everything she had told him. So that's what she did. She then had to visit the regional HQ at Buxton and talk to CID officers there.'

'And did they believe her?'

'Well, partly,' said Jackie. 'Talking to her family, it seems the police basically believed her story about seeing Wendy with this other man, but they told her she must have got the wrong day.'

'Even if they thought she'd got the days mixed up, they should still have tried to track him down. If Wendy Sewell had been meeting someone in the cemetery and knew him well enough to be putting her arms round him . . . well, surely the police should have found out who he was,' Norman pointed out.

'Yes, but she *hadn't* got the wrong day,' persisted Jackie. 'It was the first day of the school term. Jayne was wearing her school uniform and had gone looking for the dog in her school lunch break. It couldn't have been an earlier day, because that would have been in the school holidays. And in any case, Stephen had been off with a cold for the previous two days. And it couldn't have been later, because Wendy was in hospital and then died. All they needed to have established was that Jayne was in her uniform and had been at school.' This was the point which Jackie had been itching to make.

It took several more visits to Mrs Beebe and telephone calls to Lucy, in which I stressed that Jayne's testimony might be vital in getting Stephen out of jail if I could convince the authorities to allow another appeal. Eventually I persuaded them to tell me where she was. Shortly after the 1974 appeal failed she had fled the country in fear for her life and by early 1995 was living and working in a small hotel on a Greek island. I was given a telephone number.

I got through to the hotel bar and spoke with a man whose English was limited. He put me on to an Englishwoman who happened to be there having a drink. I told her my name, explained that I was calling from Matlock in Derbyshire and needed to speak to Jayne Atkins who worked at the hotel. She asked me to hold on. She said she would try to find her. I fully expected her to come back with a negative response. After waiting a good five minutes, I was taken aback when Jayne answered. I explained who I was and why I was ringing. Her first reaction was one of complete shock that I had managed to trace her. This quickly gave way to fear that if I could find her, so could anyone else. I reassured her that her family had been very concerned for her safety in all their dealings with me and wanted to protect her. She needn't worry that they were giving out her phone number at random.

She then repeated the story she had told the Court of Appeal twenty-one years earlier, standing by it in every detail. She said she hadn't known him, but had got a good look at him and had been sure she could pick him out from an identity parade.

She said she was fearful because he knew who *she* was. 'Not only did I see him, he saw me,' she said. She knew he must have read everything in the newspapers about her giving evidence to the Court of Appeal at the time, and she confirmed that there had been nasty, anonymous threats made to her family. 'I was told to keep my mouth shut or I'd end up like Wendy,' she remembered, her voice trembling. 'And after the appeal I was warned there was a contract out on me and if I opened my mouth again I'd be shot.'

It shocked me to realise that this thirty-seven-year-old woman was still living in fear for her life, as a result of a murder which had taken place twenty-one years previously.

It was around this time that I was woken by the local police in the early hours of the morning to inform me that a large skip full of rubbish, which had been sitting on the pavement outside the *Mercury* offices, had been firebombed and set ablaze.

Pulling on my clothes immediately and arriving at the offices a few minutes after 3a.m. I was just in time to see a fire crew hosing down the skip. Luckily the flames had not reached the building.

I went home and, after a few hours of fitful sleep, struggled back to the office. As I arrived I was shocked to see that the front window to the left of the door had been smashed to smithereens. It was Tuesday, the busiest day of the week with the paper going to press the next afternoon. As if I hadn't got enough to do already, I thought to myself, knowing it would have to get boarded up immediately.

I unlocked the door and, switching on the lights, saw the floor strewn with broken glass, while a brick sat in the middle of the desk belonging to the advertising manager. It must have been hurled though the window shortly after the police and fire crew had left. I was grateful that the brick had landed in the early hours of the morning rather than the middle of the day. I saw that the mess was cleaned up and glaziers were busy installing a new window by lunchtime.

That afternoon the telephone rang in my office. The caller had again come straight through on my direct line. I recognised the voice from the last time.

'There'll be more to come if you don't drop this Downing case,' the man threatened.

'So you know about the skip and the brick?'

'You'll know about more than that next time! And mark my words, there'll be a next time. You might just get blown away.'

Down went the receiver again. I admit, I was scared. It seemed that, not only was the *Matlock Mercury* building a target for attack, but I was, too.

Reviewing my progess, it was clear that the identity of at least one person, placed near the scene of the crime, was proving elusive. Who was the running man? Two of the Defence witnesses at the trial had described someone running 'ever so fast' and 'in a terrific hurry' away from the direction of the cemetery. The testimony of one of these witnesses in particular, Mrs Louisa Hadfield, had been highlighted by the judge as indicating 'someone else might have been responsible'. It seemed to me that this line of enquiry had never been pursued. Mrs Beebe had told me that her children and their friend had also talked of a man with blood on him jumping over the wall of the cemetery, although Lucy Beebe had not mentioned this to me in her recent phone call. In addition to this, Marie Bright had seen a man 'coming over the top of the wall' out of the cemetery – the same man she had seen hanging around the gates an hour or so earlier wearing a bright orange T-shirt.

I called on Louisa Hadfield, now in her late seventies and a widow. She was a wiry, if not fiery, character who didn't suffer fools glady. She walked with a stick and appeared physically frail, but her eyes gained a positive expression as she revealed the events of twenty-odd years before. The day still remained fixed in her memory, like it did with so many people on the estate. After all, the murder was probably the most dramatic event that had happened in the town in their lifetime. We sat down in the living room of her house on Yeld Road, and I asked her to tell me what she remembered.

'Everything!' she retorted, quick as a flash. 'I remember it as clearly as if it were yesterday.'

'Tell me about the running man.'

'Well, I was out walking on Upper Yeld Road with my dog, Polly, when this big healthy-looking young man came running at me like a bat out of hell. I was frightened because he was running very fast, scared-like, and the dog didn't like him one bit. She went for him, and he went up on to the grass verge and looked right into my face.' She put her hand to her face, her palm inches from her nose, and stared into it as if to demonstrate how close the man had been.

'Can you describe exactly what he looked like?'

'Yes,' she answered, 'he was over six feet tall, fair hair, youngish. His hair was long in the modern style of that day, he was a well-built lad with denim jeans and a denim jacket.'

'Did you notice what colour T-shirt he was wearing?' I asked, mindful of the reference to a bright-orange T-shirt in Marie Bright's description of the man hanging around the cemetery.

'I didn't notice a T-shirt. But something that I did notice – he had blood on him. On the left side, underneath his kneecap, and some other scratchy marks on that side too. I remember blood in the shape of a horseshoe on his jeans. I could draw you a picture. As I said, it's as clear to me as if it were yesterday. I was very frightened. He scared the living daylights out of me. I thought he was going to hit me!'

This was fascinating stuff. The judge's summing-up had not mentioned anything about the running man allegedly having blood on him. Yet it echoed what the Beebe children had told their mother. 'So where did he go?' I asked her.

'He carried on running like a bat out of hell up the road, towards Lady Manners School.'

'Did you tell anyone?'

'I told my husband about it. He said not to get involved. But it worried me. I couldn't sleep after I heard about the murder.

Eventually he said, "Right, get your coat," and we went to the police station.'

'What happened there?'

'They didn't seem too bothered. They said they'd already got someone. He'd admitted it. They took my statement and it appears others had also seen this running man. George Paling had seen him as he was about to cross the road with his grandchild and I think he gave a statement too. But he didn't want to get involved.'

'Do you remember what time it was?'

'The twenty past one Hulley's bus had just pulled up at the stop.'

'Was anyone else about?'

'Well, just before I saw this man running, I'd seen George Pearson.' I remembered that George Pearson was one of the witnesses who had given brief written evidence at the trial, to the effect that Wendy had passed him on Butts Road on the way to the cemetery some time before one o'clock.

Mrs Hadfield continued, 'George was heading down towards the cemetery, maybe five minutes or so before I saw the running man. I gather George saw the running man too. He must have done.'

This was interesting. At the trial George Pearson had certainly not mentioned seeing a man running away, especially one with blood on him. I made a mental note to speak to Mr Pearson. 'So at what point did you think this might have had something to do with the murder?'

'My neighbours, Mrs Wilson and Mrs Corbridge, told me about the attack on the woman in the graveyard at about half past three the same day. I didn't connect this man with it, though, not at the time. I never gave it a thought.'

'So when did it dawn on you that it might be relevant?'

'It must have been a day or two after the event. I was sat here like I'm sat here today.' She paused and stared ahead of her, as if staring into the past. 'As I've said before, I was so upset and bothered that my husband said, "Well, that's it, lass. Get your coat and we'll go down." And that's what we did. We went to the police, but they never said much at all. They said someone had admitted it,' Mrs Hadfield repeated, shrugging her shoulders with a sigh of resignation. It appeared to me that it was a story she must have retold many times.

'So that was the end of it, then, as far as the police were concerned?'

Mrs Hadfield gave a wry laugh and got up. She shuffled over to a heavy sideboard and retrieved a yellowing newspaper cutting from one of the top drawers. Coming back to her seat, she thrust it into my hands.

It was a report accompanied by a faded photograph from a copy of the *Derbyshire Times* some twenty years previously. I turned to Mrs Hadfield with a quizzical look.

'I was looking through the *Derbyshire Times* one day when I saw this picture. My heart missed a beat. There was the blood-stained running man!'

She leaned over and indicated a figure at the centre of a group of people. At the tip of Mrs Hadfield's pointing finger was a smiling youth with blond hair. The caption underneath did not include any names.

'This is the man I saw running away,' she said, leaning back in her chair and leaving me to study the photograph.

I continued my questioning. 'This was after the trial, Mrs Hadfield. Did you tell the police?

'Well, I was down visiting at a block of flats in the town when I bumped into Ethel Wright who was a cleaner at the police station. She was at the flats visiting her brother-in-law. Anyway, I told her all this, and she went and told them at the police station. The police phoned up that night and asked me to take the picture in the next day.'

'So did you?'

'Yes. I knew I'd seen him and I knew it was him. I went to the police station, and had to go upstairs. Bobby Ernie Charlesworth was just sat there on the phone. He was a long time and didn't seem very interested. He took the photograph and just locked it in the cabinet.'

'And did they follow it up?'

'I don't know. Even at the time of the murder, the police never came round. That's what I could never get over. All along it just looked as though you were making it up or telling lies. I hadn't told a lie. It was the truth! That's why I went and bought another paper, so I could keep this. It's been in the drawer all this time.'

I asked her if I could take the cutting away to make some copies of it. I wanted one for my files, and I thought I would send one to Stephen. She agreed, but made me promise to bring it back. After all, she had kept it safe for all these years.

'So have you ever seen this running man again?' I asked her.

'Oh, I saw him up here just a few weeks *after* the murder, before all this business in the paper. He was walking on the other side of the road, and I opened a window to let him know I'd seen him. And when he went on further, I went to the front door.'

'Do you know his name?'

'I didn't at the time. Even when I found it out much later, after the newspaper picture, it meant nothing to me − it was that *face* I remembered. I'll remember it to my dying day.'

'What is his name?'

She looked me intently in the eye and gave me the running man's name. For now, I will call him Mr Blue.

Following my conversation with Mrs Hadfield, I attempted to talk to the other trial witness, George Paling, who also claimed to have seen a man rushing up Yeld Road in the direction of Lady Manners School at around the same time. Mr Paling lived on Yeld Road, but his house was much further up towards the school.

Mr Paling was very reluctant to speak to me. Now in his late seventies, he said he had given a statement to the police and his evidence had been read out at the trial. He did not want to get involved any further.

Fortunately, in the bundle of paperwork the Downings had left with me, I found a copy of the statement Mr Paling had given the police at 11.50p.m. on the night of the attack when they visited his home.

He said that at around 1.10p.m. on the day in question he saw 'a man hurrying along the road from the direction of the cemetery towards Lady Manners School. I looked at him because he seemed harassed. He was walking as fast as he could without running, his arms were swinging and his mouth hanging open. He was sweating and he looked queer − so much so that I nudged my wife to look at him. He then went out of sight along the road.'

Mr Paling had seen this man again some five or ten minutes later as he took his granddaughter for a walk in her pushchair along by Lady Manners School. His statement said: 'As I approached the main entrance to the school I saw the same man standing in the entrance, looking towards the school, and he had his hand on the wall. He gave me a glare and, because of his whole attitude, I gave him a wide berth, although he didn't speak. I carried on walking about three or four hundred yards and then turned round. On my return he had disappeared completely.'

The description he gave of the man jumped out at me: '28 to 35 years old, about 5′8″ to 5′9″, but on the stout side, dark hair, clean shaven, flushed complexion, no hat, clean looking. He was wearing a navy blue sports shirt and trousers, no jacket. I couldn't say what colour trousers, greyish if anything. He had a good head of hair, but not long.

'Thinking about it, I can't think where he went unless it was into the school grounds.'

Reading his statement, I was very interested in the description George Paling had given. The stout, dark-haired, smartly dressed man in his late twenties to mid-thirties and of medium height was nothing like the tall, fair, denim-clad youth of Mrs Hadfield's memory. In Mr Paling's statement there was no mention of blood. Nor did the description he gave match the man Mrs Bright and Mrs Richards saw hanging around the cemetery – their man wore an orange T-shirt, Mr Paling's a navy-blue sports shirt.

So why would two men be running or hurrying up the road in a state of agitation at around the same time of day? One obvious theory is that one was chasing the other. Another is that they were rushing to an arranged meeting place or simply, independently, getting away from the cemetery as fast as they could. A third possibility, of course, was that one or both sightings were totally unconnected to the crime. And fourthly, maybe one or both of the witnesses had not given a very accurate description. Yet I visited Mrs Hadfield several times during the next few months. Now more or less housebound, she still vividly recalled that incident, and her account of it never wavered. But I was aware she was an old lady and her memory might have been fallible, or the details of the story could have been embellished with constant retelling over the years, like a game of Chinese whispers. I added Mr Blue to my list of people to talk to. He now lived outside the area, but did not prove too difficult to find.

His reaction when I telephoned and put Mrs Hadfield's allegations to him was one of stunned silence. When he eventually spoke, it was to say, 'How on earth did you manage to track me down?' He went on to deny being anywhere near the scene of the crime. Mrs Hadfield, he said, must be grossly mistaken.

Despite Mrs Hadfield positively identifying Mr Blue as the Running Man, he was never interviewed by the police.

At ten to midnight, as Mr Paling's statement was being given to Detective Constable Bagshawe, Stephen Downing had been held at Bakewell police station for around nine hours. I found it interesting that, even at this early stage of the investigation, the police had been alerted to an unidentified man hurrying away from the scene, 'harassed' and 'sweating', at a crucial time. Yet it did not prevent them charging Stephen Downing that very night.

7

'GEORGE PEARSON' WAS also a name cropping up regularly. I turned to the trial notes again – he was the witness who claimed to have said 'hello' to Wendy at 12.50p.m. near the top of the Butts, about twenty yards down from the cemetery gates. Ray Downing had been urging me to read the copies of numerous police statements from the early Eighties relating to Pearson, also in his bundle of paperwork. At that time there had been a short-lived flurry of activity surrounding this case in preparation for the second appeal. I had not yet had time to study the statements in detail, but at a glance they had seemed to be from bar staff at an inn in Bakewell. Now Mrs Hadfield had raised more questions about Pearson.

He was interviewed by police shortly after the attack because several people had mentioned seeing him around the area.

He told them he was on his way home, and had not seen Wendy again after greeting her near the top of the Butts.

In 1973 Pearson was, by his own admission, a petty crook in his early thirties, who had recently served a spell in prison and had a reputation for drinking and womanising, pursuits which led to his regular involvement in arguments in local hostelries. He was said by some women of his age group I talked to, as having 'film-star good looks' at the time.

By 1994 he was still living on the estate, had married and was separated from his wife, and was now living with a girlfriend, Janet Brailsford. I was told he had fathered numerous offspring by various women, all living in the vicinity, and that he still enjoyed a drink – or three. He scraped a living doing building jobs, gardening, or painting and decorating.

I decided it was time to pay him a visit. During the last few months of 1994 I called several times at the small house on Moorhall, but he evaded all my attempts to meet him. Some of Pearson's neighbours, observing my visits and no doubt putting two and two together, told me George had had a brief 'fling' with Wendy. They said they had heard of this from Pearson's mother.

My trips to the estate were never wasted, though. People were beginning to wait for me to appear, so they could come forward to offer encouragement and information. Somebody told me they had seen a man making a phone call at around 2p.m. on the day of the attack from the phone box outside the cemetery gates. They thought it was odd, as he had been wearing gloves. I found it incredible that, after all these years, people could remember such details and were so eager to pass them on. Keen to help solve the crime, residents on the estate said any new information they had tried to offer at the time was usually rebuffed by the police's confident boast: 'We've already got him!'or, 'He's admitted it!' I was given the impression that the police had tried to 'rubbish' Stephen Downing's reputation by describing him as a 'weirdo' or 'Peeping Tom'.

The gossip about the victim didn't abate either. Many people told me that Wendy Sewell had quite openly been having an affair with a local farmer shortly up to the time of her death. The farmer, who we will call Mr Red, lived to the north of Bakewell.

An elderly lady approached me one day and thrust an old bit of card into my hand. 'Here,' she said. 'I've kept this for twenty years. You may as well have it.' It was part of a torn cigarette packet. On it were scribbled descriptions of vehicles, and even some registration numbers. She said she'd noticed the police around the cemetery at lunchtime on 12 September, and had found out later in the afternoon what had happened. She'd written down all the makes and colours of cars or vans she'd remembered seeing in the road that morning or lunchtime and taken the registration numbers of any still parked there. 'I was trying to find a policeman to give it to,' she said. 'I expected them to come round all the houses, but they didn't.' Eventually she'd offered this to a police officer near the scene. He'd turned it down. 'See if *you* can do anything with it,' she said, before shuffling off.

Another woman told me that during the lunchtime period of 12

September 1973 she had seen a fat man sitting in a brown van near the phone box. This rang a bell, then I remembered. Mrs Marie Bright, a couple of weeks earlier, had given me the same sighting. I also double checked with the old lady's fag packet. It was there again: 'Brown van, Austin make'.

Jayne Atkins had also mentioned seeing a brownish-coloured van parked close to the cemetery on waste ground along Burton Edge near the junior school end. She had seen a large man sitting in it. That was at about five past one.

In a small town like Bakewell it is difficult to remain anonymous. When I mentioned the brown van and the fat man to others on the estate, I was told almost unanimously, 'Oh, that'll have been Syd Oulsnam.' The name seemed familiar to me. It had certainly not cropped up in the trial notes, but maybe it was one of the names Ray had fired off at me at some point when he was mentioning people seen around the area. According to my informants around town – and there was no shortgage of them – Oulsnam was a familiar figure in Bakewell and the surrounding area in 1973. Aged about thirty at the time, he was a bit of an odd-job man and his brownish-coloured Austin van could often be seen along the local roads. He lived in the Ashford area. In particular, he was frequently seen on the estate, trimming hedges and cutting grass for the district council. Many told me he preferred a supervisory role. They often saw him leaning with his elbows on the open window of his van, watching others doing the work. He also did a bit of landscape gardening. I was told he still lived locally, and thought he would be worth talking to as he appeared definitely to have been around that day. I learnt that he lived at an isolated house on the outskirts of Ashford-in-the-Water with his sister and brother-in-law. I had been given directions and drove there on spec one day after visiting Ray Downing. It was a pleasant evening as I made my way out on the small road which climbed into the hills beyond Ashford-in-the-Water towards Monsal Head, an isolated beauty spot famous for its viaduct, which straddles a steep gorge. Unfortunately I didn't get as far as the spectacular viewpoint. Following my instructions, I came across what I took to be Syd's house. It turned out to be an old white cottage with flaking paint-work, which had obviously seen better days. Next to the cottage was an outbuilding, which was being used as a garage.

The door was opened by an elderly lady who looked very similar to the TV battleaxe Norah Batty from *Last of the Summer Wine*, with her rather unfriendly expression, dark, heavy stockings and a cardigan wrapped round her shoulders. She stared at me, seemingly surprised to have a visitor. She gave the impression of being very busy and was obviously preparing a meal. She also seemed protective of something, and didn't open the door very wide. Instictively, I looked beyond her and over her left shoulder. I could see some movement in the background and then saw a man scampering about.

'Hello,' I said. 'I'm Don Hale from the *Mercury*. Is Syd Oulsnam at home?'

She looked even more surprised and nervous, as if she was not quite sure what to say. 'Syd?' she queried. 'No, he's not home.'

I looked behind her again and saw the man grabbing a jacket. He looked to be making an exit to the rear. 'When will he be back?' I asked.

She seemed even more nervous and turned slightly, trying to look behind her as if waiting for reassurance from someone else. 'Syd,' she repeated. 'No idea, he's been out all day. Don't know when he'll be back.'

I felt embarrassed for her. Although I had never met Syd, the description I had of him seemed to fit the man in the hallway behind her. I was still thanking her for her time, and handing her my business card, when a van sped out from the garage yard next to me and disappeared off in the direction of Ashford.

'Wasn't that Syd?' I asked, waving to the driver, a large portly man – I was convinced it was him.

'No, he'll be home later,' she said, sounding rather dismissive.

'That looked like him to me, Mrs . . .' But she didn't want to give her name or details, or even talk to me any more. 'Ask him to call me please,' I continued. 'You have my card and numbers. Thank you.' She closed the door and I went back to my car grinning. It looked as if there had been near panic when I first knocked on the door. It was obvious Syd didn't want to talk with me at this stage. I decided I could wait, and made a note to visit him again a week or so later if I hadn't heard from him by then.

A week or ten days later I was in Bakewell again, so took a detour to Syd's home. I parked outside the property and poked my head around the corner of the yard to see if the van was there. It was, together with a couple of other cars. I knocked on the door and heard some movement and raised voices coming from inside. This time there was a delay in opening the door.

'OK, I coming. Wait a minute,' came a shout. A minute or so later the door was opened rather cautiously, and the same old lady glared back at me. 'Yes, what do you want?' she asked.

Just at that moment I heard a car engine start and again a van sped past me and drove off towards Ashford. This time I saw the driver quite clearly and gave him another wave as he drove past. Again, I was convinced it was Syd, and noticed that he looked rather stern and uncomfortable. The van rounded the bend and disappeared out of sight. It was certainly the same man driving, and certainly the same van as before.

I turned back to look at the lady as she tried to close the door. 'That was Syd, I presume? He seemed to be in a hurry. Did he not get my message?'

The lady was in turmoil. 'Syd will be back later. I'll tell him you called,' she said.

I offered her another card but noticed she already had mine in her hand. I assumed it must have been left near the door. 'I only want a chat. Ask him to call me please?' The door closed. I got back in the car and drove through the village to Bakewell keeping an eye out for Syd and his van.

I made a couple more attempts to visit without success. Despite the odd light showing and the sound of a TV or radio in the background, no one ever seemed to be home. If he didn't want to talk there was little I could do. However, a week or so later, Syd phoned the office and asked for me. He sounded nervous and a little breathless. In the meantime I had been busy about Bakewell and again had registered interest in his name with some of his known associates.

He asked me why I wanted to see him and innocently asked, 'I gather you've been round to the house?'

I asked him what he knew about the day of the attack on Wendy Sewell in 1973. I said his name had been mentioned as one of the workers cutting grass on the estate that day, and that he might have seen Stephen Downing. I told him I understood his van had been seen in the area.

'No, not me,' he insisted. 'I wasn't anywhere near that day.' He queried what day it was, which was strange after just giving me a categorical assurance that he wasn't there.

'Wednesday 12 September 1973. It had been a cold, frosty start, and then went warm in the afternoon. Wendy Sewell was attacked at lunchtime. Does that help your memory?' I asked casually.

'No. I was miles away from Bakewell that day,' he replied, stressing the word 'miles'.

'So you were nowhere near Bakewell cemetery? So how do you explain the claim that your van was seen there?'

He again sounded nervous and uncertain. 'No, not me.' He had a distinct Derbyshire dialect and was searching for the right thing to say. 'I was miles away that day. You must be mistaken.'

I asked if he had been questioned over the murder. He remained vague and claimed he had given a statement at the time, adding, 'So had everyone else.'

'And what did you tell the police Syd? Did you tell them you were miles away?' I challenged.

'Yes, I think so,' he spluttered. 'I went to them of my own free will. I wanted to put the record straight. People kept saying these things.'

'So people did claim you were there that day?' I demanded to know. 'And you admit you were questioned by the police?'

'I went of my own free will,' he repeated. 'They said it was nowt to worry about. They already had the lad that did it. Stephen Downing. A right little pervert. He killed her.' Syd had some power in his voice now and sounded quite defiant.

I hovered for a moment to keep him in suspense. 'So, Syd, just to confirm. You were not parked near the cemetery that day? You weren't in fact parked on waste ground at the back of the cemetery? And you didn't wave to a bus driver?'

He seemed very hesitant to reply. 'Not me. No,' he said with an air of finality. My call had certain shaken him and I felt it was probably just a fishing exercise at this stage. 'So that's it is it?' he said, trying to rush me. 'I've got to get on.'

'OK, Syd. Thanks for the call. Perhaps we can talk again?' I queried. 'Shall I come around sometime when you've a bit more time?'

'Yeah, maybe. I must go now,' he said, and put down the receiver.

Ironically, when I mentioned this man to Ray, he himself claimed to have seen Oulsnam driving his van down Yeld Road away from the direction of the cemetery, heading off towards town at lunchtime on the fateful day. Having completed his morning bus run from the surrounding villages into Bakewell, picking up several youngsters bound for Lady Manners School on their first day of term, Ray had driven back to the depot.

Ray had taken a coach trip of pensioners to Chatsworth House, and had arranged to pick them up at half past three, giving them plenty of time to tour the house and take in the grounds on this bright autumn day. He had decided to go home for a spot of lunch, and drove his coach back to Bakewell.

Making a ninety-degree left turn into Yeld Road, which led to the cemetery and the council estate, Ray was slowed by a scheduled Hulley's bus coming down the hill which had reached the same junction and was turning right. Bus drivers are notorious clock watchers, as their job demands, and instinctively Ray glanced at his watch to check that the other bus was keeping time. It was dead on 1.23 p.m. Ray figured that if the daily routine had gone to plan, his wife Nita would have just been dropped off by the bus further up the road after doing some morning shopping and would at that very moment be preparing him a bite to eat. The two drivers greeted each other with a wave and a smile.

At that split second a sudden movement caught Ray's eye. A man in a brownish-coloured van sitting at the junction in front of the other bus had also put his hand up to Ray. He had mistakenly thought Ray was waving to him. On looking closer, Ray recognised the van driver as Syd Oulsnam. He thought no more of it at the time. He recalled that, when he reached home at about twenty-five past one, Nita had told him he'd just missed Stephen. He was disappointed because he had wanted his son to see the new coach. Unaware of what was happening to Stephen, Ray had gone back to work that afternoon.

Ray asked me if I had had a chance to go through all the

paperwork he had left at the office. Shamefacedly I told him I had not had time to read all of it.

'Come across anything in there about Syd?' he asked.

I had to admit that I had seen no reference to the man so far.

Ray shrugged, and then went on to give me some further, fascinating information. He explained that on 19 October 1973, some five weeks after the murder, he had received a phone call from a young man who said he had been at the same school as Stephen, and who claimed to have some information regarding a farmer, Mr Red. The man was reluctant to give his name, but Ray was sure he knew who it was.

He explained that he had been speaking to a small boy who often hung around Mr Red's farm and enjoyed helping with the animals. He said the boy had told him that Mr Red had had a 'terrific row' with Wendy Sewell on the night before the attack, and had arranged to go to Bakewell the next day to 'try to put things right with her'. He said another man, Syd Oulsnam, was going to drive him there. Mr Red had told the boy all this. When the boy had next seen Mr Red, he had instructed him, 'If anyone asks where I was that day, say I was anywhere but Bakewell.'

The alarm bells started to ring. Wendy had told Ray she had some business to attend to in Bakewell that day. My mind was running ahead.

Meanwhile Ray was continuing his story. He said he had gone to the police and related the phone call to DC Oakes that very day, 19 October. He had managed to persuade his informant to tell him the name and whereabouts of the child who he said was making the allegations. He was the son of an acquaintance of Mr Red's, who lived in the area. I will refer to him as the businessman.

Ray told me he had to rush out on a taxi job. 'Go and have a look through that bundle I left you. You might find something interesting,' he said, cryptically.

It was late in the evening, after everyone else at the *Mercury* had left for the day, that I got the chance to settle down in my office and root through the Downings' paperwork. I rummaged through the mountain of cardboard files and scraps of paper, some left originally by Ray and others collected since by my own team.

I opened a thin file labelled 'Ervin'. This was a collection of work undertaken by private investigator Robert Ervin, who the Downings had employed for some ten years after the case. Ray had told me there was a lot more of Ervin's work somewhere, but that he had lost track of the man after his retirement and now he was dead. The file contained a few copies of statements and scribbled remarks, but no mention of Oulsnam.

I noticed a file with the title 'Police Documents'. Inside was another wad of papers. On top were a pile of police statements from bar staff at a local pub apparently taken in the early Eighties, but I couldn't see any mention of him. I continued thumbing through the rest of the papers, and was thinking of picking up the phone and asking Ray what he was on about, when two names emphasised in capital letters jumped out at me: 'OULSNAM' and 'MR RED'. Here was the van driver reported as being in the area *and* an alleged former boyfriend in one fell swoop! I extracted the piece of paper from the file. It was a copy of a memo dated 19 October 1973 – a month or so after Wendy was murdered. In it, Detective Constable Oakes of Bakewell Police reports on new information:

Raymond Downing, father of the accused, has received an anonymous telephone call from a youth who went to school with his son Stephen, that he has heard from a businessman that a farmer called MR RED had a terrific row with the deceased during the evening of 11 September 1973, and on the following day a man called Syd OULSNAM of Ashford gave MR RED a lift into Bakewell. And on that day MR RED should have gone to a sheep sale but did not, in fact, go.'

Sir, Sgt Hodgson and myself interviewed MR RED during the evening of the murder, who told us that he had been to a sheep sale all day at Craven Arms, Shropshire, having left early in the morning and returned home during the early evening. This was checked out by interviewing other people who had travelled with him to the sale.

The memo ended with a reminder to check on:

(a) The businessman
(b) Mr Red
(c) Syd Oulsnam of Ashford

in order to 'see what they have to say about this new story'.

I wanted to get this straight in my head – on 19 October Ray had apparently been given a tip-off about Mr Red's movements on the day of the attack. Yet the police had already questioned Mr Red more than a month before, on 12 September, just hours after the murder. I had recently been told that Wendy Sewell had had an affair with Mr Red before she was killed. Was Ray's tipster implying that the 'terrific row' the night before her death was some sort of lovers' tiff? I had heard stories from Ray, from my deputy editor Sam Fay and, more recently from my advertising reps and from general gossip around the town, that Wendy had had 'a reputation'. She was considered promiscuous. If this memo was genuine, it was concrete proof that one of Wendy's alleged former boyfriends had been interviewed on the night of the attack. I wondered what had prompted the police to pick him up. In a small town, it is likely that the local police force would have heard the same rumours and gossip. I supposed it was not unusual that they would want to eliminate her alleged lovers as suspects.

It seemed Mr Red had had an alibi for the day in question. I wondered if any other men she knew had been questioned?

I looked for more in the file, and found another memo from DC Oakes. It appeared he went himself the very next day to the cluster of little villages where the three men on his list – the businessman, Mr Red and Oulsnam – lived. He had made the following report of his visits:

At 2.15p.m. on Saturday, 20 October 1973, I saw the businessman, and there outlined the nature of the enquiries. The businessman denied having discussed this matter with anyone, or of having any knowledge of the alleged agreement as per telephone message (received by Ray Downing). The businessman stated that Mr Red had been at the Craven Arms,

Shropshire sheep sale on the day of the murder . . . and this has been confirmed previously.

At 2.30p.m. on Saturday, 20 October 1973, I saw Syd Oulsnam, Ashford-in-the-Water, and outlined the nature of the anonymous telephone call. He informed me that on the day prior to the murder, he had been muck-carting for Mr Red and that he knew Mr Red was going to the sheep sale the following day. On completing the work for the day, Mr Red told Oulsnam not to bother going the following day as he would be in Shropshire. However, Oulsnam went up past Mr Red's house the next day (day of murder) on the off-chance Mr Red would be there, only to find that he had gone (Mr Red's car not there and no one in). Mr Oulsnam denied having seen Mr Red at all on the day of the murder or of taking him down to Bakewell.

So far as related to Mr Red (his home contacted by telephone due to his suffering from infection) he still maintains that he did go to Shropshire to the sheep sale and his statement, corroborated by others, includes such details.

DC Oakes added his own opinion:

With regard to the alleged anonymous phone call which Downing claims to have received, I would be hesitant before ever accepting that any such call had been received. In the event of any further such calls being reported, I respectfully submit that relevant statements on file be referred to, before we go casting doubt among persons already interviewed.

There was something odd about the memos. They were typed out very uniformly on lined paper, which bore no official heading.

I saw Ray the next day and asked him how he had come across them. He said Ervin had traced them years ago, but had never been able to disprove Mr Red's alibi. Stephen had done these typed copies himself. He kept a record, in prison, of everything Ervin or anyone else had discovered. Unfortunately, said Ray, Ervin had kept the original copies. They weren't in the file he had handed to me. He didn't know where the rest of Ervin's files were any more. Ervin himself had died ten years previously.

I was dismayed. An alleged police memo copied out by the convicted murderer was not going to hold much sway. 'Look, Ray,' I said, 'I need to see the originals. I'll make a few checks with my friends in the force.'

Ray shrugged and looked disappointed.

I had already been given the official line from the police that no paperwork on this case any longer existed. I thought it was worth making unofficial enquiries. So I asked one of my regular police contacts if he could do some digging, especially on the Mr Red connection. Had this man ever been interviewed about Wendy Sewell's murder? I briefly outlined the memos I was looking for, mentioning the names of DC Oakes and Sergeant Hodgson, and the relevant dates.

The following week, in the dead of night, the offices came under attack. A lighted torch was pushed through the letterbox, setting fire to some mail and the carpet. We also suffered a couple of minor break-ins, yet on each occasion nothing obvious was taken.

The warnings prompted me to remove from the office my increasing portfolio of documents relating to Wendy Sewell's murder and Stephen's conviction. I ensured that they were scattered among family members, at the bank, or in other locations.

In the meantime, I asked around Bakewell to find out more about Mr Red. I already knew he was a farmer who lived near Ashford-in-the-Water. I learnt that in the early Seventies he had several other business irons in the fire locally, and employed half a dozen or so men at any one time on a casual basis. I learnt that Syd Oulsnam was one of the men regularly employed by Mr Red. It made sense, as they both lived in the cluster of villages just to the north of Bakewell.

Mr Red's various business interests had enabled him and his wife to build a new bungalow on the farm. It seemed Mr Red was doing all right for himself. He had married in the late Sixties. His wife ran her own business from the farm. The couple had no children by the time they separated in the summer of 1973. At the time of the murder Mr Red was around thirty years old and still living on his own. I learnt that he was fit, with youthful looks for his age, and had yellowish-blond hair. He remarried in the mid-Seventies. He is not a tall man . . . only around five feet five.

With the passage of twenty-one years, I wasn't really holding out any definite hope of my contact tracing any documentation, especially given police HQ's obstructive attitude to all my previous requests. I had almost dismissed any likelihood of the Mr Red memos existing when my informant got back to me. 'Got them, Don,' he announced cheerily over the telephone. 'Where do you want to meet?'

I felt like bursting into the Hallelujah Chorus. So now I had it in black and white on Derbyshire police headed paper from 1973, straight from the police's own records . . . confirmation that an alleged ex-boyfriend of Wendy Sewell's had been questioned by police on the night of her murder.

The same source gave me a statement from one of the men who had stated that Mr Red had attended a sheep sale in Shropshire. He was James Mellor who farmed at Netherow Farm, Chelmorton, near Buxton. The statement was taken on 27 October 1973 by DC Oakes, a week after his disdainful disregard of Ray's new evidence. Mr Mellor said,

I have known Mr Red for over ten years, and he has done a bit of building for me on the farm. On Wednesday, 12 September 1973, Mr Red called for me at about 8.45a.m. at the farm. He was driving his uncle's car and, together with his two uncles, we all drove to Craven Arms, Shropshire, where we attended a sheep sale. I didn't buy any sheep but both Mr Red's uncles bought about 70 sheep between them. I don't know if Mr Red bought any himself, but he made payment with one of their cheques for the sheep his uncles had bought.

We had our dinner at a public house at the sheep sale and left, arriving back here at home at about 4.45p.m. the same day. Mr Red was with me and his uncles all day. He didn't leave the sheep sale at all. We didn't stop off anywhere on the journey there or back, other than when we filled with petrol.

This broadly corroborated what Mr Red, the businessman and Syd Oulsnam had said. I noticed one small discrepancy. Mellor said Mr Red had been driving his uncle's car. Oulsnam said Mr Red's own car had been missing from outside his home that day. I did not manage to track down the statements from the uncles who were said to have gone to the sheep sale. Nor, indeed, have I ever seen Mr Red's original statement made 'during the evening of the murder'. However, I did discover that Mellor died in 1975.

I reported back to the Downings, who were pleased with my research.

DC Oakes's memo made it clear that both Mr Red and his alibis had been interviewed some weeks *before* Ray contacted the police on 19 October. For years, until the appearance of the memo, Ray had been under the impression that Mr Red had only entered the frame on the information he had given to the police on 19 October.

And what about the anonymous telephone call that had prompted the subsequent flurry of activity?

When I next spoke to Ray about it, it was clear that, even after all these years had passed, Ray still smarted at DC Oakes' dismissive comments at the end of the memo, especially since a few sentences earlier he had admitted Mr Red had been questioned within hours of the attack. Ray added, 'I'm not surprised the businessman denied any knowledge of Mr Red and Wendy having a terrific row. It was not the businessman *senior* who was supposed to have heard the argument, but his young son.' The detective Constable had interviewed the wrong person.

I felt I had to speak to Ray's informant, the youth who had made the telephone call, even though Ray had kept his promise to keep his identity secret throughout the intervening twenty-one years. I had great trouble persuading Ray to tell me who he was. Thankfully he relented, after I explained that we would never free Stephen unless people were prepared to stand up and be counted. The man Ray named was still living locally and was, by now, in his late thirties – the same age as Stephen.

I found his number in the telephone directory. His home was in a village to the south of Bakewell. I dialled and a rough, deep voice answered. I wanted to establish I had the right man and put to him the name Ray had told me.

'That's right, mate,' he replied. 'What can I do for you?'

'It's Don Hale, from the *Matlock Mercury*. I'm looking at that Wendy Sewell murder from twenty years ago in Bakewell cemetery. I believe you used to know Stephen Downing, the lad who was done for it?'

There was complete silence on the other end of the phone.

'Hello?' I said, after what seemed like an eternity.

'Don't know the man,' he replied, this time in a quieter voice.

'But his father says you rang him with some information before the trial. Something about Wendy Sewell having a row with a farmer, a boyfriend, the night before she was attacked?'

'I don't know what you're going on about. It's not me. Whoever told you this must have got mixed up with someone else.'

I asked him if he had ever heard of Mr Red or the businessman.

'I know nothing about any of this,' he said in a nervous, restrained voice. 'Now, if you don't mind, I've got to go. Sorry.'

Ray was disappointed. He assured me I had rung the right man.

It had been an absorbing few days but I'd come to a dead end. Nevertheless, I now knew that at least one other potential suspect had been questioned at the same time Stephen was being interrogated.

Clearly my investigations were still upsetting people. More worrying than the attacks on the office was a threat I then received at home. It happened at around ten o'clock one night. Kath and I were in the living room about to watch the news. I picked up the phone to be greeted by a silence. As I was about to replace the receiver there was a menacing laugh. Then a man jeered, 'We know where you live now. You and your family had better watch your back!' I couldn't be sure if it was the same voice. I didn't wait to find out. I put the phone down. I wasn't going to engage in conversations with people like that in my own home.

The message had been clear. Stop digging the dirt. It made me feel more determined to carry on, but I had to think of my family. I told Kath what had happened. She suggested we change our phone number and go ex-directory. But she said she would support me.

Soon afterwards I was to hear of another man who had been held in the cells for several hours that night: the victim's husband, David Sewell. This rumour was confirmed by one of my police informants. David Sewell had been mentioned briefly in press reports. I was keen to ask for his version of events. He was reluctant to talk with a journalist twenty-one years later – and particularly one who was seemingly trying to defend his wife's convicted killer. I felt a great deal of sympathy for him. He sounded quite hostile and wouldn't see me at his house, but agreed to a brief telephone interview.

I told him I was investigating Stephen Downing's claims of innocence, and asked him if he knew that some evidence never put before the jury had come to light concerning the murder.

He explained, 'No, I haven't heard about any new evidence. Nothing at all. I wasn't aware there was the slightest doubt from the start. A lot of do-gooders in this country are trying to make criminals look good. I was left in no doubt and the police were left in no doubt. How you hope to prove something twenty-plus years later is beyond me.'

I said this new information might shed more light on the murder. He disagreed. 'The police went at length through the evidence at the time. They were left in no doubt.'

I asked him if he knew if Wendy was meeting anyone in the cemetery that day. It was a question I had to put to him. He must have been aware of the rumours about his wife's promiscuity, and it was obviously a sensitive subject. 'No one,' he said indignantly. 'It was a very simple and straightforward situation. Her father had died a few years earlier. They never got around to putting up a headstone for him and she simply went up there one pleasant lunchtime to have a look at the gravestones. She just wanted to get some ideas. That's all there was to it,' he insisted.

I wondered, too, if he knew why Wendy had caught the early bus that morning. He said he couldn't remember now but added, 'She was certainly here when I went to work in Derby. I just don't know why she went at that time.' He then fired back at me, 'In any case, the police were well up on this fellow and the type of offences he'd already committed. There were no end of them.'

I asked him what on earth he meant. He told me he had spoken to PC Ernie Charlesworth who had assured him they had the right man.

'I'll quote from the police,' he replied. 'They told me, "We knew what he was and were waiting for him to do something to convict him." That was said to me at the time.'

I reminded Mr Sewell, 'If we're quoting facts, in court it was made clear he had a perfectly clean record and was of good character. There was absolutely no evidence to the contrary.'

He interrupted, 'He'd made a number of attacks but police hadn't sufficient evidence to convict him. They knew what he was going to do and were waiting for him to do it. I said to the police, "It's a pity you couldn't have sorted him out first." '

These innuendos and sometimes outright claims that Stephen was a 'little pervert' had cropped up on a few occasions, usually from people who didn't know the lad. I wanted to get to the root of them. I had found nothing in my investigations so far to prove, or even suggest, any such thing about Stephen.

Had the police told others the same story Mr Sewell had just repeated to me? Neighbours on the estate had certainly complained of being fobbed off with almost identical stories when they had contacted the police with potential information. Even now, over twenty years later, this was the line the police had come out with to my reporters when the matter was first raised.

The source of most of these smears on Stephen's character seemed to be PC Ernie Charlesworth. The estate was his 'patch' and I got the impression he had liked to throw his weight around – a big fish in a small pond.

I learnt from police contacts that three years previously, when Stephen was just fourteen, he had been one of several children questioned by Charlesworth about obscene phone calls and an assault on a woman. Stephen had been completely exonerated on both counts. Moreover, he was at a school presentation when the assault took place, while the real culprit admitted the offence after his ATC badge was found near the scene. The culprit received a rebuke and was let off.

Yet I got the impression these incidents seemed to have passed into accepted police folklore. The jargon kept being trotted out: 'Charlesworth wanted to nail the little pervo bastard'.

When I mentioned Charlesworth to Ray, he rolled his eyes to

heaven. 'Oh, him . . . he's the one Stephen made his confession to . . . funny, that, isn't it?'

A couple of days later I went round to Matlock police station to see the duty inspector. He had a uniformed sergeant with him. They wanted to know why I had become involved in this case after so long. I gave them a brief résumé and explained about Ray claiming an anonymous caller might have some fresh evidence. I also showed them a photocopy of Stephen's original statement. I asked them if it was right. The inspector glanced at it and handed it back to me without comment.

'Why, then, if this is true and he hit her twice, did the Prosecution say Mrs Wendy Sewell was struck seven or eight times in a vicious, violent attack? And was there ever any evidence of a sexual assault?' I persisted.

The inspector shrugged. The sergeant looked bored.

'He found her when he returned to the cemetery after a short break when he went home,' I continued. 'He was the one who found her and reported the attack to the gatekeeper.'

'Very convenient,' said the inspector at last.

'Convenient? What do you mean?'

'Sounds like he was trying to cover his tracks,' he said.

'But several witnesses saw him leaving the area looking normal, cool and calm, with no blood on him. I believe she was attacked during his absence.'

'As I said, very convenient. Happened when he was away, did it?'

'Yes, when you look at the timings. The police said the attack happened between 12.50p.m. and 1.08p.m. This latter time was set by the gatekeeper, Wilf Walker, and his wife. They saw Stephen leaving by the main gates at this point. So did other witnesses. But in any case, if the police say it happened before Downing left at 1.08, why wasn't he in a state – sweaty and blood-stained – after attacking this woman?'

Not a flicker.

I persevered. 'One prosecution witness, Charlie Carman, was heading back to town when he looked over the hedge of the cemetery and saw Mrs Sewell walking along a path. But Stephen had spoken to

Carman further up the road, when he was going up to the shop and Charlie was heading *towards* the cemetery. In that case she was still uninjured after Downing had left to go home.' I was the only one with any paperwork. 'What are you going to do?' I asked the officers.

'Do, Mr Hale? It's up to you. You are making the allegations. It's entirely in your hands,' replied the inspector.

I looked at them in amazement. It was obvious that I was going to have to continue with my own investigation and present them with more facts. 'I have a lot of people to see and a lot of work to do but I'll be back,' I said.

I was getting up from my seat and preparing to leave the interview room when I suddenly remembered. 'What's all this about Downing being a pervert? In court it was said he had a perfectly clean record. Is there something you're not telling me, Inspector?'

He looked at his colleague. 'Just the rumours,' he said. 'It was said he'd been questioned over a sex attack years before. One of our officers had been keeping a special eye on him.'

'Not Ernie Charlesworth? You're not saying it's something to do with him? The very same officer that Downing is supposed to have confessed to?'

'I'm not saying anything, Mr Hale. Now, unless there's something else?'

'No. Not for the moment. Thank you for your time. I hope to see you again soon.' I managed a smile and left the building.

The situation with the threats, phone calls and attacks on the office reached a climax just before Christmas.

I had been out jogging on a cold, dark night, along the A6 through Darley Dale on the road towards Bakewell. I noticed a sports car parked in a lay-by close to the Red House Hotel and riding stables and St Elphin's School. It was one of my regular routes and I often noticed the odd car parked without lights in the dark in a quiet, remote area. It could have been any courting couple. A few seconds, later though, as I crossed the main A6 road heading home, the car suddenly accelerated out of the lay-by and, still without lights, skidded towards me. Instinctively I jumped on to the pavement and watched it speed past. I stopped for a moment to gain my breath but it was some time later before I realised what had happened – I'd almost been killed. At first I put it down to my own negligence – I should have been more vigilant. I didn't really think at the time that people might be trying to kill me – that would be too far-fetched. But deep down I had a niggling doubt.

I told Kath and my colleagues at work what had happened. I think I wanted confirmation of what I already feared. They all said I should report the near miss to the police.

I therefore telephoned the local CID and was promised a visit at our newspaper offices the same morning. Shortly afterwards I received a phone call to say that the detective who had been due to call had lost his car keys so would not be able to make it that day. I felt like asking if he had lost the use of his legs too, as our offices were less than a ten-minute walk from the police station.

Instead I offered to visit the station later that day to register my complaint against the unknown car driver who, I believed, had deliberately tried to run me down. When I arrived at the agreed time though, I found all the CID officers unavailable. A young police constable informed me they had all been called out unexpectedly on a 'drugs shout'. No one had bothered to let me know.

I persevered, and gave my statement to the constable. I wanted to give the police every opportunity to re-examine the Downing case and had decided on a policy of keeping them informed about everything I learned. Unfortunately, my diligence did not elicit any praise from this young individual.

All this, and I still felt I was not quite ready to go public. I had not published one story about the case to date but desperately wanted to tell the world about Downing's claims of innocence. As soon as I did this I was sure I would get support. Or at least, I hoped I would.

It was at Christmas time that I made up my mind. I would present a portfolio of evidence to the Chief Constable, John Newing, to the Home Office and to the local MP, Patrick McLoughlin. If nothing else, I was determined to make people aware of the inconsistencies and anomalies within the evidence, and make public the facts which in my mind proved that others may have been responsible.

Kath supported me, but during the Christmas break her patience started to wear a bit thin when we kept getting calls offering information about the Downing case. I couldn't switch my mind off. I was making many calls from home, following up what I thought might be new leads.

The crunch came when, on a couple of occasions, the telephone started ringing in the dead of night. Kath is a light sleeper and answered it. Both times she was greeted by long silences. 'That's it!' she told me at four o'clock one morning. 'Leave this be till the New Year.'

So that was that. I vowed to push everything to one side and enjoy Christmas with the family. We spent Christmas Day in Manchester, visiting both sets of parents, and I managed not to mention Bakewell once. We both knew it was only a brief respite, but at that point neither of us could have imagined how this case would dominate our lives over the next seven years. I was determined to get to the bottom of things once and for all. I had reached the point of no return. It was certain to make for an interesting year ahead.

Just after Christmas I received this letter.

> 26 December 1994
> HM Prison
> 7 North Square
> Dorchester
> Dorset

Dear Don,

I would like to say thank you to you and your staff for taking an interest in my case, but above all for believing in my innocence. I appreciate that it is quite an undertaking for a small paper to take on, also in view of its limited number of readers.

I hope that I am able to help you with the investigation as much as I possibly can. I trust that what I have sent will be enough to get you started. Please feel free to ask more of me. I don't see why I should sit back and let you do all the work.

The more I look at the picture of Mr Blue the more he seems to be familiar, but for the life of me I can't place where I know him from. The only possible way I could know him is from school, though I don't recall him ever being a pupil at Bath

Street Boys' School in Bakewell.

I shall look forward to reading the statements you have from witnesses. What is the reaction from Wendy's husband about your investigating the case, also her mother?

Stephen Downing

January to June 1995

8

17 January 1995

IN THE MIDDLE of January Stephen sent me a first-hand account of his interrogation by Bakewell police. I had been eager to see this, ever since reading his confession statement. I wanted to try to understand what had been going through the mind of this naive seventeen-year-old, with the reading age of eleven, who had been questioned for nine hours without a parent or solicitor present. What had finally made him change the story which he had consistently stuck to for nine hours and confess to this most brutal attack?

Stephen wrote:

A few minutes after arriving in the police station I was escorted upstairs and shown into a room on the left of the upstairs landing. It was quite a large room and one wall was dominated by two large sash windows. The sparse furnishings consisted of two desks, four or five chairs which looked like dining-room chairs and a couple of filing cabinets.

I was told to sit on one of the chairs that had been left in the centre of the room. The uniformed police then left the room and Detective Inspector Younger and another detective whose name was Johnson came in. They immediately began to ask me questions. One sat in front of me at the desk while the other sat behind my right shoulder.

They took it in turn to ask questions. This went on for between 10 and 15 minutes before they got up and walked from the room saying, 'We'll be back.' As soon as they left the room a couple of uniformed police would come in.

On other occasions PC Ernie Charlesworth would come in alone. He would position himself just in front of me and would speak as if he was my father giving me advice. He told me that if I co-operated he would do what he could to make the penalty less severe.

As I was being questioned I looked out the window and I saw a workman up a ladder wiring something up. When I asked what he was doing, I was told the phone people were installing extra telephone lines as a result of the case – and he seemed to suggest this disruption was all my fault – as if I had caused the whole town and its inhabitants to change their well-ordered and disciplined routine!

I asked on at least two occasions to see a solicitor, and I also asked to see my family. I was told that I didn't need a solicitor as I was only being questioned, and I wasn't going to be allowed to see my family, although they did inform me that they would be told where I was. That was about 10p.m., or perhaps even a little later.

It struck me that Stephen had already been at the station for about eight hours at this point, sitting on a hard chair in a bare room while Johnson, Younger and Charlesworth took it in relays to question him. I noted the reference to Charlesworth, who seemed to be playing the 'good cop', the friendly 'father figure', alone with Stephen, trying to appear chummy and conspiratorial, dangling the bait of a 'less severe' punishment.

But why was Charlesworth talking of punishment? It appeared Stephen hadn't been cautioned or told he was a suspect. He had been in the police station at least eight hours. He had written and told me that 'I was told that I didn't need a solicitor as I was only being questioned.' I underlined that phrase in red ink and read on:

I have a feeling that even then they only contacted my family because they wanted me to change my clothes so that what I had on could be sent off for forensic testing.

I believe it would be about 11p.m. when my father arrived with a change of clothing, but he was kept waiting. I knew nothing about the call to my family or of his arrival. At the time I was alone with Ernie Charlesworth. I was cold, tired and hungry and in constant pain from my back. I had got to the end of my endurance and I finally gave up. I told him I would make a statement.

Charlesworth again!

As soon as I said that, Charlesworth left the room and within seconds came back with the other detectives. They then began to question me further. Moments later my father was shown into the room. I was asked to change into the clothes that had been brought for me. Charlesworth remained by the door watching every move and I could see he was hanging on to every word that passed between me and my dad.

I vividly recall my father asking me if I had done it and I said I had. He told me that he was proud of me for having the guts to admit it, though not for what I had done. It was all so confusing. One moment he was proud and the next he wasn't. I don't think we were allowed more than about ten minutes together before he was asked to leave. He said he would be back soon and would get a solicitor.

Younger and one of the other uniformed police officers came in and I was asked to make my statement. I was asked if I would like to write it or have someone write it for me. I was deeply embarrassed at my poor spelling so I asked them to write it for me. I only learned later that this was another foolish error on my part.

I took the view that the woman would be able to tell them who it was that had attacked her or at least give some kind of description, so there would be no harm in fabricating parts of the jigsaw.

I stopped reading and again scored a thick red line under the last sentence. It was so important to remember that, at this point, Stephen had not confessed to murder, just grievous bodily harm Wendy Sewell was still alive. For a naive youth who was 'cold', 'tired', 'hungry', 'in constant pain' and 'at the end of my endurance', there was some kind of logic in his thought process. The victim would be able to tell the police it wasn't him who attacked her, so there was 'no harm' in confessing. It probably seemed a small price to pay for a good night's sleep at that point. Anything to get off that hard chair and rest his back, without having to go over and over the same questions and answers.

Stephen continued,

Younger began by asking me to tell him what happened while the uniformed guy wrote it down.

During the course of the statement being taken I was stopped, and Younger made a few 'suggestions' and led me on several occasions saying that it would mean the same but it would 'read' better. It may seem unlikely that I could allow myself to be so foolish or naive, but I only had the reading ability of an eleven-year-old. It's only now when I look back at some of the letters I wrote to my solicitor, or the forms I was required to fill in, that I realise just how backward I really was.

I guess it would be well after midnight by the time I dictated my statement and they persuaded me to believe that what they had suggested would be the best wording – if only to suit them. I was so tired in the later stages of my questioning that Younger put his hand on my shoulder twice to wake me up, or just to shake me.

I was becoming increasingly disturbed by this account. Stephen was accusing the police of putting words into his mouth. He was suggesting that he had been too naive and confused to understand what was happening. His claim of being shaken to prevent him dropping off to sleep had been mentioned in the newspaper reports of the trial. Had the jury simply not believed him? The judge, I remembered, had seemed to be at pains to point out that a confession taken under conditions of 'oppression' would have no value.

Stephen's account continued,

I think a uniformed officer wrote it down. He wrote it down in pencil and read it back to me. Afterwards I was given a ballpoint pen and asked to sign it. At the time I didn't realise the full implications of what I was signing. I hoped they would let me rest and either continue the following day or find out from Wendy who her attacker was.

If I had actually carried out the attack, I wouldn't have lied about the number of blows. A number of witnesses saw me leave the cemetery with my pop bottle in my hand and without a single blood-stain on my clothes. The police seemed to think I was capable of committing such an act and walking away calmly.

I had consistently pointed out these absurdities in Stephen's confession statement. He said he had hit her twice, but the Prosecution's own experts agreed she had been struck seven or eight times. And after that 'frenzied' attack, where was the blood on Stephen's clothes? There was hardly any. I had seen them with my own eyes a few weeks previously.

When I read the statement later I knew there were things in it that I should change, but my reading was poor and I was very embarrassed. I had been told I would be questioned all night if necessary, and I just wanted it all to be over so I could get some sleep. I know it sounds silly now, but I knew I hadn't done it and that I wouldn't be kept in for long. I was very naive.'

I took up the trial notes again, to compare the police version of the interrogation with that given by Stephen: the police evidence began in the cemetery with the arrival of PC Ball, who tried to give Wendy first aid. This was around 1.42p.m. He described Stephen as being 'very excited' and added, 'I told him to calm down.' This contradicts all other descriptions of Stephen's demeanour in the cemetery.

PC Ball said he noticed 'three small spots of blood on the left forearm, inside', of which Stephen remarked, 'These came when I turned her over'.

He claimed Stephen told him three times, 'It isn't me, honest, it isn't. Don't blame me, I haven't done it.' Stephen denied saying anything like this.

A further point of conflict concerned the pickaxe handle. PC Ball insisted Stephen had said, 'I have been using that pickaxe today, but it wasn't me . . . I had it earlier . . . just the handle.' Stephen vehemently denied ever having said this and later told the court he had, in fact, said he had not used that particular pickaxe for three weeks.

Detective Inspector Robin Younger had then taken the stand. The account Stephen had given to him in the cemetery was the same as the one he gave at trial. Younger had asked him if the marks on his arms were blood and he replied, as before, 'Yes, I got it when I turned her over.'

Twice DI Younger had asked if he had seen anyone else around and twice Stephen had replied, 'No.'

The questioning then moved on to the police station.

At 6p.m. DI Younger tried to clear up the point of the pickaxe handle. He said, 'You told one police officer you last used it three or four weeks ago and another that you used it this morning. Which is right?' Stephen replied, 'I didn't. I told them three weeks ago.'

Later, at around 9.30p.m. Younger again questioned Stephen and pointed out the blood-staining on his clothes and boots.

Why, I wondered, had it taken Younger so long to refer to the blood-staining on Stephen? I didn't really need to ask myself that question – the answer was obvious. It was because there was hardly any blood on him. I'd seen the same clothes with my own eyes. So they'd had their main suspect sitting in front of them for more than seven hours, he'd supposedly attacked a woman with a pick shaft in a vicious and prolonged frenzy, and he had a few spots of blood on him which they'd only just thought to mention.

I looked again at the summary. Soon after that, Charlesworth had taken over the questioning. Charlesworth told the court that Stephen described leaving the cemetery 'just before one o'clock'. Stephen said he had told him he left 'after one o'clock'.

It had earlier been established that Stephen had left *after* one, so Charlesworth was telling the court that Stephen had lied, the inference being that he was trying to establish an alibi.

Younger then returned. He described to the court the following exchange which occurred between himself and Stephen at this point:

'I have been making further enquiries . . . I think you know more than you say. I think you attacked her.'

'No.'

'From enquiries I have made there are inconsistencies in your story. Firstly, you have told police officers the last time you used the handle was three weeks ago. You also told them you used it this morning. Which is right?'

'I told them three weeks ago.'

'When I first saw you this afternoon you said you had not seen this woman prior to your finding her lying unconscious. Well, now you are saying that you saw her when you were going to the shop for the bottle of pop. Which is right?'

'Well, I saw her.'

'The third thing is that question of the time you got home.'

At this point Charlesworth, in the pattern that had been set, took over the interrogation. He described the following exchange to the court:

'Well, you've heard what's been said to you. When did you first see this woman and where?'

'She was walking towards the school. I saw her before I went to the shop.'

'You haven't been telling us the truth, have you? It was you who assaulted this woman, wasn't it?'

At this point in the summing up Mr Justice Nield told the jury, 'Then came this dramatic moment, as it is said, "I did do it, but I don't know what made me." Then he started to cry.'

Charlesworth had fetched Younger, as the senior officer, at this point. Younger took over. He told the court of the following exchange, which resulted in Stephen Downing making his confession statement:

'Is it correct that you are now telling Mr Charlesworth you *did* assault this woman in the cemetery?'

'Yes.'

'What made you do it?'

'I don't know.'

'How did it happen?'

'Well, I just hit her hard.'

'I believe there is a little more to it than that because of the condition of her clothing and so on. Did you take her clothes off?'

'Yes.'

'Why did you do that?'

'I don't know.'

'Did you touch her?'

'I might have done.'

'Where did you touch her?'

'On her breasts first.'

'Then where else?'

'Down here' – pointing to the lower part of his body.

'What did you do, Stephen?'

There was no reply.

'Was there anything else than just touching her down there?'

He shook his head as if to say 'yes'.

'What did you do then?'

'I pushed my middle finger up her vagina.'

'Did you attempt to have sexual intercourse?'

'No.'

'Going back to the start, what did you hit her with?'

'Well, the pickaxe handle.'

'Where did you get it from?'

'The chapel.'

'Did you follow her around the cemetery?'

'Yes.'

'Why?'

'I don't know?'

'Did you intend to knock her unconscious?'

'Yes.'

'How many blows did you hit her with?'
'Two."

The judge stopped here in his summing up to reiterate the point made by the Defence: 'Eight or more blows are spoken of by the doctor.' He also queried whether Stephen would have used or understood a 'technical' word like 'vagina'. He suggested to the jury that when they first read this in the statement they might have thought to themselves 'I don't know, this is a strange sentence . . .'

The description of the interrogation continued:

'Did you hit her hard?'
'Yes.'
'Did you realise it was dangerous?'
'Yes.'

Stephen, at this point, was asked to make a written statement. The judge drew the jury's attention to it. Mr Justice Nield reminded them, '*The crown must establish that the statement was voluntarily made and no oppression was used.*'

I was astounded by what I had just read. The confession seemed to consist of one word answers, silences, gestures, nods, blank responses, and at one point a shaking of the head which to Bakewell police signified 'yes'!

At the trial Stephen's evidence had, it seemed to me, raised serious doubts in the judge's mind regarding the method of interrogation. His summing-up went on to describe how Stephen, when asked in court why he had confessed, had replied:

I was tired, hungry and my back hurt, and I was only just able to keep awake. I have had trouble with my back for two years after a fall at school. Mr Younger, in fact, put his hand on my shoulder twice to wake me up, or rather to shake me. I signed the written statement. It was untrue. I made it because they said they would question me all night if necessary, and I did not realise Wendy was very badly hurt. My statement was read out to me. I was *told* to make it, that is the impression . . . it was not of my own free will.'

He went on to claim that one officer had said he would bet his wages that he would admit it before the night was out.

Mr Justice Nield made several pointed remarks. He reminded the jury that the questioning had gone on at the station for eight or nine hours, and continued:

As the hours wore by this young man became tired, and you may have little hesitation in concluding that if a suspect is falling asleep and having to be shaken, it is no time to continue interrogation. That is bordering, you may think, on oppression if he is not given food and the rest of it . . . what was put, you see, there was this condition of tiredness . . . one officer had said, 'Admit it. We know you've done it.' Another said, 'You will be questioned all night.' Another said he would bet his wages he'd admit it . . . Those questions would seem to indicate the suggestion of some measure of impropriety.'

However, the judge went on to point out that 'when he was cross-examined, he agreed he was not starved in the station. He also agreed he had not told anybody his back was hurting.'

Furthermore the police officers, under cross-examination, had firmly maintained that it was 'nonsense' to suggest that Stephen did not know what was going on, or that he was falling asleep.

The judge then made what I regarded as perhaps the most telling point of all. He said, 'In spite of those questions Mr Barker, on behalf of the Defence, made the comment: "*I allege no impropriety on the part of the police.*" '

Well, there you had it. If Stephen's own lawyers were, for whatever reason, unwilling to argue with the police's methods of extracting this confession, what chance did Stephen have?

I had needed to know for sure why Stephen confessed to the attack, instead of sticking to the story which he had told to everyone at the crime scene. Having read both these accounts, it was all beginning to make sense. I came to the conclusion, from what he had told me of the nature of his interrogation, that this alone would provide adequate grounds for an appeal and would constitute the 'oppression' referred to by the judge at the trial.

My research had unearthed two psychiatric reports on Stephen Downing, both prepared before his trial in February 1974. They seemed to confirm the conclusions I had come to.

On 29 November 1973, Dr A. R. Jones, a consultant psychiatrist at Scarsdale Hospital, Chesterfield, stated,

Downing was questioned by the police first of all as a witness and then as a suspect. He was then taken to the police station and questioned by the same policemen with another policeman present and this continued from about 2.30p.m. until 1.30a.m. the following morning.

On one occasion during the questioning, he was shaken by the shoulder of his jacket very briefly by one of the policemen. His clothes were taken from him, and then he asked if he needed a solicitor, but told me that the police said this was not necessary. The police then took a statement.

He became a gardener at the cemetery and had been in this employment for about seven weeks. He was probably of low intelligence. I could find no evidence of mental illness.

I interviewed first of all his mother and then his father. She described him as being a 'little bit backward', but considers that he was quite good at subjects where he used his hands, such as mechanics and art. She confirmed he lost his first two jobs because he would not get out of bed in the morning. She described him as being of a 'gentle nature', very fond of animals and frightened of spiders. She also said her son had told her he did not in fact attack this woman but had made his statement because the police kept on at him and he was almost dropping off to sleep.

His deputy headmaster described Downing as a 'lazy child with a low IQ, always late for school, and a loner'. He was not a bully and he did not bully others. He did not exhibit behaviour which suggested there was a violent side to his nature.

I asked him why he had made a statement to the police admitting this offence. He told me the policemen had informed him that he would be charged with attempted murder and he did not think there was anything else he could do.

One can imagine the possibility of a tired, frightened youth making a false confession under pressure. He said he had not been frightened or pressured except on the one occasion when the policeman shook him briefly by the shoulder of his jacket.

No one is entirely satisfied with any definition of psychopathy. If in fact Downing committed this offence, I would place him in this category and consider him to be suffering from a mental disorder as defined in the Mental Health Act. I have some slight misgivings on this score, however, in that I think it would be unusual for the psychopath to commit a major offence without previously having given some indication of anti-social tendencies of violence.

Stephen Downing was again examined, this time on 1 February 1974, by Dr J. C. M. Wilkinson, who was a consultant psychiatrist at the Pastures Hospital in Derby. His report stated,

It is not surprising from my point of view, that after being arrested and questioned for many hours, probably feeling cold and hungry and having difficulty in expressing himself, he should ultimately confess in order to escape from the worst experience of harassment he had in his life.

Having confessed, he was immensely influenced by the fact that his father, far from rejecting him, stood by him and told him how proud he was that he had, at least, owned up under very difficult circumstances.

When the victim died and Stephen realised he could not be exonerated by her naming the attacker, from what he says, he seems to have resigned himself to being a victim himself, until his father made it clear to Stephen he *did not* believe him to be guilty. Stephen Downing at this point cried and stated thereafter he had *not* committed the crime.

Stephen Downing does not suffer from any psychiatric disorder. There is no evidence whatsoever in his past to suggest that he suffers from a personality disorder, nor that he has any abnormal sexual or aggressive urges.

On the contrary, his life history would seem to indicate that it is highly unlikely that someone with his passive personality would impulsively attack a female and then proceed to sexually assault her.

These reports could have greatly added to Stephen's claims of oppression during the initial police interviews, mentioning, as they did, his 'low intelligence', 'passive personality' and 'the worst experience of harassment he had in his life', but the contents of neither report were revealed to the jury until *after* they had reached their 'guilty' verdict.

Why weren't they used as part of his defence?

I was interested to read Dr Wilkinson's assessment of why Stephen took thirteen days to retract his confession – how he was 'immensely influenced' by his father who had said he was proud of him for admitting to it – I remembered that Stephen himself had found this 'so confusing' – and how he had 'resigned himself to being a victim' until Ray made it clear he believed him to be innocent.

I asked Ray about the conversation at Risley, when Stephen had first told him he hadn't done it.

'In my heart, I knew Stephen hadn't killed this woman,' he said. 'Initially I told him I was proud of him for admitting to it, but as things progressed I became convinced he was innocent. One day during my visit to Risley I said to him, "Stephen, why do you keep saying you've done it?" At this he broke down and told us the truth.'

I told Ray that Stephen had sent me an account of his interrogation at Bakewell Police station which I hoped to use as grounds for an appeal.

Ray agreed. He said he and Nita had visited the police station several times during the late afternoon and early evening while Stephen was being held, and were repeatedly prohibited from seeing him. 'They kept saying he was just helping with enquiries,' he said. 'They assured us he would be home soon and there was nothing to worry about. We kept going back and forth but still they wouldn't let us near him. There was nothing else we could do. Eventually, we were asked to bring a change of clothing. The police wanted to do some forensic tests. We could hardly say no. It was only after he had made this so-called confession that we were finally allowed to see him.'

I believed there was much more Stephen could tell me about the day in question, especially those hours spent in the police station, if only I could meet him face to face. The next day I applied for a visiting order to Dorchester prison.

I was sick and tired of hearing various witnesses going on about the great Ernest Charlesworth. His name kept cropping up. Most people trotted out the same script. Ernie always said Downing was 'a right little pervert' and that he had been watching him for such a long time and was just waiting for him to do something. This same rubbish had been told to the victim's husband, David Sewell. Even worse, Charlesworth appeared to have dismissed a considerable amount of fresh evidence presented to him in the early days, including that of Mrs Hadfield and her claims about the running man.

I decided to confront him. I learned he was now retired and working as a part-time court bailiff. It made me smile to myself as it dawned on me that Ray and Nita had been referring to Charlesworth when they mentioned a none-too-friendly bailiff who lived in the area on my first visit to their home.

I went round to his home in Bakewell and knocked on the door. As he opened it, he could see it was me and tried to shut it again quickly. 'No you don't,' I shouted. 'I want a word with you.'

'No comment, I can't say anything,' he squealed, sounding like a frightened mouse.

I stuck my foot in the door so he couldn't quite close it. I thought, here's an old police bully too afraid to face me. I tried to talk to him. He became agitated. He refused to answer any questions.

I tried again on a second occasion. He said he had been *told* not to talk to me. He seemed nervous and was deliberately evasive. A bully often backs down when confronted and I was determined to fire difficult questions at him. I got no answer.

A few days or so later, some of the beat bobbies in Matlock were having a pop at me about Charlesworth. They said he'd sent me away with a flea in my ear. That seemed to be the tale he'd told his police mates. When I heard this again from one of my 'friendly coppers', I thought I'd try to confront the old sod again. I believed he was involved with a darts contest or something for Bakewell Carnival, where he was doing some charity work. I'd heard the Carnival Committee were meeting in a particular pub one night and decided to go along to see if I could have a word with him after their meeting.

I went into Bakewell quite late in the evening and found Charlesworth by this time propping up the bar and surrounded by some very big lads who all looked as though they were ex-job. I was fairly angry after hearing about this 'flea in my ear' stuff and beckoned to Charlesworth to come over. I told him I needed a word. He sauntered over, looking smug and confident. But when I told him he was a 'liar', he turned almost purple with rage.

There was a sudden buzz around the bar and some nasty looks were exchanged.

'Sent me away with a flea in my ear, Ernie? Is that right? At least that's what you told your police mates,' I challenged. 'I gather you didn't tell them you were scared of talking to me? Had to hide behind your front door? Refused to speak? I just want to know the truth, Ernie – you can tell me in front of your pals. What did you used to say about Downing?'

He looked daggers, as did the rest of his group. They were muttering to each other. Someone mentioned about sorting me out, and I suddenly realised they were probably *all* ex-coppers. I was already public enemy number one in Bakewell cop shop. I was anxious, though, to destroy his hard-man image once and for all. 'Come on, Ernie. Surely you can tell me the truth now?'

He swore under his breath and mumbled something about still not being able to talk about the case. Official secrets. 'It'll all come out later. Downing's guilty. He admitted it to *me*,' he said.

'So did you caution him and read him his rights, then?' I challenged.

He turned away.

'OK, Ernie, I get the message. I've not changed my opinion of you one bit. You've a lot to answer for. One day I'm going to put you on the stand. Until then, I hope you can live with yourself.'

With that I turned and left.

9

I HAVE REPORTED ON several murder cases and, quite often, the key to understanding the crime lies in the circumstances surrounding the victim. Was the murder of Wendy Sewell due to a chance encounter? If not, why had she been so savagely attacked? Who was she and who else was involved with her? Did she have any enemies? Did she have problems at home or work?

Wendy Sewell was beginning to feel like the forgotten piece in the jigsaw. It was important to tell myself continually that, although Stephen appeared to have been the victim of a terrible miscarriage of justice, Wendy had been the victim of a brutal attack.

If I needed any reminder, it came when Ray showed me police photographs taken at the scene of crime and of Wendy after the life had been beaten out of her. The horrific images will stay with me for ever. Her frail and battered body, covered in deep bruising down her back, ribs and legs – and the back of her head bludgeoned to a pulp and vainly stitched together – brought the grim reality of her death home to me. She looked emaciated, so unlike the picture of the almost plump, smiling woman which appeared in newspaper cuttings. Wendy's injuries were so severe, that it was no wonder one of the workmen had been unable to tell if he was looking at a man or woman. I thought these appalling wounds could not have come from a pickaxe handle alone. I was certain she had also been given a severe and prolonged kicking. It was an attack totally without pity. The gruesome evidence before me graphically illustrated the ferocity and intention of its perpetrator. He seemed to have had one aim – to kill this young, defenceless woman.

I believe those spine-chilling photographs marked a watershed for me. If I ever had the slightest doubt about Stephen's innocence, the pitiful sight of Wendy Sewell's crushed and broken body dispelled it. This was not the action of a mild-mannered, simple-minded youth who had stumbled over his one-word answers before confessing to hitting this woman a couple of times on the back of the head.

Reports of the trial from old newspaper cuttings portrayed the victim as a young, married typist whose lifestyle was nothing out of the ordinary. The Home Office files on the case made more interesting reading:

> The victim, Mrs Wendy Sewell, was married to David Sewell in March 1964. The marriage was not a success, however, and in September 1967 she left her husband and moved into lodgings. Subsequently, she formed associations with other men and, although she and her husband were reconciled in July 1971, and from then on lived together reasonably well until the time of her death, Mrs Sewell continued to associate with other men.

The gossip about Wendy Sewell had begun as soon as I started my investigations. In a town of just over 3,000 people in the early Seventies, everyone knew everyone else's business. Nothing much had changed since then.

Now, nearly three months later, I had been provided with an extensive list of supposed boyfriends and lurid tales of how Wendy would slip a Mars bar into the hand of the latest man to catch her eye to signal her interest in him. The scandal surrounding Mick Jagger and Marianne Faithful had obviously impressed the inhabitants of sedate, rural Bakewell in the early Seventies!

The gossip would reach me in pubs, in the street, or anywhere I chanced to meet people in the course of my work as the editor of the local paper. I had learnt to take a lot of this local rumour-mongering for what it was, tittle-tattle to pass the time of day. But, as a journalist, I couldn't afford to have a closed mind.

In fact, despite its staid exterior, in the early Seventies even a backwater like Bakewell was feeling the liberating influence of the times, albeit it had taken a little longer to reach there. Miniskirts were starting to be worn by the young ladies of Bakewell, just as their hippy-chick counterparts in the big cities like Manchester, Liverpool and London were discarding them in favour of the maxi-skirt and floppy hats. But what did Bakewell care about these places? The market stalls on Monday provided plenty of cheap, 'fashionable' clothes for Bakewell's teenagers – and their mothers and fathers.

According to former pupils of Lady Manners, which turned from Grammar to Comprehensive in 1972, short skirts, long hair, the Pill and cannabis were a way of life at the time, a permissiveness equally familiar to their affluent parents living beneath a veneer of country respectability and Barbour jackets.

Rumours began to circulate at the school of 'key parties' among the professional, middle classes and those who aspired to be part of the 'in crowd' in their small-town or village circles. The happenings at such gatherings became the subject of speculation and the cause of much whispering and tittering in the school corridors. A hushed silence would fall when an affluent pupil whose parents were meant to have participated came into earshot. The word was that their mums and dads were doing 'it' with other mums and dads to whom they were not married. Wife-swapping among the country gentry may have seemed as unlikely as an orgy at a parish council meeting, but it appears this is what was happening around Bakewell.

The common procedure at such parties, or at least the consensus arrived at by the adolescent imaginings at Lady Manners, was that several couples would arrive at a private house in one of the villages outside town, the venue of that week's party. They came from the surrounding area, and were sworn to secrecy – that was half the fun of it. Just imagine the knowing glances in the post office, village institute, and local pub the following day. The wives each threw their car key into a pile in the middle of the room. The blindfolded husbands, in turn, crawled on hands and knees to the centre of the room and retrieved a key from the heap. Everyone then got drunk or stoned and eventually each wife returned home to bed with whichever man had the key to her car. The whist drive in the village hall was never like this! This was really 'with it'. Or, as one disapproving village matron told me, 'It was all the thing at the time.'

Over the tea tables at home the adolescent musings would continue. 'Mum, guess what I heard at school today . . .' Mum would be aghast. 'Don't let anyone hear you say *that*. They'll *kill* you. Mind you, doesn't surprise me with that lot!'

Nor had the drug scene bypassed Bakewell and the Derbyshire Dales. Quite the opposite. The tiny, dark back rooms and outhouses of its old country pubs, often converted into weekend discos to amuse the local youth who had no late public transport to take them anywhere else, were a magnet for the small-time drug peddlars who flocked to the area from Sheffield, Derby and Nottingham. What better place to smoke a joint or drop a tab of acid than amid the relaxed atmosphere and beautiful scenery of the Peak District? What better places to stash and deal drugs than its secluded lanes and hills, its quiet woods and meeting places . . . places, in fact, like Bakewell cemetery and Catcliff Wood?

I do not know if Wendy Sewell was involved in these kinds of activities. If she was, then her husband David certainly was not. Locals have always made it clear to me that he was never a part of what one described as her 'active social life', preferring instead to pursue his hobby as a vintage car enthusiast. As one of the couple's acquaintances put it to me, 'If David had spent as much time on top of Wendy as he did under a car bonnet, then maybe she wouldn't have had to look elsewhere.'

The couple had met shortly after David graduated from Imperial College London, with a second-class degree in Physics. He returned to his family home in Sheffield where he met the then Wendy Crawshaw, an only child still living at home with her parents and three years his junior. David courted the twenty-year-old Wendy in his 1947 MGTC two-seater. They soon got engaged and, after their wedding in 1964, moved to a bungalow in Bakewell close to David's workplace. Shortly afterwards David quit his job and found another twenty miles away in Chapel-en-le-Frith on the road to Manchester. He was away from home from early morning till late in the evening and his young wife was left to find her own employment, and amusement, in a strange town.

She had a series of jobs, leaving one as secretary to the magistrates' clerk at the courthouse in Bakewell amid a whiff of scandal about a fling with a co-worker. It was one of many liaisons the gregarious, attractive Wendy was to form with the men among her new circle of friends. And Wendy was not short of friends. Everyone liked her. Whatever else was said by the gossips, all agreed she was a 'friendly', 'sweet-natured', 'very personable' girl.

The rumour persisted among locals in Bakewell that Wendy Sewell had been having an affair with Mr Red.

One woman told me that Wendy had confided in her that she enjoyed the thrill of sex in public places, with its attendant risk of being caught. She said Wendy was aware of her nickname 'The Martini Girl', taken from an advertising slogan current at the time, 'Anytime, Anyplace, Anywhere'. Not only didn't she mind, she was said to have revelled in the name and thought it a huge joke.

Another told me Wendy had kept a 'black book' in which she rated the performance of her 'conquests' from one to five. This apparently became a cause of great concern in business circles. It was her own peculiar joke, which may have cost her dear, I thought.

But it takes two to tango. I began to get the impression that Wendy had been passed around the local bigwigs as a trophy. Many of the names I was being given, as her alleged lovers, were men from the professional classes. I wondered if it were all true, or did it stem from mere macho boasting round the Round Table or at the Masonic Lodge? I was told one of her 'boyfriends' was a senior police officer in the Derbyshire force. She was certainly well known to the local magistrates, police and legal professionals in Bakewell through her job at the magistrates' court, and moved in their social circles.

I was starting to find all this gossip distasteful. Wendy wasn't here to answer back.

Maybe, caught up in the liberated, heady atmosphere of the late Sixties and early Seventies, she was not unlike many women of her generation. In a big city she would have been just another independent, headstrong young woman merging into the crowd with her kinky boots, pale lipstick and long flicked-out hair. In a place like Bakewell young women like Wendy – 'out on the town without their husbands,' tut-tutted one now elderly Bakewell stalwart who remembers her – well, they were bound to attract disapproving stares. It didn't seem to bother Wendy one hoot.

By 1967 the Sewell marriage had hit the rocks. The Home Office summary confirmed that Wendy moved out and rented lodgings in

Bakewell. Soon afterwards, she announced she was pregnant. I was told there was two or three men in Bakewell sweating! The rumours were that she had had a baby girl, and that the father was a Bakewell man, John Marshall, the son of a prominent local businessman and quite a few years younger than Wendy. The child, it was said, had been adopted. Wendy's lifestyle appears to have continued as before.

The long separation from her husband, and her associations with other men detailed in the Home Office summary of the case, were all kept secret from the jury at Stephen's trial. It was said in court that the Sewells had no children.

In 1971 David and Wendy Sewell were reconciled. Maybe seeking a fresh start, the couple moved into an old rambling farmhouse in picturesque Middleton-by-Youlgreave, which they set about renovating. The fresh start did not last, as the Home Office papers relate, 'Mrs Sewell continued to associate with other men.' It was from the old farmhouse that Wendy Sewell set out on her last journey to Bakewell and caught the bus driven by the father of the man who was to be accused of murdering her a few hours later.

I felt that many telling details of Wendy's final day had been overlooked at the trial. From the account Ray Downing had given me of the day of the attack, she was definitely in a hurry. On her journey in to work on the early bus from Middleton-by-Youlgreave, she had told Ray she had 'some business to attend to'. Was this business the reason for her murder? There was no mention at trial of why she should have caught the early bus, or any hint that she had an early appointment or task to attend to.

Ray told me a mate of his had mentioned seeing Wendy Sewell shortly after she had been dropped off the bus, 'heading back towards the Square from the Buxton Road end of town', before walking the few hundred yards to her job as a typist with the Forestry Commission in King Street, just off the Square in a different direction. This suggested she had made some kind of detour before going to work. Had checks ever been made on where she went?

A friendly copper had promised to try to find statements given to the police in 1973 in connection with the Sewell case. One of the first he came up with was that of John Osmaston, her boss at the Forestry Commission office in Bakewell, who had been called by the

Crown as a trial witness, once again proving that the police had lied to me when they said all the case paperwork had been destroyed. Mr Osmaston's statement contained *much* more detail than the one sentence given in the trial summary, where it was merely mentioned that Mrs Sewell had handed him a note at twenty past twelve saying she was going out 'for a breath of air'. Most notably, he told the police that Wendy had a male visitor shortly before she left the office at lunchtime. This never came out at the trial as far as I could tell, not having the full manuscript.

After describing an uneventful morning in which Wendy had already arrived when he got there at 9a.m. and then popped out as usual to get a pint of milk at 10a.m., Mr Osmaston went on to talk about the lunchtime period. 'At 12.15p.m. I asked her to get the agent to the Stanton-in-the-Peak Estate on the telephone. She said there was no reply, and I recall looking at my watch and seeing the time was 12.15. I remember saying to her that Mr Gilmore might be at lunch. However, a few minutes later she managed to get him and he spoke to me on the telephone in my office on my own extension.'

From what Osmaston said, it was obvious that he and Wendy worked in adjoining offices. He continued, 'After I had been talking to him for about ten minutes I heard someone in the other office speaking to Mrs Sewell. I only heard two or three words. Trying to recall, it seemed slightly abrupt. It was not a voice I recognised at all. I cannot say whether this person left the office, but a few moments later Mrs Sewell came into my office while I was still on the telephone and gave me a small piece of paper on which she had scribbled, "I'm going out for a breath of air." I nodded my head to her and she went out of my office, presumably out of her office too. Whatever, she had gone out of her office a couple of minutes later when I finished the phone call.'

This was vital new evidence. Why had this mystery visitor never been traced? The man was 'abrupt', he spoke only 'two or three words' to Wendy and his voice was 'high-pitched'. Was his curtness due to annoyance, even anger? Was Mr Osmaston suggesting he was speaking in a raised voice? I thought it a pity that he had never been asked about this man at the trial. Mr Osmaston's statement went on,

I crumpled up the piece of paper on which the note was written when I finished the call, and I threw it in the waste-paper bin. I can say without doubt, the writing on the paper was Mrs Sewell's. I hardly looked at her when she came into my office. I cannot say whether or not she was disturbed when she left.

I am unable to say even whether she had on a dress or trousers, which she quite frequently wears. I cannot say whether she came to work in a coat or not. As soon as I finished the phone conversation I went out for lunch. The town was busy.

I returned to the office about 1.15p.m. . . . I was surprised Mrs Sewell had not returned by then.

I remained in the office and carried on with my work, and between 2p.m. and 3p.m. telephoned the home of Mrs Sewell to see if she was there. All I could think of was that she had gone to her mother who had been ill and may have got worse.

I remained in the office until 3.15p.m. when the police told me something serious had happened to Mrs Sewell. I retrieved the piece of paper on which she had written the message, and later handed it to the police officer who called on me.

Mrs Sewell had not had a holiday away from home with her husband this year. All her leave had been taken in odd days and I notice, while I was on holiday, her leave card shows two hours per day off between 10 and 25 July between 12 noon and 2p.m. I have an idea Mrs Sewell had an interest in a wool shop on Buxton Road at Bakewell, although I am not aware of her exact connection with it.

The reference to Wendy's holiday arrangements in relation to her husband struck me as slightly curious. I wondered why Osmaston would choose to mention this? Was he implying that a happily married woman would have taken more orthodox holiday leave than the odd day here and there, or a couple of hours at lunchtime? The hours 'between 12 noon and 2p.m.' jumped out at me. Wendy had met her killer between these times. I realised my thought processes were wandering into the realm of pure speculation.

Osmaston's mention of a wool shop on Buxton Road reminded me that Wendy had been spotted that morning walking back towards the centre of Bakewell from the 'Buxton Road end' of town by one of Ray's fellow bus drivers, after getting off the bus in the centre earlier that morning. Was this shop the reason for the detour she had made before going in to the office later? What was her 'interest' in the wool shop, I wondered?

He added one further point: 'I also received a recorded mail delivery for Mrs Sewell after returning from lunch. The mail was handed to me by the postman who said he had been unable to deliver it to Mrs Sewell at home.' In a tight community like Bakewell and its surrounding villages, especially back in 1973, the postman would know everybody and almost every aspect of their daily lives. There was nothing odd about him taking a delivery to Wendy's workplace three or four miles from her home, if he needed a signature. Yet had anyone checked what was in the delivery? Was it a parcel or a letter? Again, there had been no further mention of it.

Once more I thought it a shame that Osmaston had apparently not been questioned in detail about his statement at the trial. It was providing more questions than answers. I wondered if any of Wendy's friends or work colleagues might have any clues after all these years.

Through the local grapevine I was put in touch with a woman, Joan Turner who, I was told, claimed that at least one of Wendy's friends had known who she was meeting at the cemetery during the lunchtime that she was attacked. Apparently Joan herself had even reported this to the police at the time.

I went to talk to Joan Turner at her home in Bakewell, to see what she had to say. She was a loud, jolly woman in her fifties. She said she had not known Wendy all that well although, like everyone else, she was ready with gossip about her 'reputation'. She talked of her many boyfriends and claimed she used to have a flat above a shop on Buxton Road where she 'met' male friends and posed for glamour photos. 'I think there were other women involved too,' she chortled.

I wondered if this was the reason for Mr Osmaston's oblique reference to a wool shop in his statement. When I pushed Joan for more details, she gave me a wide grin. 'Oh, I wouldn't know about all that!' She smirked. However, she said, her former friend Lesley McCrindle had been close to Wendy for five years as they worked in the same building.

In 1973 Joan was living in Ashford-in-the-Water, where Lesley also lived with her mother, Daisy, and father, 'Jock'.

Joan continued,

> Within days of the attack, one night after work, Lesley McCrindle came round very upset and with tears in her eyes. She told me she knew who Wendy was meeting.
>
> Lesley has always said it wasn't Stephen Downing who committed the murder, and always maintained Wendy was meeting someone in the cemetery. She said something about a call to the office. I'm not sure if she meant someone telephoned or called in person.
>
> Lesley and I were close friends until I told the police about this. The police questioned her and she flatly denied it. She then phoned me after they'd gone and played hell with me. The police even revisited me to check my story. I know what she said – she was very frightened and I still believe she knows who Wendy was meeting that day.
>
> I am horrified that Stephen was condemned at the scene. Lesley has always said it was not him that did it.

I soon tracked down Lesley McCrindle. I did not tell her of my conversation with Joan Turner. Instead, I said I had heard that she was a friend of Wendy's and worked in the same building. I thought she might have seen her on the morning of the attack.

She seemed interested that I was reinvestigating the case after all these years. I said I had come across the names of several people who I thought should be interviewed, or in some cases *re*-interviewed, by the police. I asked her if she knew Mr Red, Syd Oulsnam, George Pearson or Mr Blue.

'I don't know Mr Red and I only vaguely know of Pearson,' she replied. 'I know who Syd Oulsnam is, and I knew of the Blue family.

'Wendy often wandered in the cemetery looking at gravestones,' Lesley continued. 'Several people who work here know she had visited the graveyard a few times leading up to that day.'

I put it to her that she knew who Wendy was going to meet that day. I still did not tell her to who I had been talking.

She admitted, 'Wendy and I *were* very close friends. We often shared secrets.' But she denied knowing anything about a pre-arranged meeting that day. She also tried to play down the rumours of Wendy's alleged promiscuity, laughing them off as gossip.

I told her that Mr Osmaston had heard a man's voice in Wendy's office, just before she handed her boss a note saying she was going out for a 'breath of air'.

Lesley was surprised. She said she had never heard about this man before.

I asked her if she had talked to Wendy that morning.

'Yes,' she said, 'I met Wendy during the morning break and she didn't say anything about meeting anyone. We were discussing holidays and where we might like to go. I had worked with her for about five or six years and was probably the last person to really see her alive.'

I then put it to Lesley that she had been very upset and had confided in someone a few days after the attack, still not mentioning Joan Turner's name.

'Look,' she said, an air of impatience creeping into her voice, 'if I knew who Wendy was meeting that day, I would tell you. But I don't.'

I asked if the police had ever questioned her.

'A few days after the murder I received a call at work purporting to be from a police sergeant. He asked if I knew who Wendy was meeting. I said, 'No.' Later, when I mentioned it in the office, they suggested contacting the police station in Bakewell to check it out. The police said no one had phoned from there. It's a mystery.'

I thanked Lesley and got up to take my leave.

As I reached the door she called after me, 'Why don't you talk to Mr Blue?'

I phoned Joan Turner to tell her of Lesley's reaction to my visit. 'I know what she told me,' she said. 'She stood by her story. She was very frightened and said she knew who Wendy was meeting that day.'

10

I HAD MADE THE decision to nail my colours to the mast and go public with the Downing story. I was planning my first article for the *Mercury* some time towards the end of January and was in the office one day sorting through the evidence I had gleaned, when I got a very interesting telephone call. A woman asked if we could meet to talk about George Pearson and the Wendy Sewell murder. She said she was one of Pearson's former lovers.

I will call her Rita, although that is not her real name, as she is still terrified of having spoken to me. She sounded nervous. She explained she was not on the phone at home, but was calling from a phone box. She had heard on the local grapevine that I was making enquiries about the murder and had plucked up the courage to talk to me.

I arranged to meet Rita at her home. She gave me directions, but insisted I should park in the next road as she did not want anyone to know I had visited her, especially George. She stood by the window throughout our meeting, shielding herself behind the curtains, nervously looking out from time to time to see if anyone was watching the house.

'Why are you so scared, Rita?' I asked.

'I'm scared that George will find out you're here,' she replied.

'What is it you wanted to tell me?'

'George told the police a pack of lies about what he saw that day,' she said. 'At ten to one he was nowhere near the cemetery gates when he saw Wendy. He was much further down the hill by the Kissing Gate with Janet Brailsford. Wendy passed them on her way up the Butts and he said hello. George knew Wendy very well. She was well known to a lot of men.'

'Who's Janet Brailsford?'

Rita explained that Janet was another girlfriend of Pearson's. He had had an assignation with her that day and had arranged to meet her at a well-known lovers' meeting spot, the Kissing Gate, near the *bottom* of the Butts path.

'You say near the *bottom* of the Butts, Rita?' I interrupted at this point. 'Just how far away is that from the cemetery gates?'

'Oh, it's a five-minute walk,' she replied. 'Depends if you're going up or down. Probably longer on the way up.'

'How do you know this?'

'George told me all about it years afterwards. He knew what time it was when they saw Wendy because he remembered Janet saying at the time, "It's ten to one, I'd better be getting back." ' Rita explained how Janet and George had said their goodbyes and then Janet went off towards town while 'George carried on up the hill behind Wendy'.

One thing was for sure, if Wendy had been at the Kissing Gate at ten to one, it would have been around five to one when she reached the cemetery. It seemed that the Prosecution case had just had a hole shot through it. It rested on the assumption that Stephen had attacked Wendy between the time she was seen entering the cemetery at around 12.50 and the time Stephen was seen leaving the cemetery at around 1.08, some eighteen minutes. It was claimed that his trip home via the shop was merely to establish an alibi, so that he could return to the cemetery and pretend he'd found the battered and dying woman. Now it seemed that the space of time during which the attack could have happened had been reduced from eighteen to thirteen minutes.

I was very excited by Rita's new information, but wanted to hear more. 'So did he see Wendy go into the cemetery?'

She didn't know, but added, 'He told me he met Charlie Carman up there.' Rita was unable to tell me exactly where and at what time Pearson and Carman had met. She seemed to think that, contrary to his evidence read out at trial, Pearson had not gone straight home. 'I think he hung around,' she said.

Carman's whereabouts and minor part in the drama were beginning to play a crucial role in my unravelling of the crime. His written evidence to the court said he was around the cemetery gates by the phone box at 12.50 and had seen Wendy already *in* the cemetery. But Stephen claimed to have seen him some twenty minutes *after* that, walking *towards* the cemetery. Now Pearson was also meant to have seen Carman. If Rita was telling the truth, neither Wendy nor Pearson could have arrived at the cemetery gates at the top of the Butts before five to one. If he 'hung around', there was no telling what time Pearson had seen Carman. If it was some time after one, then it would lend weight to Stephen's story about seeing Carman. Could Charlie Carman have got his times so badly mixed up? What a pity he wasn't here to ask.

'So if he didn't go straight home, what did George do when he reached the top of the Butts?' I asked Rita.

'I don't know where he was going. I think he hung around the estate, went along Yeld Road and, after heading back towards the cemetery, he said he saw a man running away.'

'What!' I exclaimed.

'He saw a man running away from the cemetery. I'm sure he told me that.' She bit her lip, turning her head and throwing a quick glance towards the window.

'Have you ever told anyone this before?' I asked.

She wrung her hands, looked straight at me and slowly shook her head. She was visibly upset. 'George would kill me if he knew I was talking to you,' she whispered, choking back a sob.

I reached into my pocket, pulled out a clean handkerchief and handed it to her. 'Did he know this man?' I continued after a few seconds.

'He never said.'

'Did George see Stephen Downing at any point?'

'I'm sure he said something about seeing Stephen going into the cemetery *after* Wendy had been found by someone else.'

I was astounded by what Rita was telling me. 'Try to remember exactly what he said,' I coaxed.

'I can't. It's so long ago,' she replied wearily. 'But I know pretty soon afterwards he went down to the Castle Hotel in Bakewell and told people Wendy had been attacked. He said she had head injuries.'

'How on earth did he know?'

'I can't quite remember. I think he said he had seen someone and they told him – one of the workmen in the cemetery I think. But I remember him saying it wasn't Stephen.'

The only time the workmen had left the cemetery was to phone the emergency services. I supposed one of them could have told Pearson. But something struck me as odd. How would the workmen have known who the injured woman was so 'soon afterwards'? One of them had even been unable to say if it was a man or a woman lying there on the graves. Mr Pearson certainly had some answering to do.

'And he told Charlie Carman and Jock McCrindle too,' Rita added, while I was still pondering her last bombshell.

'Where was Charlie Carman at this point?'

'He was back at work in Bath Gardens. I think the gardeners' afternoon shift started at one.'

I had heard Jock's name before. It was Lesley McCrindle's father, the gardener and part-time photographer from Ashford. Once again it struck me what a small world Bakewell was.

'Rita, I'm going to have to see George. Is there anything else you can remember him saying?'

'No. Only that Stephen never did it. He's often said that. Please don't tell George I've said anything. Or Janet.'

'Janet?'

'Yes, Janet Brailsford. I told you, she's the one he was meeting that day Wendy was attacked. He lives with her now. She'll probably be there if you go to see him.'

I promised her that I would not tell George or his girlfriend about this visit, but stressed that to get Stephen out of jail she might have to give evidence to a court. She agreed she would do it, if necessary.

If Rita was telling the truth, then it threw up several interesting questions about her former lover.

Why did he not tell the police and the trial the whole truth about his movements, and all he had seen?

Who was the running man he claimed to have seen? Mrs Hadfield had insisted Pearson must have seen the blond-haired youth running up Yeld Road. She had seen this running man at 1.20, and said she'd seen Pearson five minutes before on Yeld Road heading in the direction of the cemetery. That would also add weight to Rita's theory that Pearson was 'hanging around' the area, and not at his mother's house, at ten past one.

Who was the person who found Wendy, before Stephen Downing stumbled across her? The report of Pearson seeing Stephen go into the cemetery *after* Wendy's battered body had already been discovered by someone else was dynamite, if true. Nothing like this had ever come out at the trial. It would place Pearson close to the cemetery some time between Stephen leaving at 1.08 and returning between 1.15 and 1.20 – the period during which I was certain the attack had taken place. What else had Pearson seen?

Who told him Wendy had been attacked? At what time was Pearson back in Bakewell town centre, telling people that Wendy had been attacked in the cemetery and had head injuries? More importantly how did he know so 'soon afterwards'? Why did he maintain with such certainty over the years that Stephen Downing was innocent? Maybe Pearson was sure Stephen was innocent because he knew who the guilty person was.

The timings thrown up by Rita's account of Pearson's movements raised some serious questions. I recapped, scribbling times and names on my pad: the prosecution maintained the attack had happened within an eighteen-minute period between Wendy entering the cemetery at 12.50 and Stephen leaving at 1.08. Rita's account would put Wendy in the cemetery some five minutes later, and I believed I had shown that other evidence concerning Carman, and the sightings of Wendy leaving work, backed this up.

I armed myself with a stopwatch and asked Ray Downing to accompany me to the Kissing Gate. It was on the Butts about halfway up between the town and the cemetery. Rita said Wendy had passed Pearson and Janet at this very spot at 12.50p.m. I could see why it was a lovers' meeting place. It was an old wrought-iron gate and marked an old entry from the Butts path into Catcliff Woods, but now led into a housing estate.

Ray and I set off. I tried to walk at the pace a healthy thirty-two-year-old woman would have kept to. I began to get a little out of puff, so slowed down slightly. Ray was panting for breath, but the point of my exercise would have been lost had I stopped for him. To make matters worse for himself, he had insisted on talking during our climb, telling me more about George Pearson. He said that several neighbours doubted whether Pearson had ever continued on to his mother's house that day after reaching the top of the Butts. They had been chatting on street corners in the bright autumn sunshine and had not seen any sign of him on any of the routes he would have to have taken. 'So what was he doing?' gasped Ray in one final flourish as we reached the wrought iron cemetery gates. I looked at my stopwatch: five minutes and twenty seconds.

If Rita was right, Wendy would have arrived at the cemetery more like 12.55p.m., not 12.50p.m., and a few minutes here and there could make a huge difference to Stephen's claims of innocence. The gatekeeper, Wilf Walker, and other witnesses, had been in no doubt that they had seen Stephen walk past these very cemetery gates on his way to the shop and then home at 1.08p.m., leaving at most only thirteen minutes between Wendy entering the cemetery and the time Stephen left. I reset my stopwatch. I needed to test these thirteen minutes against the account given by Stephen in his confession, the statement on which he had been convicted. According to the Prosecution, Stephen had seen Wendy, gone to the store to get the pickaxe handle, followed her around the cemetery, carried out the attack, undressed and sexually assaulted her, returned to the chapel to collect his pop bottle and put on his jacket, and calmly left the cemetery witnessed by several people.

My starting point was the unconsecrated chapel, some 260 yards from the gates. I started the watch. I allowed Wendy two minutes to have been in the cemetery before Stephen saw her. The Prosecution version says he spotted her on the lower path walking *towards* the main gate. It is likely that she would have strolled around for at least two minutes as, at some point, she must have turned round and retraced her steps. In his *own* account to me Stephen said he first saw her walking towards the Garden of Remembrance at the far end, some 400 yards from the gate, after which he had gone into the chapel store to stoke up the fire and collect his pop bottle. Jayne Atkins had also noticed Wendy *in* the Garden of Remembrance when she was near the far end of the cemetery looking for her dog. When Stephen went outside again, he said Wendy was walking along the lower path in the direction of the consecrated chapel and the gates. This walk to the Garden of Remembrance and back would have taken Wendy much longer than two minutes, more like eight, as she was wandering along looking at headstones, according to Stephen. But at this point I decided to stick to the Prosecution's version, which made no mention of such a walk.

In his confession Stephen said he had watched Wendy. I added on another minute for him to have observed her on the lower path and then made the decision to attack her.

I could not recreate his next action as the old chapel store was locked, but I allowed another fifty seconds for Stephen to have entered, then selected and picked up the murder weapon.

So far my total was three minutes and fifty seconds – from Wendy having entered the cemetery to her would-be attacker standing ready with the weapon in his hands.

I then followed the most direct route from the unconsecrated chapel, to the spot on the lower path near the consecrated chapel where Wendy had been attacked. I walked along the middle path, and then crossed diagonally over rough terrain through the gravestones to reach the lower path. I did not rush, as Stephen was meant to have attacked Wendy from behind and would have had to creep up on her in order not to attract her attention. It took me two minutes and thirty seconds. So far a total of five minutes and twenty seconds.

The violent attack on Wendy, with seven or eight blows being struck, plus the subsequent sexual assault after undressing her, must have taken at least five minutes. I had read in one of the newspaper reports that Mrs Sewell had a black belt at judo. Surely she would have put up a struggle? From photographs I had seen of Stephen, he was not a particularly tall man. He had also, I remembered, complained of having a bad back, which had plagued him during the hours of police interrogations. By now I already had an accumulated total of nine minutes and twenty seconds.

I then retraced Stephen's route back to the unconsecrated chapel, where he had gone to collect his pop bottle – another one minute and thirty seconds. I deduced he would have gone a little quicker on the way back, if he had just violently assaulted a woman. A running total of twelve minutes and twenty seconds so far.

A further minute to have gone into the chapel for the pop bottle and composed himself, then the 260-yard walk from there to the main gates, which took me two minutes and thirty seconds. Ray told me that if I were to time Stephen's walk I would need to reduce my pace as his son had a slow and ambling gait. I remembered that the trial witnesses had said he left the cemetery looking the same as usual, perfectly normal and not agitated, certainly not running as one might have expected. So I added a further twenty seconds.

That gave me a final time total of fifteen minutes and ten seconds for Stephen to have done all the things he was meant to have done, and I felt I had erred on the side of caution. The initial few minutes from Wendy entering the cemetery and Stephen deciding to attack her would most likely have taken longer than the two minutes I had estimated, especially if the sightings in the Garden of Remembrance were true.

I was still concerned that other witnesses, apart from Pearson, had given different times for seeing Wendy in or around the cemetery. At the trial Mrs Hill said she saw Wendy enter the cemetery gates at 12.45. Yet Mr Read said he saw her leave her office in King Street at 12.40. Even Linford Christie could not have got up *that* hill in five minutes! Moreover, the two joiners, Messrs Lomas and Bradwell, roughly confirmed the time at which she left the town centre. They saw her, just having entered Butts Road, at 12.45p.m.

It was looking as though she *had* entered the cemetery at more like five to one. Granted, Charlie Carman had said he saw her *in* the cemetery at 12.50p.m., but from what Stephen and Rita had told me, Carman probably passed the cemetery much later than this, one o'clock at the earliest. If Stephen were to be believed, Carman was walking through the housing estate at 1.08p.m. Moreover, if Pearson really had been a few minutes behind Wendy climbing the hill and then 'hung around' the area, it would put Carman around the scene a bit later, as Pearson had seen him too. Then it struck me. Rita had said the gardeners' shifts started at one o'clock. Had Carman lied in his statement to the police because he was late for work?

There were clearly some major time discrepancies within a handful of key witness statements. I remembered that, in the trial summary, the judge had made it clear that all timings given by witnesses should be taken as approximate.

To me there seemed some doubt about the time Stephen had spent away from the cemetery. It was said Stephen had left around 1.08p.m. and returned between 1.15p.m. and 1.20p.m., when he had been spotted by Wilf Walker re-entering the gates. A few minutes later he had called on Mr Walker, saying he had found an injured woman. This would give him between seven and twelve minutes to walk from the cemetery gates to the shop, then to his house, chat to his mother, change his boots, and return again to the cemetery. I estimated he would have been away from the cemetery for at *least* twelve minutes to have done all that. As the time of 1.08p.m. for his leaving appeared undisputed, I was sure it was at least twenty past one when he returned, probably a bit later.

I studied all my notes again. Mrs Hadfield claimed she saw Pearson heading back towards the direction of the cemetery at 1.15p.m. and that minutes later, when she saw the running man, Pearson must have seen him too.

Rita said that 'soon afterwards' Pearson was in the Castle pub, and also with Carman and another gardener in Bath Gardens in the centre of Bakewell, telling everyone about the attack. I decided to see if this other gardener, Jock McCrindle, was still alive. Then I remembered that pile of police statements sitting unread in my office, relating to Pearson, and taken from bar staff at a Bakewell pub. Could this be what they were all about? Maybe they held the clue to the time at which Pearson was back in town talking about the attack? I made a resolution to read them as soon as I got a spare moment, and there weren't many of those nowadays.

I noted from the trial notes that it had taken twelve minutes before a policeman arrived. It was claimed by the workers in the cemetery that PC David Ball began asking questions before checking the victim, then spoke to other officers on his radio and only afterwards decided to call an ambulance. If this was true, it beggared belief. I couldn't believe it, but still found myself wondering why it had taken so long to get medical attention when a woman had been brutally attacked and lay dying. Surely the ambulance should have been called as a matter of priority, even before the police? It was 1.55p.m. before the ambulance arrived, over an hour after the Prosecution alleged that Wendy had been attacked – or by my estimate, three-quarters of an hour. I wondered if she might still be alive today if medical aid had reached her sooner.

Unfortunately many of the witnesses were now dead, including some of the workmen, Wilf Walker and his wife, and Charlie Carman. In the trial notes there were some discrepancies between their accounts and that of Stephen: whether he spoke to Wilf and his wife, whether he said he was wearing gloves, whether he said he was worried about losing his job, whether he said there looked like being an identity parade, whether he spoke to Carman as he walked to the shop. How could all my questions be answered after twenty-one years? It was very frustrating.

I wanted to find out just exactly what Pearson had been saying about the attack on the afternoon it had happened. How and when had he found out the details? From further copies of police statements provided by informants, I read that Charlie Carman had said he first heard of the attack from George Pearson at about half past three in the afternoon while he was working in Bath Gardens. I found out that his fellow gardener on the day, Jock McCrindle, was alive and living in Ashford-in-the-Water. He was a semi-professional photographer and advertised occasionally in the *Mercury*. I wanted to see if he recalled George Pearson's conversation that lunchtime twenty-one years ago.

Jock McCrindle was none too pleased to see me. In fact, he became extremely aggressive and told me to sling my hook in no uncertain terms. I was somewhat taken aback as I had approached him in a polite and non-confrontational manner with what seemed to me a harmless question. I simply wanted to know if he could corroborate or refute the claim by one of Pearson's ex-girlfriends that Pearson had informed him and Charlie Carman of the attack on Wendy Sewell while they were at work in the centre of town.

I was wasting my time. McCrindle told me to mind my own business. I could not understand why he should be so sensitive about my visit. I thought maybe he was annoyed at my questioning of his daughter Lesley. I remembered Joan Turner telling me he had been a close friend of Wendy's mother, Margery Crawshaw, who still lived in Bakewell. As a result, it appeared, he had known Wendy.

Having drawn a blank with McCrindle, I wanted to determine what, if anything, Pearson had been saying in the bar of the Castle Hotel that lunchtime. According to Ray, about six months after the murder, two women who worked at the hotel, Cynthia Smithurst and Yvonne Spencer, told him they had first heard of the attack on Wendy from George Pearson on the day it happened. They told him George had been in the bar that lunchtime. They finished work at 2p.m., so they knew he must have mentioned it before then.

In the early Eighties there was a resurgence of interest in the case, largely due to Ray's persistence in trying to unearth new information. Robert Ervin was also collecting new evidence in preparation for a second appeal. It appeared that Cynthia and Yvonne were interviewed by the police. Statements were also taken from the hotel's proprietors, Arthur and Muriel Duplock, along with their son, Robert.

These statements were part of the huge pile of documents Ray had collected over the years. But when I went through them with one of my police informants, I was astonished when I discovered the truth about them. The statements had actually been written up in the Eighties, based on notes taken in 1973 – and the dates were a fabrication. I must say I found some of the contents strange, too. The attack on Wendy was constantly referred to as a 'murder' even though Wendy had not yet died, and descriptions of hoards of journalists staying overnight at the Castle Hotel in Bakewell because a young woman had been assaulted did not ring true.

Yvonne's read: 'It was during the lunch hour that my friend Cynthia Smithurst told me that someone had been battered in the cemetery. I was working in the kitchen at the time. I remember saying "How do you know?" and she said, "George Pearson's been in and told me."' Her hours of duty, she said, were 8.30a.m. to 2p.m.

Cynthia's read: 'I finished cleaning the bedrooms about 1.45p.m. and went into the bar. I remember seeing Yvonne in or around the bar, and also Arthur, Muriel and Robert Duplock. As far as I can remember, given that it was about eight years ago, someone in the bar said, "There's been a murder in the churchyard," or words to that effect. I cannot remember who said this.' She said her normal hours of work were from noon until 2p.m. Of George Pearson she said, 'I am certain he was in the bar.'

The two statements broadly back up what Ray Downing claims to have been told by the same two women in 1974. However, the statement of the proprietors' son, Robert Duplock, contradicts their version of events. As he recalled, 'My parents had gone out for the day to Brighton visiting relatives. As far as I can remember, the first I heard of the murder was towards the end of the lunchtime closing on the 12th. Lunchtime permitted hours were from 10.30a.m. to 3p.m. and, as far I can recall, it was towards 3p.m., perhaps 2.45p.m., that someone came into the pub and said something like "there's been a murder in the churchyard". I cannot for the life of me think who came in and said this, nor of any other persons who were in the hotel at the time. Thinking back, I seem to remember that all the women who worked at the hotel had left at around 2p.m. I remember thinking when the murder was mentioned that it was a pity they weren't there because they would have liked to hear such gossip! I feel sure that if the girls had heard of such a murder earlier than myself, then they would have told me about it. They didn't, though. By the evening reporters had booked in at the hotel and gossip surrounding the murder was rife.'

Robert's parents, Cynthia and Arthur Duplock, confirmed that they had been hundreds of miles away at the time, visiting Mrs Duplock's parents in Brighton. Arthur Duplock stated, 'I positively recall that this was the day that Wendy Sewell was murdered as, on our return to the Castle Hotel at approximately 1a.m. the following morning, I saw that the pub was still lit up, and press reporters were in the bar of the hotel. This was the first that I had heard of the attack on Wendy Sewell.'

I couldn't help thinking it was odd that the gentlemen of the press had arrived so quickly and booked into the hotel. It didn't make sense. At this stage it was still only an assault. News desks would never send reporters all the way from Manchester, Derby or Sheffield to investigate an assault on a young girl in a country graveyard, let alone pay for them to stay in the local hotel overnight.

The police had been back to the two barmaids shortly afterwards to see if, perhaps, they were mixed up about the time they heard of the attack. On reflection, Cynthia had stated, 'It may be that on the day that Wendy Sewell was murdered Mr and Mrs Duplock had the day off and left Robert in charge. If this was the case, I would most likely have stayed behind to help . . . it could be any time up to 3p.m. that someone mentioned the murder.'

Yvonne Spencer stood by her story, but she too was persuaded that she might have got the times mixed up. In her second statement she says, 'It could have been said after 2p.m., and more like 3p.m. which is closing time . . . on occasions I worked later, particularly if the Duplocks had the day off . . .' When I spoke to one of the former barmaids, she told me she had no recollection of making a signed, formal statement to the police.

Both women were adamant that they had heard of the attack on that day. As both lived near the cemetery, they remembered seeing lots of police activity around the area. They were both neighbours and good acquaintances of the Downing family, which the police implied might somehow have tainted their evidence. The officer who interviewed them actually said in his report that they might 'with the best will in the world, have told Ray Downing what he wanted to hear'.

Over the years Ray and Nita Downing had found themselves in an almost impossible position. Let down badly, as they saw it, by the local police, Stephen's solicitors, the local press and politicians, they had attempted to do their own detective work to prove their son innocent and, in addition, had hired the services of the amateur sleuth Robert Ervin. This involved Ray and Nita talking to their neighbours. If anyone had seen anything on the day it would most likely have been the folk who, like the Downings, lived near the scene of the crime. Others came to them, those frustrated at having been turned away by the police at the time with the glib reason 'we already have our man', those who over the years had harboured suspicions of their own, those who knew and respected the family and had racked their brains to try to remember any relevant clues to what had happened.

If any of this threw up useful information, it was duly reported to the police. Yet invariably the involvement of the Downing family in obtaining this new evidence from among such a small, close community immediately led to it being viewed as suspect. I learnt from police informants that, at the time of the appeal in October 1974 when Jayne Atkins had travelled to the Court of Appeal in London to give evidence in support of Stephen, there had been a feeling that the Downings had encouraged the teenage girl to give her evidence. It is true that they and Jayne's family, the Beebes, were friends and neighbours from the estate and Nita Downing had accompanied Jayne and her mother Margaret Beebe to the police station when Jayne went with new evidence in March 1974. Since then, police officers had told me that Ray Downing especially had been his own worst enemy, muddying the waters in many instances by talking to potential witnesses, and approaching people in Bakewell with questions relating to the case. But what were Ray and Nita meant to do? No one in authority appeared to be helping them, or cared about what happened to Stephen.

The police re-interviewed George Pearson in 1981. He stuck by his earlier account, and added that he had first heard of the attack between 4p.m. and 5p.m. while he was in Bakewell Square. He said, 'It is possible that I went into the Castle before it closed at 3p.m. on the day of the attack, but I couldn't have spoken to anyone about it because I didn't know it had happened at that time. I did not see any activity at the cemetery during the afternoon to make me think anything had happened there and, although I did go back into town from my mother's house, it is quite likely that I walked down Moorhall, Yeld Road and South Church Street which is the opposite direction to the cemetery.' He also told the police that he had never been out with Wendy Sewell, nor had she ever been to his home.

After evading all my earlier attempts to see him, in early 1995 Pearson contacted Ray Downing to say he was willing to speak with me. I once again made my way to the council estate and the small house on Moorhall round the corner from the Downings' and along by the shop. Pearson met me at the door – he had obviously been looking out for me. He was a scruffy-looking, stocky individual in his mid-fifties with a rakish Jack-the-Lad appearance. I remembered that I had been told he had 'film-star looks' when he was younger. Considering his reputation as a ladies' man, I supposed it might have been true. By now he had a sizeable paunch and thinning hair.

He showed me into a rather bare living room and introduced me to his girlfriend, Janet Brailsford. She sat on a sofa, smoking a cigarette and coughing. She seemed shaky and gave me a weak smile. George, too, seemed nervous but both received me politely.

When I asked him if he'd seen anyone else around the cemetery that day, he said he had seen no one apart from Wendy. He certainly denied seeing Mrs Hadfield or a running man and said he had always believed that it was Stephen Downing who found Wendy. He wasn't aware of anyone else being around at the time she was found, but how could he know when he wasn't there at that time? He insisted he had gone straight to his mother's house after walking up the Butts and had seen no one on his way back to town. He said he had not seen Stephen Downing *at all* that day.

But he was adamant that Stephen was innocent. He could give no precise reason for this belief, other than saying he was 'not quite the type'. 'He's a quiet lad, bit of a loner,' he said. 'He must have had a hell of a time in prison. I know. I've been there,' he added.

I pressed him further, to remember if he'd seen anyone else. Eventually he said he did have a fuzzy recollection of someone leaving the cemetery to phone for help. 'I think they said Wendy had been attacked,' he recalled.

I asked which of the workmen, but he shrugged and said he couldn't remember. He couldn't recall any conversation with anyone in Bath Gardens, or in the Castle bar.

So Pearson had denied or was vague about everything his former lover, Rita, had told me. I had promised her I wouldn't mention our conversation to George and I remained true to my word.

Throughout, Janet had sat on the sofa, chain-smoking. She fidgeted nervously during the brief moments she did not have a cigarette between her fingers. She almost jumped out of her skin when I turned to her and asked if she could tell me what time Wendy had passed her and George on the Butts that day.

She did, though, say that she *had* been at the Kissing Gate with George on the day in question. 'I remember,' she spluttered, between a bout of coughing, 'she passed us and then I said, "Oh, look, George, it's ten to one, I'd better be getting back down to Bakewell."'

When I told George I'd heard Wendy Sewell was once his girlfriend, he immediately denied it, but said he had known her very well and was friendly with her. Bakewell, after all, was that sort of town. I noticed Janet had looked up quickly and glared at George when I asked this question, and wondered if there was still something he wasn't prepared to tell me in front of his current girlfriend.

It was one of many conversations I was to have with George. Each time I was more frustrated and confused than the last. Pearson always adopted an air of active interest and helpfulness, answering all my questions, but changing his story from one meeting to the next. As he and Janet spent most days propping up the various bars of Bakewell's pubs and each other, I was not sure how reliable any information was that came from him. Yet throughout, drunk or sober, he was adamant about Stephen's innocence. I got the feeling that his certainty came from knowledge, a knowledge that he was unwilling to share with me.

Lucy Beebe contacted me again on several occasions in January to add further pieces of information. She was able to relate how she and Pam had been in the cemetery playing with Ian at around 1.10p.m., but had then gone out through the hedge towards their homes and left the little boy on his own. On a further occasion she told me that she and Pam had seen a blood-stained person jump over the wall from the cemetery and make off. She then gave me a telephone number for her brother Ian. She had persuaded him to talk to me.

When I spoke to Ian Beebe in January 1995, he was in his mid-twenties. Although his memories of 12 September 1973 were clouded in the mists of early childhood, he was adamant that he had experienced something 'horrific', and some vivid details remained with him. He explained, 'I was only about four at the time. I went out of the house on my push-bike and was going into the cemetery by the main gates. Pam and I were playing a game of hide-and-seek. I was pedalling up and down the paths when I saw this lady slumped on a gravestone. She was covered in blood and groaning. It really gave me quite a start and frightened the life out of me.'

'Are you sure it was a woman, Ian? At the time, your sister says you told her it was a man.'

'I panicked – I must have been in shock. This arm came over the gravestone. It was definitely a woman covered in blood. I might have said a man at the time, I can't remember. I think it was because of the long hair. Everyone had long hair in those days. I couldn't really speak.'

I recalled that one of the workmen who had given evidence at the trial, Herbert Dawson, had also shown some confusion as to whether the person drenched in blood and lying on the gravestones had been a man or a woman. How much more confusing it must have been for a four-year-old boy.

'Did you see a man at all?'

'Pam said there was a bloke with blood on him.' He paused for a while and seemed to relive his fear. 'It was dinner time and my mother let me stay off school for a long time afterwards, and I had nightmares. It took me a long time to get over it. Probably only when we moved. I couldn't go back into the cemetery again.'

The jigsaw of what the children claimed to have seen was starting to fit together.

About two weeks after my conversation with Jayne Atkins, Alan Taylor contacted me again. He had begun to take a real interest in the Downing case. When I told him I had spoken to Jayne, he asked if I could give him the details of her whereabouts, so that he could speak directly with her. At first I was reluctant to give him the information. Eventually I agreed to contact Jayne to see how she felt about doing a television interview. To my surprise, she agreed on condition that her exact location was *not* disclosed. Alan called her the following day, and she permitted him to do a taped interview over the telephone. That same evening it was broadcast on Central Television's regional news programme, over an old photograph of Jayne. She added nothing to my own interview with her, but reiterated her claims in support of Stephen Downing, while a voice-over updated viewers on other developments in the case.

To my horror, however, Jayne Atkins telephoned me a few days later in a blind panic. Despite my assurances to her that her where-abouts would not be disclosed, she informed me that her interview with Central Television had been broadcast on Greek TV and her cover was blown. Now everyone knew where she was. She said she would be forced to move on again. I did not understand. Despite repeated requests by the police to reveal her address, I had constantly refused. A check with a reliable police source confirmed that the police and Home Office had been tipped off by someone about her exact whereabouts. Had this same person also tipped off the Greek TV station?

Another good contact, this time at the Home Office, seemed to know more about this than he was prepared to say, but he pointed out that it would not take too much ingenuity to trace telephone calls out of the Central studios in Nottingham to a destination somewhere in Greece. He also added that photographs and a pirate news video from regional TV shows would not be too difficult to obtain or market abroad, given the right incentive. Alan Taylor assured me that he had told no one else from Central TV of Jayne's whereabouts, although he agreed it would not be too difficult for anyone to trace his call. He said Central TV had not sold the interview on to any other company and the broadcast in Greece must have been an enhanced pirate copy. It seemed I was not the only one who wanted to keep tabs on this particular witness. Both my police and Home Office informants had hinted that someone else in much higher authority was interested in Jayne.

'What did you make of her?' I asked Alan Taylor, the next time we met.

'I spoke to her at length,' he replied. 'I can't totally dismiss her claims. She's not the sort of person to embellish or distort. There's no doubt she was a crucial witness. OK, it took her a long time, but even so, her troubled childhood should not be forgotten. It can't have been easy for her to come forward with her story.'

I agreed. It had taken great courage for a teenage girl with a troubled home background, from a rural backwater, to make her first trip to London to appear in such august surroundings as the Court of Appeal before three bewigged judges. In doing so, and in telling all she knew in order to try to help free Stephen Downing and see justice prevail, despite anonymous threats to her family, she had done what many in Bakewell had been afraid to do. Many older, more respected pillars of the small society had kept their own counsel, and in fact continued to do so for twenty-eight more years. A teenage schoolgirl with no standing in the community had demonstrated what real courage and decency mean.

I was trying to tie up some loose ends before publishing my first article on the Downing case. As a result, January was turning out to be a very busy month.

I wondered if Wendy's fingernail scrapings had been taken. If she had fought and scratched her attacker, it would be possible with modern DNA techniques, to match them to him.

I had already been told early on in my enquiries that all exhibits, police paperwork, and the murder weapon had been destroyed. My police informants had disproved that by regularly coming up with copies of old witness statements and internal police notes from the case. I decided I wouldn't get anywhere if I didn't ask, so again I put in a formal enquiry to police headquarters about possible fingernail scrapings from Wendy Sewell. I got the reply that none were ever taken. One officer at police HQ told me it was probably because her nails were too short.

I went to Bakewell one day to try to find out more about John Marshall, the man who was allegedly the father of Wendy's child. I had half a dozen very good contacts who had lived all their life in the town and, like everybody else, had spent it keeping their ear to the ground. It was that sort of place. There was an old Derbyshire saying which went ''Ear all, See All, and Say Nowt' – the local variation on the Three Wise Monkeys. The first two commands I could go along with.

Marshall, I was told, was only about nineteen when Wendy became pregnant; she was some seven or eight years older. His family owned Broughton's department store in King Street in Bakewell, an established family outfitters and general store which sold traditional, well-made clothes meant to last for years and also had the contract to supply the pupils of Lady Manners with their school uniforms. It was a business which young John was destined to inherit one day. His family's plans for him did *not* include taking on the responsibility of an illegitimate child with an older, married woman. John, it appears, was quickly despatched to the army. It seems army life suited him. I was told he even bragged of being a member of the SAS.

While I was in Bakewell talking about the Wendy Sewell murder, I was astounded to learn that five men from the Bakewell area had been pulled in for questioning over the killing of Barbara Mayo, a young student from London who was found murdered in Derbyshire after hitching a lift up the M1. I remembered this case well – the murder had been high-profile nationally in 1970. Two young women, found murdered in the area, just three years apart. I wondered if there could be a connection.

Things suddenly seemed to be getting very serious. I was working alone, and most of my investigations into this case were being conducted in my own time. I wondered if I was beginning to get out of my depth. My fear was compounded by a resurgence of threatening telephone calls, mostly to my home.

Kath and I had still not got around to changing our number, despite good intentions. For one thing, I was reluctant to go ex-directory because of my job. It would be inconvenient. Most people who wanted to get in touch with the local newspaper editor were not wanting to discuss a murder. But I had to put my family first. The number was changed in January. I reported the renewed threats to the police at Matlock but, as before, I was disappointed at their apparent lack of interest.

I was still waiting for my permit to visit Stephen Downing in prison, when on 22 January a further letter arrived from him with answers to some of the questions I had previously asked. He wrote back, using my questions as headings:

WHAT CAN YOU TELL ME ABOUT THE MAN WHO THREATENED YOU?
I only saw the man who threatened me from the back as he ran off into the woods. He was wearing denim trousers and jacket, and I could see he had on a lemon-coloured T-shirt. From the back view I calculated he would have been around 5 feet 10 to 6 feet 4, heavily built though not overweight, and agile for his size. I didn't see his face, but I feel it must have been someone who knew me because he knew I had a sister.

I would say he had a local accent. That is to say, I didn't

notice anything to indicate he was an outsider. His voice was fairly deep in tone, though this could have been distorted as he spoke through clenched teeth in a vicious manner. There was no laughter or any other comments, save the ones I have already written to you about.

I didn't notice any body odour, aftershave or similar preparation, or smell of tobacco . . . although I was a smoker at the time so would probably not have detected it on another person.

As for the sharp instrument I felt in the small of my back, I had the impression that it could have been a knife. However, a knife was not used in the attack on Wendy Sewell. The police found two splinters of wood from the pickaxe shaft, each said to be around six inches in length. He could have pushed one of them into my back. There is nothing in the trial papers to indicate that they were tested for fingerprints. I don't think the shaft itself was tested either. I would not dismiss the possibility, either, that the two blood-stains on the back of my T-shirt might also have come from a splinter of wood if that was used, or from someone poking their finger into me. I don't know how far apart the stains are, or their size.

WHY DID YOU TELL NO ONE ABOUT HIM AT THE TIME?
I didn't tell the police or my solicitors because I thought I would eventually be released, and I was frightened because the man had threatened the same would happen to my sister if I told anybody.

WHEN DID YOU FIRST TELL SOMEONE ABOUT HIM?
The first person I told was my father in February 1974 after I had been convicted. I think he told my solicitors.

WHY DID YOU WAIT THIRTEEN DAYS TO RETRACT YOUR CONFESSION, AND WHAT PROMPTED YOU TO DO IT AT THAT POINT?
I strongly believed that I would not be kept in Risley for very long, before being released. I know that this seems rather silly, but I was that naive as to believe it. It was several days before I realised that I was not going to be let out. And with Wendy

Sewell dying, it had reduced my chances of the police finding out who was really responsible as she was not able to tell them.

This was quite devastating for me. It was like not being able to swim and getting thrown in the deep end. You believe someone will come along and save you, but when they don't you realise it is up to you to do something.

I had been terrified of saying anything about the man who threatened me in case the same happened to my sister. A few days after my arrest I had asked my parents to get police protection for Christine, on her way to and from school and so on. But the police had refused.

When I realised I was going to be held in prison and couldn't do anything to protect her, I had to change my plea so as I would be released and could watch over Christine. That's when I changed my plea . . . I broke down and cried and told my father I hadn't done it. Even this failed to get me released . . . but at least the truth was out. I certainly wasn't going to go back to taking the blame.

At last I felt I understood.

11

AFTER FIVE MONTHS of investigating the case, I now felt
ready to go public and run my first story. I prepared a file on my
initial findings to present to Derbyshire police and in late January ran
the first of many exclusive reports.

Matlock Mercury
27 January 1995

INNOCENT OR GUILTY?

The Home Secretary is to be asked to reopen the file on
Stephen Downing, the teenager convicted of the Bakewell
cemetery murder of Mrs Wendy Sewell in September 1973. A
portfolio containing new evidence is to be presented to the
authorities by Stephen's parents Ray and Juanita Downing in a
bid to secure his freedom . . .

After recapping the facts of the case, and Stephen's trial and subsequent appeals, the report went on to give a detailed account of my
investigations since September.

It put forward evidence that perhaps should have been placed
before the jury – but never was – like the psychiatric reports attesting
to Stephen's 'low intelligence', which went on to say it was not
suprising he had confessed to the attack after 'the worst experience of
harassment he had had in his life'. These reports were only made
known to the jury *after* they had reached their verdict. There was also
Mr Moss's forensic report, which had categorically stated that the
blood-staining on Stephen's clothes matched his version of events
and not that of his confession statement.

The method of interrogation was brought into question. A

teenager with the reading age of an eleven-year-old had been asked to sign a statement which he was unable to read properly, allegedly written for him in pencil, after nine hours of continuous questioning during which time he was denied access to a solicitor or his parents, and maintained he was cold, tired, hungry, in pain from a back injury and almost falling asleep.

It explained how the jury were unaware that Stephen had told police he saw and spoke to Charlie Carman who was between the shop and the cemetery heading towards the town, while Stephen was on his way home. Charlie told the jury he saw Wendy alive and well in the cemetery as he continued on his way to town. As this point was further on his route, it follows that he saw Wendy uninjured *after* Stephen had left the cemetery.

It continued in the same vein, relating how the jury were unaware that Stephen Downing claimed to have been assaulted and threatened by an assailant, who then ran off into the woods. The description he gave of this man matched that of a blood-stained man seen by one of the trial witnesses running away from the scene like 'a bat out of hell'. The article pointed out that the identity of this running man remained a mystery. It also reminded readers that Jayne Atkins alleged she saw a woman matching Wendy Sewell's description embracing a man in the cemetery, after this same witness had seen Stephen Downing leave by the gates. Her evidence was dismissed by an appeal court because she had not come forward before the trial, yet she stood by her story.

Anomalies about the number of blows struck, and Stephen's 'calm' and 'normal' demeanour as he passed by witnesses at the main gates, were also highlighted.

New allegations were made that Wendy Sewell might have had a prearranged meeting at the cemetery that day. The article focused on her final hours and included the facts that she had had a male visitor that morning at work, and that her boss had heard someone speaking to her in an 'abrupt' manner in her office just before she left for a 'breath of fresh air'. The article told of her secret past, and how the jury never knew that her marriage had been troubled, that she had numerous affairs and had a baby during a period of separation from her husband.

My story ran on to some inside pages together with photographs of Ray and Nita, the blood-stained clothing, the scene of crime, aerial shots of the site and pictures of Stephen in prison. Although my name was on the article, Jackie and my other colleagues at the *Mercury* had also made a valuable contribution.

With the heading 'Innocent or Guilty?' I was trying to turn the readers into a new jury, presenting them with a host of new facts, challenging them to see what they would have made of this new evidence – and whether it could throw doubt on the conviction.

The story attracted widespread publicity on several television and radio networks, and encouraged a tremendous local groundswell of support. Initially, this support seemed rather surprising, given the brutal nature of the attack and the passage of time. I had gained many new friends, but the story had struck a nerve with certain individuals – I had also collected a few enemies.

Calls came thick and fast over the next few days. Most were supportive and offered praise for my efforts. The odd one or two were more threatening and again criticised my involvement.

Quite unexpectedly my enquiries began to elicit rumours that reflected my own thoughts about a potential link to the murder of Barbara Mayo. It was being said around town, according to two of my regular Bakewell informants, that one of the men I was raising questions about had been quizzed in the past over the Mayo killing. The name being mentioned was that of Mr Red.

In Matlock, several Derbyshire police officers smiled sarcastically when they saw me in the street and indicated I had now put the cat among the pigeons. They made it plain that headquarters had placed me on the black list. It was nothing new and I was certainly not going to lose any sleep over their non-involvement. Other officers, that I had come to know and respect, offered their congratulations for such a daring article and expressed a desire to sort things out. The police at headquarters, however, still seemed uninterested and hostile.

28 January 1995
HM Prison
7 North Square
Dorchester, Dorset

Dear Don,

Thank you for the copy of the *Matlock Mercury*.

I should like to express my sincere gratitude both to you and your team for putting together an excellent article. I understand from my mother that it has sold 150 copies over and above the normal circulation in the local shop. At least it proves that a great many people are showing an interest, even if it is only to see if they are linked with it, as I suspect there will be a few that are worried that their names might appear.

Stephen Downing

30 January 1995

It had been a pig of an evening. I watched the wind and rain battering the bay window of my living room. I kept looking at the clock, hoping the weather would improve. Jess, my five-year-old blue merle collie, watched me, her head between her paws as she lay at my feet, looking up with sad, sorrowful eyes pleading for her evening walk. I pulled back the curtains further as if to explain, but she seemed determined.

Unlike the rain, I relented I had a simple plan. Take the car the half-mile or so to the local park opposite the small cinema, check out the forthcoming films in the foyer, then give Jess her run. The latest blockbusters usually reached Matlock's tiny screens several weeks after their London premieres, by which time the blanket newspaper and magazine coverage of plots, stars and special effects gave the locals the impression of already having seen them. Nevertheless, it was a night out, something a bit different from the pub and a Chinese takeaway.

As I turned sharp left into Steep Turnpike, the street adjacent to the cinema, I almost clipped the back wing of a dark-coloured sports car parked awkwardly on the corner. My slow speed, as I busied myself wiping the windscreen, had avoided a minor collision, something I could do without on a night like this. I manoeuvred the car into a parking bay at the back of a convenience store, and noticed the clock on the dashboard showed 9.45p.m.

It was cold and dark outside, the only brightness coming from the neon lights at the top of the cinema shining down on the hoardings and illuminating the front of the building, while across the road in the park a few tired, forgotten Christmas lights still glowed tackily, reflecting in coloured streaky patterns from the wet pavement.

I looked both ways before crossing. The rain was now driving horizontally into the side of my head. Part of my face went numb from the extreme cold. On my side of the road was a lay-by. It was normally full of parked cars but, on a night like this, was completely empty. This was also the widest part of the road and, with the lay-by, it was rather like crossing three lanes of traffic.

I was halfway across the road before I realised the danger.

The first screech from the rear wheels of the fast-moving vehicle as it accelerated from a standing start on the greasy road surface alerted my senses, that split second of prior warning giving me a fighting chance.

An unlit high-powered sports car had sped round the corner, crossed the central white line and begun to accelerate towards me out of the shadows. For an instant I froze, unsure whether to dodge back or go forward. I could feel my heart pounding and an acute tightness in my throat.

I thought I would be safest in the far lane and made to scurry quickly across, but the car was coming fast. It was now or never. I launched myself with arms outstretched on to the hard, wet pavement at the far side of the road. It was an instinctive, desperate dive. I rolled over and over with the momentum, until my back and my head thumped against the cinema wall.

The car clipped the kerb about a yard in front of me and continued its manic ascent of Steep Turnpike. Its spray hit me in the face, and the smell like rotten eggs from its catalytic converter made me feel nauseous. With swimming vision I saw the car skid, first one way then another, the wheels spinning crazily before the driver finally regained control.

Then I passed out.

'You were lucky! You were very lucky!' repeated the shrill, surreal and rather elderly voice into my right ear.

I felt dazed and my head was throbbing. It was like one of those moments when you are startled awake from a dream, slowly open your eyes, then pull back the bedclothes over your head and disappear again into the warm and comfortable land of nod.

'Are you still in one piece?' It was that voice again. I recoiled with a start, lifted my aching shoulders, shook my head and cursed at this persistent nuisance. I could still hear her talking . . . somewhere. Apparently I wasn't dreaming.

'Are you OK?' – that same voice.

I was gradually coming round and rubbed my eyes in disbelief. I was wet through, bleeding and I hurt. I stared aimlessly down at my bloody hands. I must have been knocked out cold for a few seconds.

'How are you feeling?' I tried to focus on the source of this relentless inquisition. I sat up square on the ground and grabbed at a drainpipe. I attempted to pull myself up. I seem to recall trying to stretch out an arm towards the old lady's sleeve. She appeared fuzzy, out of focus and her arm looked as though it was swinging about. I was not sure if her bony frame could support my weight, but my legs were wobbly and my head still spinning. Staggering to my feet, I regained my bearings and gently pushed the woman aside to glance up the steep road.

Surprisingly I could still see and hear the car climbing into the distance, its engine roaring. I had been out cold for just a matter of seconds. I watched as the driver turned on the lights before the car disappeared into the gloom of the deteriorating night. 'Yes, I'm fine,' I finally replied. I staggered to my feet, clutching at the old woman's coat. My legs were still like jelly. 'At least I'll be fine in a minute.' I didn't really feel at all fine, but I was wary of alarming her.

'I don't suppose you happened to see anything?' I asked hesitantly. I was breathless and my body shook. I let go of the woman's coat as a shooting pain caused me to clutch at my right elbow. I could feel the gash in my jacket, right through my jumper and shirt and the skin and flesh underneath. I must have taken the full impact of my dive on my right-hand side. My hair was saturated and something other than water began to trickle down my face and into the corner of my mouth. 'Ouch!' I yelled out involuntarily, as my fingers explored my bloodied matted hair, finding a small, deep cut on my forehead. My collar was already pink and stained from the gash and, as I brought my hand down, the rain washed the blood from my palm.

At that moment the first house from the cinema began to pour out and, despite the fact that the rain continued to belt down, a small crowd had soon gathered to stare at us: the odd couple, an elderly woman and a bedraggled, bruised and bleeding man with torn jacket and trousers.

I was confused and having serious doubts about what had happened. Had I been careless? Had something been prearranged? Who else knew I would be there? Had someone followed me from my home? Could I trust friends and work colleagues? Had someone let something slip?

A shout interrupted my wandering thoughts. 'Hey, look! It's that bloke from the *Mercury*,' roared a gruff voice from the back of the crowd. 'Excuse me, I'm coming through.' A short, thickset man in his early thirties pushed his way to the front of the assembled group. 'Hello, remember me?' he began, enthusiastically. 'You're Don Hale, aren't you? That bloke from the *Mercury*? You did a piece on my lad, remember?'

The rain was rolling down my face. As I wiped it away, pinky-red streaks appeared on my hands and wrists. My eyes were still trying to focus properly as I looked into the eager face smiling at me, arms sticking out squarely from his shoulders as if a large coat-hanger was keeping them in place. His face seemed vaguely familiar and in my dazed state I remember my gaze became transfixed on one cauliflower ear. All I really wanted to do was return home.

'So what's gone off then, youth? Has someone been knocked down?' asked a young woman who had joined my interrogator, slipping an arm proprietorially through his as if to announce to the crowd that they were a couple. I turned my gaze to her and winced in pain with the slight movement. She was dressed in a short coat and even shorter skirt and I noticed her legs through her tights turning bright pink in the rain.

I was about to reply when the old lady gave a nudge to my ribs with her umbrella, prodding me out of the way. 'This gentleman . . .' she explained, pointing back towards me, 'a car tried to run him over.'

This sent a sudden buzz of excitement through the crowd and people began chattering excitedly. 'Run him over! Did you hear that?' I heard a bystander enquire.

My interrogator persisted, 'That piece on my lad, remember? You're Don Hale, aren't you? Editor of the *Mercury*? You wrote about my lad . . . Brian Barrett. It was on the sports pages about two weeks ago. The picture and write-up are still on his bedroom wall.'

'Oh, yes. I remember,' I muttered softly. The man's voice sounded far away.

He seemed satisfied with my mumbled recognition. His partner smiled at me in sympathy and urged him to move away. He was not satisfied, though, and resisted any attempt to be moved on. 'So,' he demanded, 'what the bloody 'ell's been going on 'ere, then?' He was now standing even closer, almost on my shoes, and stared straight into my face.

'Bloody 'ell,' said another male voice from the middle of the damp throng. 'You say you're from the *Mercury*. That'll be about that murder investigation you've got on yer front page this week.'

At any other time such enthusiasm for my newspaper would have been music to my ears, but not on a night like this, with an unwanted audience and feeling groggy.

'Oh, it's nothing.' I sighed. 'I must have just slipped. It was dark and wet, and I probably didn't look properly when I crossed the road.'

My answer seemed to disappoint the drenched crowd. There was some additional chatter.

I felt an arm support my elbow and heard a woman's voice enquire, 'What's going on? Are you OK?' I turned and was relieved to see a face I knew instantly. One of my neighbours and a group she was with had been among the last to leave the cinema. 'Are you injured? I didn't realise it was you.'

She could see I was in pain. 'It's all right, I'll see to him, he'll be

OK,' she announced. The crowd began to disperse. 'I'll see you tomorrow, then,' she shouted to her friends, with a forced lightness in her voice, dismissing them with a casual wave. 'Let's sort you out,' she said briskly, turning back to me.

Then she started, as she felt a tap on her shoulder. 'Excuse me, miss, but I saw what happened. Someone definitely tried to run him over. I'm sure of it.' The elderly woman was still standing there.

'Er, yes, thanks for all your help, Mrs . . . er . . . I'm really grateful,' I stuttered, my words and thoughts still garbled.

'Yes, thanks so much,' my neighbour replied to her. 'He'll be fine. I'll take him home. I live near him.'

With that she rested my arm across her shoulder, asked where I was parked and steered me back across the road. 'Give me your keys,' she demanded.

'It's OK, I'll drive.' I replied.

'Keys!' she insisted. I fumbled for the right-hand pocket of my waxed jacket and realised there was a gaping hole where it should have been. I found the keys eventually in the lining and gave them to her.

My neighbour had driven back on to the A6 and around the traffic island in the centre of town before she spoke again. 'So what on earth happened to you?' she demanded. 'You look really awful!'

'Thanks, I've certainly had better days,' I replied mournfully.

'You're not answering my question. That woman said someone tried to run you over. Is that right? Are you OK? Do you need to see a doctor?'

'No, don't worry, I'll be all right. Let's head home. It was probably my fault. I fell awkwardly on to the pavement.'

She sighed. The explanation did not satisfy her, but she realised it was the only one she was going to get.

I continually replayed the moment in my head on the drive back, but was too sore and confused to reach sensible conclusions. I wanted to play it down. Was I being paranoid? Had I been careless, as I told everyone? I kept asking myself the same old questions. I remembered the dark-coloured car parked by the corner of the main road, without lights. I couldn't stop turning it over in my mind. It was the second time it had happened. Then there were the threatening phone calls.

I picked up that week's *Mercury* after my concerned neighbour had dropped off me and Jess at home. As I stared at the headline, 'Innnocent or Guilty?', I wondered if the bystander outside the cinema had been correct. Had my report attracted unwanted and sinister attention, resulting in the events of tonight? If I were truthful, I already knew the answer to that question.

The following morning as I walked down the hill towards the *Mercury* offices on the edge of the town, I felt certain that the office girls would have been told about the previous night's escapade.

'Well, how are you, then?' demanded Elsie, as I walked through the main door towards my office.

'Fine,' I replied.

Jackie was staring at me. 'God, you look a bloody mess!' she exclaimed.

I carefully felt my way around the desk and sat down with a bump. I had a sticking plaster over a deep cut above one eye and my right arm and elbow were throbbing with pain. 'Yes, I feel it. I had a bit of an argument with a racing car last night . . . as no doubt you've already heard.'

'My sister was at the pictures,' explained Elsie. 'She saw you after the fall.'

'Hit and run again?' asked Jackie.

'Well, sort of,' I blustered. 'Except it didn't quite hit. I somehow managed to leap clear, but it was close – and I'm paying for it today,' I added, rubbing my aching shoulder.

About an hour passed before Sam approached my desk. 'Well, come on. Spill the beans. It's that Downing case again, isn't it? I knew it! When you told me last September, I knew there was something in it. And then that man phoned.'

The other reporters had stopped tapping away at their computers in order to listen.

'I'm sorry to disappoint you but I really don't know what it's all about.' I sat on the edge of my desk, folded my arms and began to explain in more detail what had happened the previous night. 'This car just came out of nowhere. It had no lights. A dark-red Mazda sports car, I think. There may have been only one person in it, perhaps two. I remember seeing what looked like a young person crouched over the wheel. Long hair. I couldn't really tell if it was a man or a woman.'

'Look,' Sam said forcefully, 'a few weeks ago you were nearly killed. Then there was last night. What do you have to do before you finally accept that it's connected, end up in some morgue? You must tell the police.'

'Tell them what? I saw the police last time and they weren't interested. I've no more evidence,' I said.

Jackie, too, seemed genuinely concerned. 'Show them your arm, your coat, and what about that old lady who saw it? There's your evidence,' she shouted across the room. 'Tell them, Don, please. If you don't, I will!'

'OK, OK, I'll see them,' I finally conceded.

Later that day my phone rang. I picked up the receiver. 'Hello, who is it?'

It was Gill at the front desk. She said she had an anonymous caller on the line. 'Don, they won't give a name. Do you want me to put them off? Tell them you're busy?'

'No, I'll take it, thanks, there may be a connection. Is it a man or a woman?'

'A man,' she replied, 'and he sounds a bit aggressive. He sounds as if he's in a pub, or a bookie's, there's a lot of background noise.'

I pressed the button on my phone to take the call. 'Hello, Don Hale, editor, here. Can I help?' I asked calmly.

The editorial office suddenly went very, very quiet. All the journalists were listening as I took the call. They began to huddle around. I waved them away and mouthed that it was OK.

'Yes, Don Hale speaking, I'm the editor . . . Yes, I know about that murder story . . . Really, that's interesting. What exactly do you mean by that? . . . Can you explain? . . . Well, let's book the last week in June and first in July . . . I appreciate your call. It's been most helpful. At least it's proved we don't have a crazy driver on the loose in Derbyshire and that I'm probably on the right track regarding Mr Downing. Would you have attempted anything if the right person had been in prison?' There was a pause. 'Well, thank you. Tell your boss he *should* be concerned. Tell him the net is slowly closing and a file has been handed to the police.'

I replaced the receiver and punched the air with delight. 'Yes! Yes!' To Sam's alarm I rushed out to the front desk to see if the receptionist who had answered the phone had gleaned any further information from the anonymous caller, but she had nothing to add. I returned to the office, still with a wide grin across my face, the pain of my injuries temporarily forgotten in my excitement.

Jackie, Phil, Norman and Sam were standing around my desk waiting for an explanation.

'Was that him?' asked Sam.

'What did he want? What did he say?' Jackie too was very close to my desk and almost trampling on my feet with anticipation.

There was a buzz of excitement in the office as I recounted the conversation. 'Slow down, everyone,' I said. 'Yes, that *was* someone who claimed to know about the hit and runs last night and last month.' I took a deep breath. I still felt weak and shaky and sat back down in my chair before continuing. 'He told me not to meddle in affairs that didn't concern me and that there wouldn't be a next time or I'd be blown away.'

'What was that about being on the right track?' asked Sam.

'That's when he went very quiet,' I replied. 'He hadn't thought of that one, then I think the penny finally dropped. He obviously wasn't the driver or the top man, just someone phoning for someone else. And there wasn't much between his ears.'

'And what was all this business about last week in June and first in July?' demanded Norman.

'He said I'd got two weeks to live unless I dropped the Downing story, so I booked those two weeks with him!' I could not help grinning, much to Jackie's annoyance.

'You can't joke with people like that!' she exclaimed.

'Look, if they seriously wanted to kill me they could have done it at any time. It's hardly Fort Knox in here, is it? And everyone knows I'm always out jogging. It could be a crank – someone who's read this week's story.' I tried to appear relaxed.

'Rubbish!' said Sam, who had known true fear in his Second World War army days. 'A man threatens your life and you remain calm! How could a crank know about the other attempt in Darley Dale? Only the police knew about that – apart from us.'

The room went quiet again, as everyone pondered his words.

I broke the silence. 'I still feel that if they really wanted to kill me, they would have done so *before* I went public and prepared a file for the police, not now. It would only bring it down upon them if anything happened to me.' I had already conceded privately that handing the file of my findings to the police was probably going to be as much use as throwing it to my dog Jess to chew.

'You're a tricky devil. You're actually pleased about this call, aren't you?' added Sam in exasperation.

'So you'll go to the police?' reiterated Norman. 'Tell them about last night and this call?'

'Oh, don't start! I'll go.' I stretched my arms into the air, then winced at the sudden, sharp pang. 'It still hurts,' I admitted, half expecting some sympathy and clutching at the new source of pain.

'See, told you. What they do next time could hurt even more, so please go to the police station *now*,' pleaded Jackie. 'Do you want me or Sam or Norman to come with you?'

'No, I think not.' I snapped back.

The conversation settled down but the atmosphere remained strained. The tension was diffused by Gill popping her head round the door of the editorial office. 'Sorry to interrupt, Don, but there are some people in reception. Can you come and have a word? They're threatening to storm in here.'

'What do they want?'

'They're from the Women's Institute. They want to know why their report hasn't gone in again this week. They're after your blood!'

'Well, my dear, there's not much of it left. They'll have to stand in line.'

Later that day I walked slowly up the flight of stone steps to Matlock police station, still smarting from my injuries of Sunday evening. I recalled with dismay that I had already climbed these same steps on several occasions over the past four months to report on other matters concerning the Downing case. Each time I had come away feeling it had been a complete waste of time.

My heart sank as I pushed open the heavy swing door into the reception area. The only officer visibly on duty was a young constable, who had dealt with my first report of a possible hit and run attempt the previous month. So it was with some misgivings that I prepared to relate what I believed was a further attempt to mow me down.

The PC turned his back on me the moment I entered and simultaneously reached for a ringing telephone. I was left studying the noticeboard for a full ten minutes, the usual standard appeals and warnings about drink-driving, drugs, Neighbourhood Watch, Pub Watch, cycling proficiency tests. I tried to eavesdrop on the PC's conversation. It sounded like an internal call, someone of the same rank as he never used the word 'sir' throughout. He seemed quite laid back as if he was prepared to go on chatting all afternoon and I heard my own name mentioned a couple of times.

Sheila Davies, the station's civilian receptionist, came in. She had been there for some years and, although very polite and efficient, had a frosty attitude towards the media, which she had no doubt picked up from her force colleagues. 'Are you being seen to?' she enquired.

'Apparently not.' I snapped back, in a voice laden with sarcasm. 'Your colleague seems very busy.' I immediately regretted transferring my annoyance on to her.

'We're a bit short-handed at the moment. What's the problem?' she asked, unruffled by my irritability.

I gave her the name of the detective I wished to speak to. I had talked to him about the case on several occasions and he had tried to co-operate as much as he dared. He gave me 'off the record' explanations about police actions at the time of the investigation, but said he was 'under pressure from above'. It had become evident that his relationship with me was being scrutinised and censored from the force's county headquarters. He was certainly not a man to do anything which would jeopardise his own career.

'Is he expecting you?'

'Well, if his grapevine is as good as mine, yes.'

She picked up an internal phone and glared at the constable who was still deep in conversation, before turning her back on me completely. 'Hello, CID? Reception here. It's Mr Hale from the

Matlock Mercury to see the detective.' There was a long pause. 'Oh, thank you. I'll tell him. He'll be right down, Mr Hale. Please take a seat.' She gestured towards a row of uncomfortable-looking orange plastic chairs.

'Many thanks.'

About thirty seconds later the constable put down the telephone and called Sheila over. They had just begun a whispered conversation when the security lock buzzed on a door leading from a corridor into reception and the detective appeared. He ignored the PC and Sheila and walked straight past the reception desk towards me. 'Don, how are you?' he greeted me, holding out his hand in welcome. 'Come through. What can we do for you?'

'It's about a hit and run attempt last night,' I replied, speaking deliberately loudly as we passed back through the security door.

As we headed towards an interview room off the corridor I could hear the PC remonstrating with Sheila, telling her to refer all serious complaints from the public to him and not take it upon herself to ring CID directly.

'I bet he wishes he'd put that phone down earlier.' I could not help sniggering.

The detective grinned. 'You shouldn't encourage him, Don. You know he hates journalists.'

He pushed open the door to the bare, narrow interview room, clicking on the switch which jolted the fluorescent tube lights on the ceiling into life. One of the four was reluctant to come on at first and we both stood patiently waiting as it flickered a few times before pinging into action. The stark yellow glow made the dirty cream peeling paint on the walls and frosted-glass windows look even more dingy and a slight smell of disinfectant did nothing to dispel the unwelcoming ambience.

We sat on hard wooden chairs at opposite ends of a dismal Formica-topped table, with one short leg ensuring the compulsory wobble.

I had not been in this particular room before. 'Is this where you grill all the villains?' I asked.

'Of course, Don. Why do you think I've brought you here?' he joked, as he opened a drawer and took out a folder of blank statement sheets.

'What do you want me to admit to, then?' I challenged him. 'No, only kidding. I thought I was Stephen Downing there, for a minute.'

'Less of the frivolity, Don. What really brings you here? And sorry about this room, by the way. The CID office is being decorated.'

'Hope they make a better job of it than they did in here,' I mocked, looking around and added, 'It's about last night.'

'Last night?' the detective asked. He was about to pull out a pack of cigarettes, but remembered that I disliked smokers. 'Oh, sorry, Don. I'll have it later. It's a dirty habit. You mean the cinema incident?'

I looked at him in surprise. 'So you have heard?'

'Only from a "special" who came out from the first house. And then in a brief report from one of our guys who was sat in his car keeping an eye on the nightclub next door.'

'Next door! Then he must have seen everything that happened?'

'Not really. He said it was all over in seconds. This is all confidential, you understand? He heard a car screech, then saw someone sprawled on the pavement. He didn't know it was you. Probably wouldn't know you anyway. He's down from Derby division for a few days. He couldn't get a good look from where he was parked.'

'Well, why didn't he go in pursuit?'

'Come on! He was in plain clothes on surveillance. He had orders from Derby to watch that club.'

'That's more important, is it? Watching to see who goes in and out of that club, rather than a potential hit and run?'

'OK, I take your point. But as I say, he's Derby. We don't have a say. Anyway, you're OK, aren't you?'

'No thanks to your lot.'

'Look, I'll get us a cup of tea. You look as if you could do with one.' He went out to the canteen across the corridor and a few minutes later I heard his footsteps on the hard floor outside. He reappeared with two plastic cups. 'Two sugars, isn't it?'

'Yes, that's just the job.'

The detective took down the details of the incident outside the cinema the previous night, and the threatening phone call at the office the next day. He added comments about the similar incident near the riding stables in Darley Dale the previous month. Then he promised that both these alleged hit and runs *would* be taken seriously. Both, he confirmed, would be notified immediately to headquarters. 'Check under your car each time you need to use it and don't open any suspicious packages at the office for a while,' he warned me. 'If in doubt, call the police.'

12

FROM DAY ONE of my investigation I tried to keep the police and the Home Office fully informed of my progress.

During January and February 1995 I prepared two separate and detailed submissions to send to the Home Office on behalf of Stephen Downing. I believed my submissions contained a considerable amount of new information that demanded some explanation. I said I hoped to be able to prove reasonable doubt against Downing's conviction and trusted that, whatever the outcome, Downing would soon be considered for parole.

The West Derbyshire MP, Patrick McLoughlin, presented my first submission to the Home Office at the end of January 1995, while I handed in a copy in person at Derbyshire police headquarters in Ripley for the Chief Constable, John Newing, the following week.

By the end of January 1995, the following information formed the basis of my case to call for the re-examination of Stephen Downing's conviction for murder. I have to thank the unnamed, but unwaveringly supportive, police officers whose information enabled me to compile much of this information from old police reports which I was officially told had been destroyed.

The submission is only presented here as a summary, as my original document ran into 30 pages.

The method of interrogation constituted oppression:
- He was questioned for around nine hours without a guardian or solicitor present, even though he requested a solicitor on at least two occasions.
- There is confusion in police reports over the times he was cautioned and charged.

- He claims his statement was written for him in pencil and signed by him in ink.
- He claims parts of his confession statement were suggested to him and altered.
- He had to be shaken to keep him awake.
- He said he was cold, tired and hungry and in pain from a spinal injury.
- He said he was told he would be questioned all night if he did not admit it.
- Psychiatric reports confirm his poor reading ability and his reading age of an eleven-year-old at the time. The contents of these reports were not made known to the jury until after they had reached their verdict. He probably could not have read, written or fully understood his statement.
- He claims officers were betting their wages that he would confess before the night was out.

The contents of Stephen Downing's confession, which he later retracted, do not fit the known facts:
- Downing said he struck Mrs Sewell twice, yet it is undisputed that she was struck seven or eight times in a 'frenzied attack'.
- Forensic testing on the pickaxe handle was also consistent with an extremely frenzied attack, which contradicted Downing's confession statement.
- Downing said he had sexually assaulted her by inserting his finger into her vagina. Although the police were happy to use this as evidence they knew there was not a scrap of forensic evidence to back up a sexual assault.
- Is 'vagina' a word Stephen Downing would normally have used or understood?

The forensic evidence:
- Minute spots of blood on the trousers and other clothing, some of which could only be seen under a microscope, match Downing's explanation that, as he backed away from the victim, she raised herself up and shook her head, spraying minute particles of blood through the air. This explanation was not accepted by the Prosecution. A report compiled for

the Defence backed Downing's version, but the expert who had written it was not called to give evidence.

- With such a ferocious attack, Stephen's clothing would have been extremely blood-stained. The ambulanceman who attended to Wendy was covered in blood and had to destroy his uniform. Yet several witnesses noticed Stephen leaving the cemetery after the attack was claimed to have taken place and none saw any signs of blood-staining about his person.

- There is confusion over whether Downing's fingerprints were taken, as it was assumed he had been wearing gloves. No evidence regarding his fingerprints was put forward at the trial. His fellow workmen who gave evidence at his trial said they remembered him telling police he had been wearing gloves. Yet Downing's statement taken on the night of the attack, clearly says his gloves were in his back pocket and forensic experts at trial described how blood could have got on to his gloves in his back pocket. There would have been more blood on his gloves if he had been wearing them when he turned her over.

- It was not made clear at trial that the victim moved from the path where she was attacked to gravestones several yards away and adjacent to the path. Nor was it explained *how* she moved, or was moved.

The timings:

- Downing was seen by witnesses leaving the cemetery at 1.08p.m. appearing calm and with no obvious signs of blood-staining. Neither of these things would have been possible, had he just carried out a frenzied attack as alleged. After his return, only one witness out of the six who described his demeanour said he was in an excitable state. The others maintained he was calm and normal.

- Jayne Atkins saw Wendy Sewell in the cemetery with her arms round another man, just minutes after she had seen Stephen leaving at 1.08p.m. I believe I have shown that, contrary to what was asserted at appeal, her evidence is reliable.

- One witness, whose evidence was read out at trial, claimed to have seen Wendy Sewell walking in the cemetery. It was not stated at trial that Downing claimed to have seen this same person at an earlier time *after* he had left the cemetery.
- From the known movements of Wendy Sewell and Stephen Downing, he would have had at most thirteen minutes to follow the woman around the cemetery, go to the store to collect the murder weapon, carry out the attack as described, return to the store and collect his jacket and pop bottle, stoke the fire . . . then walk 260 yards to the main gates. The prosecution case claimed he had eighteen minutes.
- Jayne Atkins and her mother, Mrs Margaret Beebe, both heard a cry for help *after* Downing had left the cemetery.

The scene of crime procedures:
- Local residents have complained that no routine house-to-house enquiries were made at the houses overlooking the cemetery.
- The area was not cordoned off, according to local residents.
- No search was made in the adjoining woods for the victim's personal possessions or tights.
- Local residents have complained of offering information to the police e.g. registration numbers of suspicious vehicles in the area, suspicious people in the area at the relevant time . . . and of being turned away.
- Downing was allowed to continue working with bloody hands, before being taken to the police station.

The new witness statements:
- Recent statements by Stephen Downing highlight facts not presented to the jury:

1. There were blood-stains on his jacket, yet he clearly describes how he collected his jacket from the store just prior to leaving the cemetery at 1.08p.m. At the time he was meant to have carried out the attack he was not even wearing his jacket. The stains could only have come when he returned and found the body.

2. He himself was threatened after he returned to the cemetery and was warned not to say anything or else the same would happen to his sister. He saw his assailant disappear into Catcliff Woods and was able to describe him. Although this did not come out at trial, there is proof that he told his Defence team about this threat shortly after the trial. He has given reasons why he did not mention this earlier.

- Recent statements from witness Jayne Atkins, whose evidence was rejected at appeal on the grounds that it was not 'reliable' because there had been an 'excessive delay' in her coming forward. These new statements explain the circumstances in which she came forward with new evidence and demonstrate there was not an 'excessive delay'. Her statements prove that she could not have got mixed up about the day in question, when she alleged she saw Wendy Sewell in the cemetery with her arms round a man behind the consecrated chapel, near to the spot where she was attacked. He is not Stephen Downing.

- A man was alleged to have had a 'terrific row' with Wendy Sewell on the night before the attack and arranged to meet her the next day to 'put things right'. He was questioned about this before the trial, but gave an alibi and was believed.

- This same man fits the description of a man seen hanging around the cemetery up to an hour before the attack, according to two new witness statements.

- A man seen running away blood-stained from the scene was positively identified to the police shortly after the trial. This witness has again repeated this man's identity in a recent statement given to me. Despite her reporting this to the police, the man has never been interviewed.

- A new witness claims she was told by a friend of Mrs Sewell's that the murdered woman had an assignation with someone in the cemetery that day.

- A new witness has come forward to say that one of the people who gave evidence to the trial told 'a pack of lies' about his movements that day and about the time he saw Wendy heading for the cemetery.
- Two further witnesses, one a child at the time, have spoken of a man running away from the direction of the cemetery at the critical time. One noticed he was blood-stained.
- One witness, then a child, has spoken of seeing a person covered in blood on a gravestone.
- A new witness statement shows that Mrs Sewell may have had some business to attend to that morning before she went to work.

Other considerations:

- Although Mrs Sewell was not on trial, her background was never mentioned in court. It was evident she was well known to a number of men. She was married to David Sewell, but had a child five years previously with someone else, during a period of separation from her husband.
- The man talking to Mrs Sewell in an abrupt, high-pitched voice in her office just before she left work at lunchtime has never been traced.
- At least two of Mrs Sewell's known associates were questioned about the murder of another woman three years before Mrs Sewell was murdered.
- Downing retracted his statement thirteen days later. His revised statement was never checked or accepted by the police.

The medical reports, forensic reports, together with the Home Office Summary and social reports relating to Stephen Downing, which backed up many of the above points, all formed part of the submission.

Dear Don,

Thanks for sending the copies of the proposed submission. I have read it several times so that I am familiar with the contents.

It puts across a strong argument to support and uphold my claim of innocence. Hoping that your time-honoured efforts will not have been in vain.
Best regards,

Stephen Downing.

13

Early February

IN FEBRUARY 1995, perhaps in response to my article, an anonymous letter arrived at the offices of the *Matlock Mercury*, purportedly from a woman who had been in the vicinity of the graveyard at the time of the attack on Wendy Sewell. Its contents suggested that the letter writer was the woman who Ray Downing claimed had tried to contact the *Mercury* and the *Star* the previous year, which had prompted his visit to me in the first place.

It was received on 2 February, and stated:

> Just after Easter, I wrote to the editor of the *Daily Star* in London. I informed him that I had recently returned to the Bakewell area after living away for 20 years and that on 12 September 1973 I had met a male friend on the pretence that we were taking our children back to school (Bakewell Junior School).
>
> After seeing our children into school, we went down towards the cemetery and started to walk along the path towards Burton Edge. On the waste ground there, we saw a parked van with the driver sat in it. As we knew him, Syd Oulsnam, we retraced our steps and entered the cemetery near the beech hedge and walked along the top footpath. On reaching the chapel which the council used as a workshop we saw the groundsman, Stephen Downing, walking along the main drive towards the main gate.
>
> We heard voices coming from the direction of the other chapel near the wood. We saw two people, Mr Red and Wendy

Sewell. They appeared to be arguing. At this point we saw another person, George Pearson, walking towards them. We also heard voices coming from the direction of Burton Edge and saw two women talking somewhere near no. 4.

We decided to leave the cemetery by the bottom gate and walk through the wood. As we walked towards Butts Road we heard a lot of shouting, then all went quiet. My friend climbed up the bank and looked over the wall. He said that someone was lying on the ground and went over the wall to see what had happened.

Someone was running away from the scene. We think it was George Pearson. When I looked over the wall I told my friend that Stephen Downing was coming back down the main drive. He climbed back over the wall. In doing so, he dropped his wallet from his pocket. As he looked over the wall, he saw Stephen had arrived on the scene and was bending over Wendy Sewell with his back to us.

My friend went to pick up his wallet. Stephen Downing got up and jumped back. My friend put his hand on Downing's shoulder and said something like 'Don't turn around or we'll say you did it and think of your sister'. We then ran back into the wood.

I am writing this in the hope you can look into this and clear this young man's name and put the right one behind bars.

Three of the men I'd been chasing all mentioned in the one letter!

The letter raised many interesting questions, the most glaring being the sighting of Wendy in the cemetery arguing with our old friend Mr Red near the area where she was attacked. This fitted with the account given by Jayne Atkins, except Jayne had stumbled on Wendy embracing a man, not arguing with him. Both my mystery correspondent and Jayne had reported seeing Stephen walking towards the cemetery gates at the same time as these sightings occurred.

If the letter were genuine, then the anonymous woman and her male 'friend' could clear Stephen Downing's name. Here were two

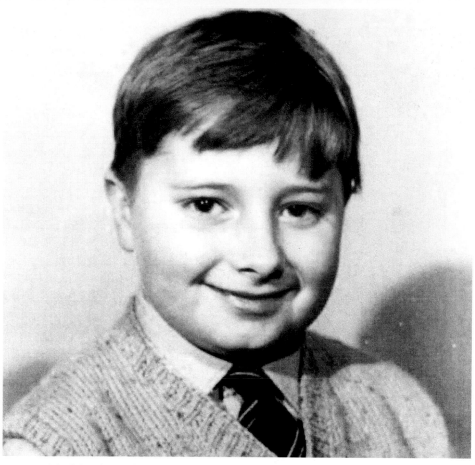

1 (*above*) Stephen at Junior School   2 (*below*) Stephen as a long-haired 70's teenager

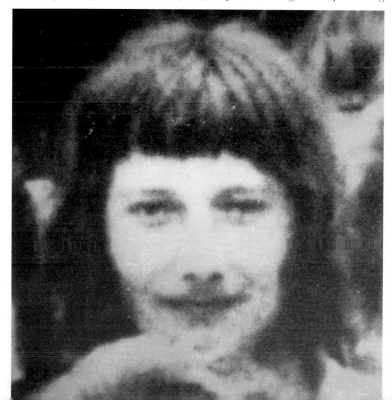

3 A radiant Wendy on her wedding day in March 1964

4 An aerial view of the cemetery where Wendy was murdered

5 (*above*) The Kissing Gate where Wendy passed George Pearson on her final walk

6 (*below*) Workmen's pick-axe handles in the unconsecrated chapel

7 (*above*) The bottom path where Wendy met her death

8 (*below*) Wendy's clothes at the scene of crime

9 (*left*) The heavily bloodstained pick-axe handle used to bludgeon Wendy to death

10 (*below*) A police chalkmark shows blood on the grave of Anthony Naylor at the crime scene

11 (*above*) Don at work at the *Mercury*

13 (*right*) Stephen, with *Mercury* staff, reads about his freedom (Don took the picture)

12 (*below*) Stephen's family in the cemetery 27 years to the day after the murder

14 (*above*) Broad smiles from Nita and Stephen after the appeal verdict

15 (*below*) Freedom at last – Don and Stephen stride the hills above Bakewell

more people to add to my growing list, who apparently saw Wendy alive and well *after* Stephen had left the area for a break. The letter writer corroborated Stephen's own story about being threatened from behind as he leant over the injured Wendy, and of his assailant warning him not to turn round or else something would happen to his sister. But she seemed to show that this man was *not* the murderer, as I had previously thought.

George Pearson's name had again cropped up. If the events described in the letter were true, he probably saw the anonymous courting couple discover Wendy lying on the path. This would fit in with what his former lover, Rita, had recently told me.

And other witnesses on the estate, including Ray Downing and Jayne Atkins, had mentioned Syd Oulsnam or someone of his description parked or driving in his van near the scene.

The writer said there had been 'a lot of shouting' at one point. Mrs Beebe had mentioned hearing a cry some time after one o'clock. So had her daughter Jayne.

I wondered if one of the women talking on Burton Edge could have been Pat Shimwell? She'd told me she was chatting to a neighbour outside her house when Stephen left the cemetery at about ten past one. She might have still been there.

All the pieces of the jigsaw seemed to be fitting together.

On the other hand I had to accept that the letter was most likely to have been a hoax to implicate people in the crime – either maliciously, or because they believed them to be guilty, or simply to create confusion and throw me off the trail. When I showed George Pearson the letter some time later, he hotly denied the allegations it made against him. That was the problem with anonymous letters. As hard evidence, they were ultimately useless.

I sighed heavily and put the letter aside. I had this week's edition of the paper to get out that day and I had another major story about the Downing case on the front page based on my recent letter from Stephen in Dorchester prison.

Matlock Mercury
Friday, 3 February 1995

ADMITTED ATTACK TO PROTECT HIS SISTER

Bakewell man Stephen Downing has claimed that he only admitted to the attack on murder victim Wendy Sewell in 1973 – to help protect his sister!

In an exclusive interview this week, Downing confirmed why he originally decided to take the rap for a crime he has since maintained he did *not* commit and why after 22 years behind bars he now regrets his panic-driven action.

Downing said he had admitted it to protect his sister's safety. And he claimed he himself had been assaulted immediately after finding the body in the cemetery . . .

The report went on to describe how Stephen had retracted his admission of guilt in a conversation with his father a few days after being charged with murder. It told how he had then, shortly after his trial in February 1974, explained to Ray Downing something he had never told the police – that he himself had been threatened by a man in the cemetery and told to keep quiet. And that he had been scared to tell anyone because the man had told him his sister Christine would come to harm if he spoke out.

I jumped up when she reared up and I jumped back and leaned against a gravestone. She fell back. At this point a hand was placed on my back and someone said, 'Don't move. We will say you did it – remember the same will happen to your sister.' He then added 'Have you got it?' or 'Have you found it?' I heard rustling and turned around, but only saw the back of someone going down the slope and into the woods. He had a denim jacket over his head. I thought he was wearing a lemon T-shirt.

The response to this report was just as overwhelming as to that of the previous one, although thankfully I did not have to leap out of the path of any speeding cars this time.

As before, the telephones never stopped ringing with messages of support and with information or requests for meetings from people who thought they might know something, or who had been waiting for the opportunity to get something off their chests for over twenty years. Once more I was astounded at the depth of feeling aroused by this case in Bakewell and the surrounding area.

Perhaps prompted by my second report in the *Mercury*, another anonymous letter arrived ten days later on 13 February. In it the writer confessed,

> Had I not been young at the time, I would have placed more importance on any information given to an inquiry.
>
> Wendy was known to me and I had seen her prior to this incident date accompanied by a man in the wooded area, located down from the cremation Garden of Remembrance. This person was *not* Stephen Downing. Stephen would have been instantly recognisable as the young man who had once got me some water for flowers and who I had seen at other times.

She said that during this period she used to visit a farmer's wife in the Peak District, and her letter went on,

> She would quiz me if, or not, I knew anything about Wendy, who was apparently having a relationship with her husband.
>
> I did not know him to speak to but had, on occasions, seen Wendy with him in a van. It occurred to me on reading an article in a paper that a witness had come forward seeing a blond man run away. I believe he was blond-haired.
>
> I understand only too well anonymous letters are of little value and would be prepared to sign a witness statement, given an assurance that it will be kept confidential – even from other witnesses.

In the following weeks, an anonymous phone call came to the offices of the *Matlock Mercury* from a very frightened woman. It was passed straight on to me. She claimed to have written one of the anonymous letters and said she had further information which could help to free Stephen Downing. She said she used to help with Mrs Red's business on the farm. The woman sounded quite young, probably in her twenties or thirties. This was obviously the writer of the second letter. She knew all the details of Mrs Red's business, which I, too, had learned about from my contacts in the Bakewell area. The caller's story rang true so far.

She continued, 'Mr Red's wife became suspicious that he was becoming involved with a very attractive young woman from Bakewell. She said her name was Wendy Sewell. She asked me if I could keep an eye out and let her know if I saw them together. She thought Mr Red used to meet Wendy around the edges of the farm and wanted me to watch out for them as I rode around the lanes. I often used to see them together. Sometimes they were in a Land Rover, other times in the fields.'

'How old were you at the time?' I asked gently.

'I was in my early teens.' That put the woman in her thirties.

'So what did you do?'

'Well, one day I saw them kissing. I think he saw me watching. You can imagine – I was a young girl in this situation. I was terrified after that. He kept giving me these stares when he saw me around the stables. I knew his secret! I didn't want to be involved any more.'

'Did you tell his wife?'

The woman said she had to go. I could hear voices in the background. It sounded more like an office than a home. 'There's someone on another line,' she said. 'I'll call back.'

True to her word the woman called again a couple of days later. She told me more about Mr Red. 'He was an arrogant bully!' she said. 'Quite a few local men used to come to the farm looking for work. He had this take it or leave it attitude towards them. I think most of them were frightened of him. There were some pretty heavy-duty-looking friends used to come to the farm, too. I don't know who they were.'

'What kind of work did he give people?'

'Oh, this and that. Building, driving and deliveries . . . he seemed to have some kind of hold over work contracts with the local council for trimming hedges, grass verges, wall repairs, transport, that kind of thing.'

My mind immediately turned to Oulsnam and the hedge-triming and grass-cutting he had been doing on the estate in 1973. Was he one of the local men employed by Mr Red at that time? They lived in neighbouring villages. It was quite likely.

I asked the woman if she would be prepared to meet me. She refused point blank. She said there was nothing more she could tell me and was not prepared to make a statement. Sadly, no amount of coaxing would change her mind.

I did manage to trace her call, though. I had heard several background references to quarrying while she was talking to me. I had worked out she was on a reception counter or a switchboard. I rang around the local quarries. On my fourth call, bingo! The same woman answered. I told her who I was and asked her if she had just phoned me. She denied it. I knew it was her.

She called once more after that, to tell me she wouldn't be able to speak with me any more. She said she was too scared of repercussions and didn't want to end up like Wendy.

14

February 1995

IN EARLY FEBRUARY I received an astonishing phone call
from someone claiming to be an assistant to the curator at Derby
Police Museum. In a strong Derbyshire dialect he said, 'Eh up, youth,
is it you that's looking for this murder weapon in the Downing case?'

I could hardy believe my ears and wondered if it was a wind-up. It
was not the usual 'police speak'. 'The pickaxe handle?' I asked.

'Yes, that's the one. It's here. I'm looking at it right now. It's one
of our prize exhibits. It's even got a brass plaque: "Stephen Downing,
Bakewell cemetery murder, September 1973, victim Wendy
Sewell".'

I was astonished. Then I wondered if it were a hoax.

'Do you want to pick it up?' he asked.

'No, no! You're saying this pickaxe handle is in the Derby Police
Museum?' I checked, still wondering if there had been a mix-up. 'I
was told it had been burnt.'

'No, mate, it's not been burnt. It's here. Looks a bit discoloured
but it's one of our best displays. It's here all right. Been here for years.
We're quite proud of it. One of Derby and County's quickest
convictions,' he said.

'Don't touch it,' I told him. 'And don't tell anyone else about it –
and especially don't say you've spoken with me. I'll try and make
some arrangements for collection. Many thanks.'

'No problem, mate,' he acknowledged casually. 'Just wanted to put
you right.'

'Much obliged,' I said, putting down the phone.

I sat down in disbelief with my face between my hands. This was potentially crucial evidence and vital for any appeal. Just like the Prosecution paperwork, it had turned up despite continual claims from the force that all exhibits and documents relating to Downing's case had been burnt or destroyed. I told Norman, Jackie and Sam, and enjoyed their equally surprised expressions.

Another informant rang from police HQ a few days later. He told me there was a clear palm print on the heavily blood-stained wooden shaft – which was certainly not Stephen Downing's. There was also, he said, a blood sample on the handle which belonged to neither Stephen nor the victim, Wendy Sewell. So whose was it? It suggested the assailant might have cut himself during the attack on Wendy. This was exciting stuff and a real breakthrough.

My contact said hairs and fibres might also have been found on the weapon. These, added to the blood sample and palm print, could now help to identify a third person – possibly the real killer – and I hoped it would be sufficient for the police to use their much heralded DNA techniques. My informant was as intrigued as I was, but warned, 'The palm print might be a red herring.'

'What do you mean?'

'Looks like it could belong to one of our lads. A PC who was left hanging about was told to bag up the bits and bring them back to the shop. He probably picked up the whole lot and just did as he was told.'

I tried to picture the scene. A young bobby left alone for hours in that cold, desolate cemetery, stamping his feet and trying to keep warm as darkness fell. I immediately thought of cross-contamination and wondered if the bloody murder weapon had been placed in the same bag as Wendy's clothing. Vital clues could have been obliterated. 'He didn't put everything in the same bag, did he?' I asked incredulously.

He was uncertain as to how many bags were used. 'You have to remember, Don,' he replied, 'at the time no one knew this was a murder. The case notes from the first couple of days that I've got here are still referring to it as grievous bodily harm.'

I had already noted from other paperwork leaked to me by police contacts that the Home Office forensic scientist had not attended the scene of crime, working and preparing his analysis from a base some

twenty-five miles away. This report had been sent to me anonymously. There were obviously police officers at Derbyshire HQ
wishing me well. It made up for the rest. Friendly contacts within the
force remained only too willing to feed occasional snippets of
information through the system. I had four very reliable informants
among the Derbyshire police who have remained supportive
throughout my enquiry.

A little later that month I got another call to say that, contrary to
what I had been told by Derbyshire police HQ the previous month,
fingernail scrapings *had* been taken from the victim, Wendy Sewell.
They still existed. They had lain in police vaults for twenty-two
years. 'So you see, Don, what you were told was wrong. The trial
exhibits haven't all been destroyed.'

I told him that Wendy's fingernail scrapings had never even
appeared on the trial list of exhibits. Yet I had always thought it strange
that none were taken from her, considering the brutality of the
attack. Surely she would have scratched and clawed at her assailant?
Once again, it was my hope that, with DNA technology, the
scrapings and the murder weapon could be vital in linking Wendy to
her attacker.

My informant rang a few days later to add that records showed
Downing's fingerprints had *not* appeared on the blood-stained shaft
of the pickaxe handle and there had been nothing obvious in
Wendy's fingernail scrapings to link her to Downing. This, at least,
seemed to indicate that Stephen's fingerprints *had* been taken.

My exclusive story in the *Matlock Mercury* ran with the angle of
'DNA LINK: MURDER CLUES'. The report encouraged the local force
to use their high-tech DNA expertise to help eliminate people from
their enquiries. I believed that not only could it help clear Stephen's
name,but it could establish a clear and definite link to someone else.

The national press now began to show an interest in the Downing
case. In particular, Frank Curran of the *Daily Star* regularly telephoned or met with me to keep abreast of any updates. As explained
earlier, I had contacted Frank when Ray Downing first got in touch
with me the previous September.

Frank, Alan Taylor and Brian Collins from Central Television, and
Rob Hollingworth from the *Sheffield Star* began to conduct their

own independent enquiries and faced similar hostility and threats from certain quarters. Frank and Alan in particular helped to keep up the pressure. They interviewed the family, key witnesses, potential suspects, police officers and other interested parties. They agreed that there were too many inconsistencies in the original evidence to have produced a safe conviction.

The first major Downing story to hit the nationals was Frank Curran's front-page lead in the *Daily Star* in February 1995: '22 YEARS IN JAIL — BUT IS HE INNOCENT?' The sub-heading claimed 'Love Cheat Wife's New Clues to Murder Case' and the introduction explained how 'A cheating wife has given police clues which could prove a convicted killer who has served 22 years is *innocent*. The "silent witness" says she knows Stephen Downing did not batter a woman in the cemetery.' The article went on to give details of the anonymous letters I had received earlier that month.

But it was Frank's second story the following week that really caused the muck to hit the proverbial fan. On 13 February 1995, picking up on my DNA article and talking to his own contacts within Derbyshire police, Frank Curran had another major page lead on the story:

Tell-tale fingertip scrapings could prove that Stephen Downing has been wrongly jailed for 22 years.

Typist Mrs Wendy Sewell was murdered in Bakewell in 1973, but in her struggle scratched her attacker — his skin was under her nails. Now the four suspects will be tested to see if their DNA matches. The *Daily Star* has discovered the scrapings have lain in police vaults for 22 years. But the evidence was never given in court. It would have cleared Stephen as his blood group did *not* match.

For some unexplained reason gardener Stephen's Defence Counsel was not told of its existence. The *Daily Star* has discovered two other vital pieces of evidence which point to a miscarriage of justice.

(a) Several fingerprints were found on the bloodstained murder weapon — a wooden shaft — but none were Stephen's.

(b) Experts told police that the killer was almost certainly right-handed. Stephen is left-handed.

Stephen, 39, has spent 22 years in prison and last night was still in Dorchester jail. Downing, then aged 17, with a reading age of 11, was arrested minutes after finding the body where he worked.

New suspects were recently named by a cheating wife who was in the cemetery with her lover when Wendy was killed. She wrote anonymously to a local paper telling how she saw Stephen arrive *after* Wendy was brutally attacked . . .

Frank then went on to describe four men placed at the scene that day by the anonymous letter writer and others. He gave detailed descriptions of Syd Oulsnam, Mr Red, George Pearson and Mr Blue, and told of alleged sightings of them around the cemetery that day. He stopped short of naming them, giving them letters instead.

My telephone was red-hot after the *Mercury* report – and then later with Frank's revelations in the *Daily Star*. Readers were checking in to compare notes and to see who was who. Names were offered to put faces to the four whom Frank had named merely as A, B, C and D. Informants in Bakewell told me that alleged suspects were panicking. They had definitely recognised themselves from Frank's piece.

On the afternoon of 13 February came one of the most surprising and bizarre phone calls I have ever received in connection with the case. Syd Oulsnam phoned in. He admitted he thought he was the person described as Suspect A in the *Daily Star* report. He asked, 'What does DNA mean?' and also demanded to know, apparently in all innocence, 'If my vehicle was involved, how could it link me with the pickaxe handle?'

I couldn't believe my luck. I explained, as best I could and in simple layman's terms, the intricacies of DNA. I argued that if Syd, or anyone else, had touched the murder weapon, or if the forensic evidence contained hairs or fibres from his vehicle, the police would be able to determine these facts.

It was obvious Syd was in complete turmoil. As in our last conversation, he at first denied being in the Bakewell area that day.

'I've told you, I was miles away,' he bleated. 'I already gave the police a statement telling them that I was nowhere near.'

I told him that I had new witness statements from people on the estate who had seen his van up there that day. What's more, they had seen him in it. 'I can tell you its registration number, where it was parked, for how long and exactly what you looked like in 1973. There's no doubt it was you, Syd. What's the point in lying about it?'

At first, Syd continued to deny any involvement.

'So *prove* where you were, if you weren't at Bakewell cemetery, then.'

'It was a long time ago,' he replied weakly.

'Well, with DNA and these new statements, *I* can prove where you were,' I told him.

He still denied it.

I put the pressure on and told him, 'Look, Syd, eventually new DNA evidence is going to free Stephen Downing. Then there'll be murder and conspiracy charges brought against other people. It would be best for anyone who knows something to talk now.'

The mention of DNA had really got him on the run. 'OK,' he eventually relented. 'I'll admit it. I was up there near the cemetery.' He sounded almost in tears.

'What were you doing up there?' I asked, fully expecting the reply 'cutting grass'.

'I took Mr Red up there.'

My heart missed a beat. 'What time?'

'We got there about half past twelve.'

'What happened then?'

'We waited around for a while near the gates. Then I drove to some waste ground at the back of the cemetery and parked up.'

'What were you doing there?'

'We were waiting. I had nothing to do with it!'

'To do with what?' I asked.

'That murder. Wendy Sewell,' Syd replied.

'Look, Syd, I just want to know what happened. You could well be in the frame for this at present. Let's help to clear your name,' I explained, using a softer voice.

'I never got out of the van!' he replied, obviously in a panic.

'No, no, Syd. I'm not saying you did. Just tell me what Mr Red did.'

He paused. 'Mr Red went somewhere.'

'Where?'

'I don't know. Mr Orange was waiting for us.'

'Who?'

'Mr Orange [his name for this book].'

'Who's he?' This was a name I hadn't heard before.

'He's a friend.' I decided to check out Mr Orange later.

'Did Mr Red take anything with him from the van?' I enquired.

'He took something from the back.'

'What?'

'I don't know.'

'What kind of things did you carry in the back?'

'Tools and suchlike.'

'Were there ever pickaxe shafts in the back of your van?'

'*Yes.*'

'So when did you next see Mr Red?'

'I met up later with him in town,' he said.

'Why didn't you wait for him?'

'I can't remember.'

I pushed him further. 'Come on, Syd, try.'

Eventually he replied, 'I remember hearing a shout or something, then I drove off.'

'What time?'

'About twenty past one, I suppose.'

'Were Mr Red and Mr Orange meeting anyone else up there?' I asked.

'I don't know.'

'Was Wendy Sewell ever a girlfriend of Mr Red's?'

'*Yes.*'

'Do you know anything about Wendy and Mr Red having a row the night before?'

He said he thought they had. 'I think', he added, 'they wanted to put things right.'

Eureka! I thought, after I put the phone down. For once I hoped the police had tapped my call. For weeks I'd been hearing strange nosies and clicks on my direct line and home phone. Kath and the boys had heard them too. I wondered if they were also monitoring the homes of potential suspects and witnesses.

I hadn't mentioned Mr Red's name. Syd had volunteered that information. He'd now placed them both at the scene, which confirmed they'd both given false alibis to the police in the past.

He'd confirmed the connection between Mr Red and Wendy and the row the night before . . . probably the one overheard by the son of the businessman that Ray had been told about twenty years before.

I now knew that at least two of the men I was interested in were acquainted.

Other details began to fit into place. Jayne Atkins and her mother, Margaret Beebe, had both mentioned hearing a cry at around the same time as Syd. Ray Downing had seen Syd at 1.23 driving down the road away from the cemetery towards town. I'd always assumed all this, but until now had never known for sure.

One new piece of information was, of course, the name Mr Orange. Here was a fifth man allegedly placed at the scene . . . to add to Mr Red, Oulsnam, Pearson and Mr Blue. Again I asked around the Bakewell grapevine. It appeared Mr Orange lived by himself, somewhere on the edge of the Peak District, and kept himself pretty much to himself, preferring to live and work alone. He was described to me as a tall, slim, fit-looking man, now aged around fifty. That would have made him in his late twenties at the time of the murder. I was told that back then he had had blondish hair, but was now fair and turning grey. 'Quite nondescript' was one phrase used. He occasionally did odd jobs for Mr Red, and sometimes drank in Bakewell's pubs.

A few days after Syd's panic-stricken phone call to me, a reliable informant from Bakewell, who ran a business in the town, told me he had heard that Syd had been speaking to me.

'What makes you think that?' I quizzed him.

'He was only bleating about it the next day in the pub to all his mates,' he answered. 'He said he'd been talking to the editor of the *Mercury* and had been forced to admit the truth. He's shitting himself now. Dead worried about all this media coverage you've stirred up. They all are.'

Over the next two weeks I tried twice to talk to Mr Orange, setting up meetings in pubs through people who knew him. Both times he failed to show.

15 February 1995
HM Prison
7 North Square
Dorchester
Dorset

Dear Don,

It really is amazing the power the press has on people. I never would have thought for a minute that one of the four suspects would have come forward to tender evidence, perhaps even against his own friends.

I find it equally hard to believe that the police have allowed vital evidence to remain in a vault for almost 22 years. It seems that they were desperate to secure a conviction and a fast one, with little regard for who shouldered the blame.

It has often been said that the truth will always prevail and it now looks as if I am on the path that proves, yet again, the adage is true.

It wasn't until the *Daily Star* took up my plight in a bid to establish my innocence that I began to have reservations about the kind of reception I would get from my fellow inmates. Any fears I had can certainly be laid to rest.

This has become big news and a buzz of excitement ripples through the wing at mail call, with a number of eager lads jostling to be the next in line to read the following instalment in what has become Dorchester Prison's very own soap opera. Even staff are wishing me well in the fight to have the Home Secretary exercise a Royal Prerogative of Mercy.

The wealth of evidence contained in the dossier would appear to offer the Home Secretary little choice in what action he can take. Whether or not Mr Howard will view it as a case of Hobson's choice remains to be seen.

Stephen Downing

I had been busy rechecking original statements, cuttings and further background information on the case, and liaising with probation officers, Parole Board officials and civil servants at the Home Office. I had twice visited the CID offices at Matlock police station with anonymous letters and the envelopes in which they had arrived. Although, once again, the police had not seemed particularly interested, I was determined they should be given every opportunity to make their own enquiries and check the items for fingerprints.

I was receiving support from many quarters. Stephen's childhood friend, Richard Brailsford, who had tried to rally enthusiasm for the campaign on several occasions over the past two decades, was inspired by my efforts and the publicity being generated. Ironically Richard was the brother of Janet, the girlfriend of George Pearson. It brought home to me once again what a goldfish bowl Bakewell was. With renewed vigour Richard set about collecting signatures for a petition calling for the release of Stephen and a re-examination of the case. Like me, he was soon to learn the dangers of meddling in the affair. He too received telephone threats at his home. He was told by one anonymous caller that Stephen would be a dead man if he was ever released.

Because of the potential dangers, I now decided to deal with the main investigation on my own. I didn't want anyone else's life threatened. The warning from the detective at Matlock police to check under my car and not to open suspicious packages still rang in my ears. I instructed my staff *not* to take any unnecessary risks and, in particular, *not* to meet anyone after dark and always to tell someone else where they were going. My family were already well-trained in this respect.

16 February 1995
HM Prison
7 North Square
Dorchester
Dorset

Dear Don,

Please excuse this letter being handwritten, only I'm not really in the mood for typing after hearing of the threats to you,

Richard Brailsford and his family and also against me if I am released. What is really bugging me is not knowing if my family have also been receiving threats. It is not something my mother would admit to me if asked. Can you enlighten me?

If my family are under threat too, do you think the police will give them round-the-clock protection and move them to a safe house? The last thing I want is for one of them to answer the door and take the full impact of a shotgun. I don't want that to happen to anyone, not just my family. I know that it sounds rather dramatic and something you would come to expect in a film script, but I am desperate to know that they are safe.

Stephen Downing

In mid-February, just a fortnight after I submitted my evidence to the Chief Constable and the Home Office, I received a very interesting call from a contact at Derbyshire Police Headquarters in Ripley.

My source explained that in the past few days top-secret documents had been forwarded from the Home Office to Police HQ, containing confidential information about the Downing case and other murders. The main file, marked 'Jigsaw Murders', contained details of unsolved killings in Derbyshire and neighbouring counties going back thirty years.

He said a Home Office co-ordinator had been appointed to oversee developments, under the control of a commander from CIB2, a new special Complaints Investigation Bureau unit based at Scotland Yard. The commander had apparently suggested that Derbyshire police put two detectives full-time on to the cases in the county contained within the 'Jigsaw' file. My informant said the gossip in the office was that the commander would send 'a couple of his own boys' to sift through the Downing paperwork. He said it was being rumoured that the original scene of crime procedures had been a bit 'iffy', and that HQ was getting worried about repercussions.

The mention of CIB2 was enough to strike fear into the hearts of the most hardened police officers. Its job was to monitor complaints against the police, but it did not officially exist, although it was rumoured to be linked to Special Branch and MI5. Several newspaper editors took a keen interest in CIB2, as its hand-picked team appeared determined to find out which police officers were tipping off the press, and to plug these 'leaks' in the system. It was my belief that any investigative journalist who began to cause ripples would automatically come under the scrutiny of CIB2.

My source added that he had seen a copy of my recent application for a visiting order to see Stephen Downing in Dorchester Prison. He said it must have been sent to Police HQ either from the Home Office or direct from the prison.

15

ICONTINUED TO CORRESPOND with Stephen Downing and spoke with him regularly on the telephone. I was also able to communicate delicate matters via his parents and family who frequently contacted him at Dorchester prison. Although I wanted to concentrate on particular aspects of the original police interrogation and evidence, it became obvious that Stephen, at times, just wanted to pour his heart out and needed comfort from magazines and star photographs. He was in the midst of a recurring nightmare. I provided his only probable lifeline. A simple youth from a simple background, he had been a young innocent thrown into a difficult and dangerous adult world, and, more worrying, one which he had been forced to accept.

I pushed him again to write and explain about his early hours of detention in 1973 and received the following account:

> I was led downstairs after giving my statement and locked in one of the holding cells. My bed was a large wooden bench about 6ft by 3ft. It had a filthy blanket tossed over one corner and from the smell of it I would say it hadn't been washed since the day it was first put there. The only other item in the cell was a toilet – a true luxury for its day, as I was to learn later.
>
> Even though I was fairly snug in this dimly lit cell, sleep was impossible. At intervals of about fifteen minutes I was asked if I was all right. I said I was. Then Charlesworth and another PC came in. They asked for a sample of pubic hair and head hair. They told me they were being taken for forensic analysis.
>
> Soon after this I was taken back upstairs to the same interview room. Fingernail scrapings were then taken with the pointed

blade of a surgical knife. This operation was not without some pain and discomfort – enough to cause me to pull my fingers away. I was told it had to be done and to keep still but I think the sadistic sod took great pleasure in my pain.

As each fingernail was scraped, the contents were put into a separate envelope and labelled. With the tips of my fingers still stinging and spots of blood showing beneath my nails I was returned to the cell. About another half an hour went by and another two visits were made to make sure I was OK.

The next interruption was again to take me away from my cell and any hope of sleep. 'Where to now?' I wondered. But my question was soon answered. I was bustled into a van and taken to Buxton police headquarters. On my way out I caught a brief glimpse of the station clock and it was about 3a.m. I was pushed out of the door to be met by the cold and black of early morning. A yellow transit van with black one-way windows waited at the kerb. I was flanked by two police officers and driven away to Buxton.

I think it took us about twenty minutes to get there. The Buxton police centre was brightly lit and seemed a hive of activity. I was beyond sleep now as I was taken to the counter and fingerprinted. A small sink was mounted on the wall to the side and I was told I could wash the ink off in that. After several attempts I gave up. My fingers seemed as black as when I had started. I was then taken along and put in a very large cell. The door slammed behind me and I was left there with my thoughts.

It was several days before I realised that I was not going to be let out and when Wendy died it reduced the chances of the police finding out who was really responsible.

As I started to grow used to my surroundings I realised this cell was worse than the one at Bakewell. Although much cleaner, the only means of sleeping were on an angled concrete slab topped in wood and no more than two feet wide.

My dress boots were taken from me and I was asked if I had a tie or a belt. I hadn't either. I was then given a rub-down search. About ten minutes later I was disturbed again and was given a full examination by a doctor. Then I was left alone for a few minutes before some blankets were thrown at me – with apologies they didn't have any pillows.

The cell was freezing cold and I couldn't see any heating pipes or radiators. It must have been hell in winter if it was this cold in September. I counted seven blankets and folded two up as a makeshift mattress to help take some of the hardness out of the wooden bench. I used two more as pillows and three to cover myself up.

I don't know how long I lay there before I fell asleep but it wasn't long. I woke to the sound of the door being unlocked and a pint-sized mug of lukewarm tea and a blue plastic plate with two burnt slices of toast were thrust at me. There was a knob of margarine and a spoonful of marmalade on the edge. I asked for a knife only to be told they were not allowed. I turned to see the door slam shut again.

The margarine was rock hard so I just ripped off pieces of toast and dipped them in the marmalade. Time dragged slowly by. It would be late morning when I pushed the bell button on the wall and waited. The door finally opened and I asked if I could use the toilet. They showed me where it was. I was told it was a good job there were only two of us in the cells, otherwise it would have meant a longer wait.

I remembered not to leave it so long the next time before ringing in case I had a lengthy wait. They told me lunch would be served in an hour. It was too uncomfortable to lie down again, or even to sit. I spent much of the time pacing my cell like a caged animal. I had not been asked to remove my boots when I returned from the toilet, so at least my feet were warm. I wrapped a blanket round my shoulders like a Mexican poncho to keep my circulation going.

Lunch arrived on another blue plastic plate. It consisted of fish and chips and some hard peas. To follow I was given steamed sponge and lukewarm custard. They gave me a plastic spoon and took my breakfast stuff away. They then asked me if I wanted to use the toilet again as nobody would be available to take me there again till after 2p.m.

As I left my cell I was asked where my boots were and I told the sergeant I was wearing them. He looked down and gave me a bit of an ear-bashing about how I was not allowed them in case I used the laces to try and hang myself. So on returning to my cell they were taken away again.

It was deathly quiet in the building. I set about my meal and began to chase the peas round the plate. The sponge was like rubber but I forced myself to eat, not knowing when my next meal would arrive. Afterwards, I again wrapped myself in my blankets to keep warm and lay down on the bench. Sometime after two o'clock I began to hear muffled voices and realised other policemen were now on duty.

The hours dragged by. I remained locked up apart from the odd toilet visit. I was wakened by the unlocking of my cell door.

Breakfast arrived once more on a tray and it was placed on the end of my bench. Toast, marmalade, margarine and tea. It was now Friday and I was to make my first appearance before the magistrates at Bakewell town hall.

I was handcuffed and taken back to Bakewell police station where again I was put back in the same cell. I thought my case was to be heard about ten o'clock so, after being recuffed, I was marched 400 yards through the streets of my home town in full public view to the town hall. We sat through a few applications for extensions to pub licensing hours, then it was my turn.

Very little was said by the police or my solicitor, Paul Dickinson, who had met me shortly before I left the police station. The magistrate turned out to be my former headmaster, Harry Schofield. Without any further ado he remanded me to Risley remand centre for a week. The cuffs were put back on and I was then escorted through the streets again back to the cell at the police station.

My parents and sister, who had been present at my court appearance, were brought to my cell and locked up alongside me. We were allowed about an hour together before they had to leave. It was an emotional meeting and I cannot remember what was said, but I know they were supportive and wished me luck before they had to go.

The drive to the remand centre, near Warrington in Cheshire, took just under two hours. And when I got there it became obvious to me why anyone who has had the misfortune to spend time at Risley, even for just one night, will never forget the experience and will know how it became known as 'Grisly Risley'.

When we arrived at the reception area at the remand centre, I stood sandwiched between two police officers. A fat screw sat behind a high counter.

'Name,' he barked.

'Stephen,' I replied.

'Stephen what?' he went on.

'Stephen Downing,' I explained in all innocence.

'Anything else?' he snapped again.

'Just Stephen Leslie Downing,' came my reply again. That was when one of my escorts gave me a nudge and whispered, 'Call him sir!'

'Don't prompt him, sir, let him learn the hard way,' said the screw, who now fixed me with a look of complete contempt.

One or two other particulars were taken. The few pounds which my father had given me and which the police had brought with them were passed through a slot in the top of the desk. I was told that they would be kept with my private belongings. I was then ordered into another room and told to strip off. As I did my clothing was all noted on a property card before being tossed into a cardboard box.

Wrapped in a towel I was given my prison number, 797501, and told to go to the stores for some clothing and then to go on to the bathhouse.

The kit I was given was not my size, but when I asked if it could be changed my request was denied. 'Nonce coming through,' bellowed one of the screws. Of course the word meant nothing to me but a few moments later a scream rang out from the bath area. I entered to find this guy standing in front of me naked and lobster red from head to toe.

I asked one of the others what had happened to him and I was told he was a 'nonce' and that he'd slipped getting into the bath. I was new to this kind of language but I was told a 'nonce' was someone who had raped a woman or molested a child. A scalding hot bath awaited each one that came through. The tap was left running so the bath overflowed and the water remained at the same excrutiatingly high temperature.

If the 'nonces' didn't like that they had the alternative choice of a hose-down which consisted of a naked fire-hosing from a water jet so powerful that they couldn't stand up. The victims would 'dance', spending more time on their backsides because it was impossible to keep their footing on the slippery surface of the bath house.

I recalled Stephen had mentioned this incident to me during one of our telephone calls. At the time he had become upset when I asked him if anything like that had ever happened to him. He had skirted around the subject. I knew from visits to other prisoners of the red-hot 'sheep dip' or, alternatively, a hose-down. When I interviewed other prisoners they claimed warders would turn a blind eye to this type of punishment. I was sure that, in twenty-one years of imprisonment, Stephen must have seen, and experienced, many horrors of prison life. If he chose not to talk about them, who was I to insist otherwise?

His account continued,

I was shown the scalding bath as a warning to behave, but an ordinary bath was reserved for me on that occasion. The threat was made, however – behave or you'll get the same treatment. Before I climbed into the bath I was asked by one of the bath-house orderlies if I wanted to buy anything from the canteen with my cash.

I asked what I could buy and I was told it was things like tobacco, toiletries or stationery. I was shown a list of the items available and their prices which hung from the bath house wall. I ordered 100 cigarettes, soap, toothpaste, shampoo and a bottle of orange cordial. I was told by the orderly they would be delivered to me on the following Tuesday.

I enjoyed the bath, my first since having being taken into police custody. There hadn't even been any facilities provided for washing and shaving at Bakewell or Buxton. After bathing I dressed and collected my bedding along with a set of plastic cutlery, plate, bowl and mug. I was then put into a large holding cell with about twenty other blokes.

Concrete slabs topped in wood ran around the walls with some in the centre of the cell between support pillars. Some people spoke but I was happy to sit in silence. The walls were covered in graffiti and in places slices of bread had been stuck to them with knobs of margarine. From time to time, some of the occupants would spit on the floor which was covered with dirty paper and fag ends.

After about two hours a screw appeared and read out some names – mine was one of them. We took it in turn to go before the doctor who asked if we were well. That was the extent of our medical examination. When the last man in our group came out of the doctor's office, we were all taken to the hospital. I found out there that I was considered a suicide risk so I had to be kept in the hospital so I could be watched every minute of the day and night.

The ground floors were made up of offices, ordinary cells, punishment cells and segregation areas. On the next two floors were wards, two on each floor with a room for a doctor, psychiatrist, psychologist, probation officer or dentist and an ante-room where you waited to see them. I was put in Ward A on the top floor. The ward had partitions throughout with two beds in each section, making room for twenty-four beds in all.

But because of chronic overcrowding, several camp beds had been erected in the centre of the ward, so now there were fifty-two of us sharing a space for half that number. Conditions were extremely cramped but we made the best of it and morale was high. There was about a six-inch clearance on either side of my bed and about twelve inches at the head of it before the next rows of beds started.

There was a TV near the entrance which was switched on from five o'clock in the evening until nine. We all had to be in bed, or at least lying on it, by 10p.m. On one side of the entrance were the toilets and wash basins and on the other was a bath. We could use the bath up till 9p.m. although the toilets could be used at any time.

I was too timid to make friends, so any conversation, no matter how trivial, was started by another inmate. I soon got to know people and we spent time playing cards or watching TV. In less than a week, all the extra beds were removed and I was moved to one of the proper hospital beds which overlooked the exercise yard. It may not seem like much but it was great to be able to sleep in a real bed again.

The time passed quickly and soon Friday came round. I was checked through reception and told to get back into my own clothes before being handed over to the police who took me back to Bakewell for my regular weekly court appearance which was followed by a visit from my family.

I reminded them to ask for a hospital visit when they came again. That way, we would not have to try and talk through the mesh of a heavy wired glass on a closed visit.

We had a two-hour visit and my mother would bring a carrier bag full of goodies with her – and the same on Friday when I went to court. I'd started work as a cleaner and received the princely sum of 30p per week. This was a fixed wage regardless of the work. I then moved on to the kit store, then dirty laundry before getting a job working on the hotplate serving food.

Because there was no way of making tea back on the ward we would fill-up several orange squash bottles with diesel [prison slang for 'tea'] and then top up the tea urn with hot water from the tap in the washing area. It was still prison policy to put bromide in the tea, which was thought to reduce any sexual urges. The bottom of the tea urns would be about an inch thick with sediment. We took the bottles of tea back with us and stowed them away in our lockers until later on.

The tea would be cold by 11p.m. so the bottles would be put into sinks full of hot water and topped up later. It would take about half an hour to get the tea hot and by then it had taken on a muddy-brownish colour. Later, I became friendly with one of the night staff and would hunt out some paperbacks for him. In return, he let me make two mugs of tea for my mate and me by letting me boil his kettle.

After travelling for thirteen weeks to the magistrates court, I was finally committed for trial. This put an end to my weekly excursions. However, my family began to visit me on the Friday at Risley as well as on the Monday. I would sit on the edge of my bed and watch for them to be escorted from the gate, then wave as they approached and dash downstairs to greet them properly.

Exercise was compulsory but I found that I could often get out of it by washing my hair as they called us to file out. Winter was now closing fast and I was one of the first to weave my way to the front when a pile of pullovers arrived on the table.

One of the worst nightmares I had while still on weekly visits to the magistrates court was to pick up a dose of head lice. They gave me some shampoo from the sick bay but it didn't help and I had to have my long hair cut off. They shaved my head. It had taken me over a year to grow it long – and suddenly it was all gone in just a few minutes. It was a sad day for me.

Our regular discussions and correspondence provided a channel for Stephen to vent his feelings. I was gradually gaining his confidence and trying to look for any other information that might prove beneficial to his case.

His account answered specific questions about his trial. Once again, I needed to gauge his own reaction and memory of events.

He continued,

My trial was at Nottingham Crown Court in February 1974. To make it more convenient, they transferred me to HMP Lincoln. I was again put in a hospital. This time it had a single cell, number 13. I was there for two days and then moved to number 9, which I shared with two other men who were up on charges of murdering a prostitute. They told me they strangled her for the money she owed them.

In court, the clerk introduced each member of the jury and I was invited to say if I objected to any of them. I didn't. The clerk then read out the charge and said that if I wished to plead guilty to manslaughter, the court would accept this and award me ten years. I was then asked how did I plead and I told them 'not guilty'.

I remember very little of the trial itself, except for the feeling of humiliation at being the focal point of everything. Looking back, I didn't feel the Defence put up much of a fight. Reading over the contents, there were a vast number of avenues that could have led to further investigation and cast doubt on the Prosecution case. The jury heard all they were going to hear and were eventually asked to retire and deliberate.

I was led downstairs to one of the cells to await the verdict. The jury was out for less than ten minutes to deliberate! I had lit a cigarette and only smoked about half of it when the door reopened and I was told the jury were coming back. I sat in the rear of the dock and the clerk told me to stand before turning to the foreman. He asked him if he'd had time to consider. He said he had and passed him a piece of paper. The judge slowly unfolded it and handed it back to the clerk. They had found me guilty by a unanimous verdict!

They asked me if I wished to say anything before sentence was passed. I was too numb with shock to say anything. I think I said no and then just shook my head.

On 15 February 1974 prisoner number 797501 Stephen Leslie Downing was taken down from the dock at Nottingham Crown Court. He had just been told by Mr Justice Nield that he was unable to sentence him to anything other than a term of imprisonment to be served at Her Majesty's Pleasure. This sentence only applies to offenders under the age of eighteen and technically has no time limit. It can be reviewed by the court at any time or, on the other hand, can last as long as the justice system wishes – even for ever.

But at that moment the length of the sentence was the furthest thing from Stephen's mind. He just wanted to see his family and, as he was led to one of the holding cells beneath the dock, his wish was granted, albeit fleetingly. His mother, father and sister were there to greet him and reassure him that he wouldn't be in for long and that he should never give up hope.

Twenty minutes later he was on his way back to Lincoln prison where he stayed for a couple of days before being transferred back to the remand centre at Risley to await the final decision on the prison where he would start his sentence. I could tell from regular personal contact that his early experience of prison life had affected him very badly. He naturally struggled at times to understand his situation but had learnt to adapt to circumstances.

His account continues,

My arrival back at Risley was tinged with a touch of sadness as I was told that I was to be located in a hospital cell rather than go back to the main ward. Despite my protests they said they were not prepared to take the chance of having me attacked by one of the other inmates, as news reports on TV had mentioned I was in for murder and the sex murder of a young woman at that.

I did not understand what all the fuss was about as I had never hidden any of the facts of the case from the other prisoners – and I knew I was innocent.

I was told I had to stay put and that meant I also lost the job I enjoyed doing. Now I was to be a humble cleaner on the ground floor. I didn't get to see the TV any more either and a pot served as my toilet in the night.

The only means of entertainment that I hadn't had before was piped radio from the wing office and even then it was what the screws wanted to listen to, mostly Radio 4 or Radio 2 for the cricket. On Sunday, though, we always had the Pop Charts on Radio 1.

My time as a cleaner on the ground floor lasted for about two months and then I was transferred to D Wing and given a single cell. After a couple of days I was put to work in the shop where you were issued with a curved bladed knife and you stripped the plastic sleeve from electrical copper wire.

I was then told to join another lad at a table away from the wire stripping where we were each given a large blunt needle and were told to thread thin elastic on to papier mâché masks. It was part of an assembly line for toy soldiers and cowboys and Indians.

I had already been a witness to the kind of punishment the screws were prone to administer when I was in the hospital cell. A Korean who only knew a few words of English had been kicked black and blue because he couldn't speak our language.

I was also to find the same kind of rough justice administered to the bloke I worked with. He had run out of parts to assemble so he asked the shop instructor for some more. There were none in the shop so the instructor went off to the store to get some. In the meantime the discipline screw came over and ordered him to carry on working. He explained that the instructor had gone for some more parts and even dropped in a couple of 'sirs' along the way, but that still wasn't good enough.

The screw ordered him again to get back to work. He couldn't. I was just as idle but was left alone. My mate explained once more that he couldn't work until the instructor came back. Before the screw returned to his seat he leaned close and said he would see him later on the exercise yard. Moments later the instructor returned with the parts and we carried on working.

11.00 hours came and we filed out of the workshop into the exercise yard and began to walk round in an anti-clockwise direction. We had been walking for quite a while and I began to think the screw had only been bluffing when all of a sudden my mate's name was called out. He went over and was taken inside. I later learnt that six screws had taken him into his cell and given him a good kicking.

The cells were a complete contrast to any part of the hospital accommodation. They were furnished with a bed which usually had most of the springs missing, but I was lucky because there was only one missing from mine. I was also lucky that only some of the panes of glass in my window had been smashed.

Why there was a locker in the cells was beyond me as all we had was a plastic cup and the few items we could buy with our 30p wages. The only clothes we had were what we were dressed in. Some of the cells had steel tubular chairs and I managed to acquire one from an empty cell. My family had bought me in a small radio so I was able to listen to some music when I felt like it.

Prisoners on D wing like the others were given association about once every ten days which would be from about 17.00–19.00 hours. A couple of newspapers would be available, along with darts, TV, cards, dominoes and chess, or you could just sit about chatting.

It was during one such evening that I was approached and asked if I would like to sell my radio. At first I said no, but when I was offered three-quarters of an ounce of tobacco I changed my mind and said yes. I was given the tobacco and the guy said he would collect the radio on the way back from association.

The word soon spread around that I had tobacco and I was the constant focus of attention until I had given it all away. He came and got the radio and it was only then that I regretted having agreed to sell it, because I had ended up with no radio and no tobacco.

The following morning while I was at work the door to the workshop opened and in marched a body of staff, the Chief, POs, SOs and a large number of screws. It was my name they called out.

I got up and went over to them, having just managed to compose myself to do so. Everyone must have seen me shaking with fear as to what was on the cards for me. It was the Chief that spoke to me. He asked me if I had a radio. My fear grew and in an almost inaudible voice I managed to say 'No'. He then went on to ask where it was.

It was pointless to lie as they evidently knew all about it, so I said that I had sold it. During the course of the question and answer session I explained that I had no tobacco left and now regretted the whole episode. He said that the bloke I had sold it to had been discharged that morning. His cell mate had grassed him up to the screws but he had gone before they were able to recover it.

He then asked me if I was aware of what I should get (by this he meant being taken away and given a bloody good kicking).

I said that I was, with which he suggested I take it as a warning and sent me back to work.

I told my family what I had done during a visit – I was back to having these again for no more than 15 or 20 minutes every 14 days – and they brought me a new radio on the next visit.

About a month later I was called to the PO's office and he asked me where I would like to be transferred to.

I explained that I didn't really know anything about any other prisons, so he said he had worked at Swinfen Hall and that it was OK, so I said that was fine by me. I knew I wouldn't be sorry to see the back of Risley and with it, I hoped, the harsh regime.

A regime which also allowed them to punish prisoners by putting them in a concrete cell with a concrete slab with a mattress for a bed and a concrete seat. The only light came from a filthy 60-watt bulb that shone through the two inch thick glass tiles set in the ceiling. The switch was outside so you couldn't control when the light was on or off.

There was no heating in the cell and the only means of warmth was a single fire blanket. The occupant would be put in naked and two cell doors closed behind him. Then another cell door about six feet away was also slammed shut. In the cell within a cell, cut off from the rest of the prison by three locked doors, it was possible to do all the shouting and banging you could without being heard.

You would be in there for three days and the only meals were bread and water. The ration was three slices of bread and a pint of water for each meal. The only form of sanitation was a bucket in the corner which you only emptied after the three days' confinement were up. There were no means of washing during this term of punishment.

It was shortly after my eighteenth birthday when I was transferred to Swinfen Hall at Lichfield in Staffordshire – I was glad to see the back of Risley.

Stephen Downing's 'career plan' at 'The Queen's Pleasure' read like some graphic travelogue of horrific venues. He had been to at least ten different prisons since September 1973 – including high-security establishments at Wakefield, Gartree, Nottingham and later Dart-moor. He even saw Moors murderer Ian Brady at Gartree and faced his steely, vacant expression from just a few feet away in a prison exercise yard.

I had received a copy of Downing's prison records from a very helpful and supportive contact at the Home Office. I didn't admit this to the authorities, or to anyone else, at the time – or once again they would have demanded the name of the supplier. The police and Home Office always seemed more interested in my sources of information, rather than dealing with the facts.

The summary of reports on Stephen Downing made interesting but depressing reading. They confirmed his state of mind and limited intelligence in the early years. They showed the sheer horror he experienced in the early years at being sent to these adult punishment institutions as a childlike youth of just seventeen.

His prison summary at Swinfen Hall was typical. Downing arrived in May 1974. The first report prepared two and a half years later, described him as,

> a dull, lifeless and emotionally immature young man, who never displayed any feelings but could be stubborn at times. On arrival he had been at a loss, moving around like someone in a dream. He would not speak unless approached and even then would only answer in monosyllables. He had eventually found a comfortable niche and since then had been content to remain in the background, not making any real attempt to improve himself, or to make use of the facilities offered.
>
> His work effort was poor and he continued to give the impression he was on another level and was oblivious to what was going on around him. He was polite and friendly enough in his dealings with staff, though with little to offer by way of conversation.
>
> His continued denial of guilt for the offence precluded him from gaining true insight. Overall, he made little progress, though he was better able to cope generally.

The fact that Stephen was continually in denial of the murder was constantly highlighted. This meant major battles with the Parole Board hearings. His Parole Board reports were excellent. Often he was described as a 'model prisoner' but, time and time again, his unwavering protestation of innocence was considered the one obstacle preventing his release or transfer to more open prison conditions.

His casework officer's report from 1994 was a typical example:

Downing has done over twenty years in custody, I believe due to his denial of the offence. Until he admits to the offence, it is impossible for anyone to comment on his attitude to the offence or degree of remorse shown.

Downing's behaviour has been exemplary. He shows good moral standards that would be commendable in a normal social environment. He is friendly and communicative to both staff and other inmates. I find no abnormalities in his attitude towards women. He has a respectable outlook. No concerns have been voiced and his attitude towards women has been commendable.

The Local Review Committee report added, 'Downing continues to maintain his innocence. He would benefit from a period of more open conditions.'

The life officer's report continued in the same vein:

It is well documented that Downing denies the offence and, therefore, there are obvious difficulties in addressing this area. Downing's behaviour has never been a cause for complaint. After all these years he has developed the best way to cope with prison life and does so very well. There is some doubt, however, as to advancement to category D status due to his denial of the offence. It must be said that his behaviour shows that he has matured and now does *not* present a risk to the public. I feel that despite his denial of responsibility, he is ready for a more progressive move to more open conditions.

His personal officer, Mr Revynk, also confirmed, 'Downing's approach to women was quiet and reserved. He established a sound and perfectly acceptable working relationship with all female staff. He was always polite, co-operative and courteous.'

A host of other prison reports were similar in nature and description. Yet he was constantly denied a face-to-face hearing with the Parole Board due to his denial of the crime. The government steadfastly barred him from directly putting his case for release, or transfer to an open prison, unless he changed his mind and admitted guilt.

Throughout the years Stephen had made several applications for his case to be heard and had been turned down. Unless he admitted to murder and sexual assault and agreed to submit to treatment programmes, he would not be judged to have shown remorse and therefore would be considered a danger to the public if he were released. It seemed that this ludicrous Catch 22 position could never be resolved.

Soon after I took up his case he made it clear to me that he would *never* admit to murder or sexual assault and would *never* agree to go on a sex offenders' treatment programme. He would prefer to end his days in prison. He sent me a dossier of all his written representations to the Parole Board over the years. The various worthies and notables on the numerous Boards which had judged his case over the years had still never met this charming and, by now, self-educated man face to face because he was always refused an oral hearing. He highlighted what he considered to be some of the more ludicrous comments written about him in various psychological and psychiatric reports each time his bi-annual Parole Board Review came up. He found it particularly frustrating that his denial of the crime should be considered somehow deviant, dangerous or deluded.

While in Gartree prison in 1983, it had been suggested that Stephen had 'almost come to believe the story of his innocence'. Stephen had commented indignantly, 'I don't *almost* believe the story of my innocence. I *do* believe it because it is true.'

Stephen was always annoyed at the attitude of so-called experts towards his 'unrealistic' and 'inappropriate' desire, upon release, of finding a job in the film industry, an ambition he had often mentioned to me during his conversations. Again, in 1983 he had written, 'I do not see it as unrealistic in wanting to enter the film industry. It is only because people writing the reports do not have an interest in working in the film industry that they feel it justifies them criticising those who do. I am sure that many people who have entered this business have had to contend with just as much ridicule.'

In 1990, while still at Gartree, Stephen was reported as being 'mature and well-balanced'.

By 1993, at the same establishment, he was considered 'out of touch with the real world'. He had written, 'Reporting staff are now saying that I am immature. Yet in 1990 I was considered mature. Presumably these observations are made by the same reporting staff!' He added, 'I don't think it is unfair to say that I am out of touch with the real world when one considers the length of time I have been away.' And he pointed out, 'I would say that I have received no instructions or assistance with rehabilitation.'

These last comments made me very angry. This man had been locked away for decades, had spent all his adolescent years and the prime of his life in jail and the authorities had the audacity, insensitivity or just plain ignorance – call it what you will – to describe him as 'out of touch'. Most people under those conditions would have become stark raving mad by now.

While his latest parole report was being considered, Stephen and some other current and former inmates of the Verne prison at Portland in Dorset, had been questioned over alleged obscene telephone calls to a female member of staff out of hours. This had happened in late 1994, soon after I began my investigation into his case. While enquiries were being made into this telephone incident, Stephen had been transferred, in November 1994, to Dorchester prison in Dorset. Dorset CID, reputedly acting on reports from an anonymous source, made extensive enquiries. Many of the calls were said to have come from a phone not generally available to the majority of prisoners and to have been made after lock-up. The police later claimed to have traced, and even recorded, some of the conversations.

When I learnt that Stephen Downing was one of a number of prisoners under suspicion, I immediately contacted the senior investigating officer at Dorset police. I was sceptical of the authorities' motives in casting doubt on his character in this way, so soon after I had begun such a vigorous campaign to prove his innocence. I wondered who the anonymous source was who had tipped off the police. I was told that Downing was one of several who had been questioned, in his case because his offence had originally been described as a sex attack.

He had written to me in despair, while these investigations were continuing.

> 22 January 1995
> HMP
> 7 North Square
> Dorchester
> Dorset

Dear Don,

I was pleased to read of the progress that you are making. I don't want to dash anyone's hopes of success, but can't help feeling that the whole thing will be a wet squib. With all this now coming on top of me, I can't help wondering if I will ever get out. I feel that I am eventually going to be told that the Parole Board thinks I should go back into the category B system and go through the whole lot yet again. I'm sorry for being so depressed!

Stephen Downing

When it became obvious that Stephen did not have access to the particular phone from which the calls emanated, not to mention the fact that he would have been locked in his cell at the time they were meant to have been made, the inquiry against him was suddenly dropped. He never received any explanation or apology.

The inference, though, had come at a critical time, when his bi-annual parole review was under way.

23 February 1995
HM Prison
7 North Square
Dorchester
Dorset

Dear Don,

The Princess Royal is due to arrive at 1.45p.m. Most places have been given a lick of fresh paint. The cells on the two landings will have new picture boards installed, with clear instructions that nothing offensive is to be put on them!

Two new floor polishing machines have been bought at a cost of £1000 each and several gallons of industrial floor cleaner and polish, not to mention 50 litres of highly concentrated industrial degreaser. I saw a large roll of heavyweight carpeting which I can only assume is laid in the cells.

I was hoping that with the weight of all the evidence as well as the MP's backing I might have been released in time for Christine's birthday on 4 March. I was able to enjoy it last year on the home visit. Still I can always make up for it with a party at a later date.

My father was telling me that George Pearson was chatting to him in a very friendly fashion the other day. I couldn't help thinking how naive he must be if he thinks he's not wanted for questioning. And Syd Oulsnam was parked near to where my father was. He was watching him out of the corner of his eye while pretending to read the paper. Apparently he made off with his head down, so he must suspect something is afoot.

My sister informed me that you had printed another good story this week, along with the cartoon of me making tea for HRH and guests. I will look forward to reading that tomorrow lunchtime with my fish and chips.

Stephen Downing

Making the decision to see Stephen in jail had been easy – but the mechanics of the visit proved frustrating in the extreme, like almost all of my encounters with the authorities. At first the prison refused to allow Stephen to send me a visiting order. Eventually, after several phone calls, they changed their minds and I received one allowing me a twenty-minute visit. It would have given me just enough time to say hello, shake him by the hand, sit down, then get up again and say goodbye.

So I tried again. In the next series of calls I explained to the powers that be at Dorchester jail that the round trip from Derbyshire to Dorchester was several hundred miles and that it was a long way to travel for just twenty minutes. I also explained the growing amount of support for the Downing case locally. I wasn't sure if this had a positive or negative effect. But after much cajoling and many consultations at the prison the authorities relented – they said they would allow me a one-hour visit.

I drove down to Dorchester late in the afternoon on 22 February 1995. It was a bitterly cold day. When I was about three hours into the journey the weather deteriorated. What started out as heavy rain soon changed to sleet, then snow and after all that a thick, swirling fog descended, reducing visibility to almost nil, which caused me to miss my turn-off on the motorway. I eventually arrived at my hotel around midnight.

The following day I met Stephen's solicitor, Simon Lacey, who worked for a local firm that represented many people at the prison. The meeting only lasted about an hour but at least I was able to get a few tips on the local prison system – tips which were to prove invaluable.

At two o'clock that afternoon I reported to the visitors block. The waiting room was packed to overflowing – mothers and children mainly. The kids were crying and running amok. Almost every adult was smoking. It was like hell on earth – and that was only the waiting room. I couldn't help wondering what the jail itself would be like.

I couldn't find a seat so I stood outside in the fresh cool air waiting for the call to enter. Soon the visitors were asked to register and hand in their VOs. I approached one of the prison officers and handed him my permit. 'You're that reporter bloke, aren't you?' he asked.

I looked at him, rather taken aback. Word must have got around fast. 'Yes,' I replied. 'I'm Don Hale from the *Matlock Mercury*. I'm here to see Stephen Downing. It's all been arranged.'

'Not with those, you're not,' came the gruff reply. The prison officer was pointing to the package of goodies I had brought down with me from Stephen's family and friends. 'Anyway, we'll have to see if he's free. He might not want to see *you*.'

I was loaded with books, magazines and various other things Stephen had requested. I had already gone through each and every one of the items on the telephone with prison officials several days previously and had been given permission to take them in. But the man at reception had other ideas. 'You'll have to leave them all here,' he said. 'Put them in a locker if you like but they can't go in.' I explained about the telephone conversation but I quickly realised it was like talking to a brick wall. 'You don't have to go in, you know,' said my tormentor. 'Nobody will bother if you don't turn up to see him. He'll understand.'

I was having difficulty controlling my temper, but I knew if I didn't I would be playing right into this awkward bastard's hands. 'What's the point in getting permission to take things in, only to have you refuse at the last minute?' I asked.

The officer suddenly looked as if he was auditioning for the part of the Straw Man in *The Wizard of Oz*. He couldn't seem to understand the question and stared at me blankly. 'Wait there, please,' he said finally, without a flicker of emotion. 'All visitors come with me,' he shouted into the packed office. The babble of conversation reached fever pitch as dozens of people poured out to join the assembled group and walk up the slight incline towards two very large wooden gates. The prison looked like a medieval castle standing on top of a hill.

I let the others go first and then began to follow. 'And where do you think you're going?' the officer bellowed.

'I've got a visiting order to see someone,' I replied. 'You've just checked it. Don't you remember?'

'You'll go nowhere until I say. Stay there and I'll go and check. As I said, he might not want to see you.'

I was getting nowhere fast. 'And what about these papers? Stephen has to see them,' I shouted.

'Stay there! I'll come back,' the officer replied.

I watched the group of visitors stagger slowly up the hill and disappear through the gates. I remembered I had been told I would be allowed a minimum of twenty minutes and a maximum of an hour for the visit. It was now ten past two – there were only fifty minutes left if the prison authorities were going to adhere strictly to the letter of the law.

Another ten minutes passed. Not a sign of any other visitors or of anyone else for that matter. Eventually another prison officer came down from the gates. He had no cap on and was wearing a short-sleeved white shirt. 'Excuse me,' I said. 'I've been waiting to be taken up to see a prisoner.' I mentioned the other officer's name and number, and explained in detail what I had been told.

'I should wait in there then, pal,' said the officer, pointing to the waiting room. I walked back down the driveway again, entered the reception cabin and started to read the notices stuck on the wall, which laid out all the conditions that have to be fulfilled to get a visit. I assured myself I had followed the procedure down to the last detail.

Then, as I paced back and forth in mounting frustration, a woman appeared as if by magic from behind the counter. She had a damp cloth and started to wipe the table tops. A few coffee cups had been left half full and there were some empty crisp packets and various other wrappers and containers on the surfaces. The woman started to put real effort into her every wipe. 'Can I help you, dear?' she asked, obviously inferring that I was in her way. 'Are you visiting someone?'

'Yes, but I was told to wait here,' I replied.

'I should ignore that, it's nearly twenty past,' she said. 'Go on up to the gate – they've probably forgotten all about you.'

'I think you're right,' I agreed. Once again I left the reception cabin and marched determinedly up the hill towards the gates. They looked even larger and more forebidding the closer I got to them. In fact, they looked to me very much like the gates of Nottingham Castle. There were a series of heavy black studs around the edges and a large bell set into the wall at the side. I pushed the bell and waited.

I could hear some movement and then some cursing on the other side. Finally, a small half door within the main door opened and a big, burly officer popped his head out. 'Yes,' he shouted. His mouth was full of food and he sprayed half-digested fragments all over me. He had a half-eaten meat pie in his hand.

'I'm here to see a prisoner,' I replied wearily.

'You're too late and you need a VO,' came back the answer as bits of food continued to shower the area.

He was about to shut the door and disappear when I shoved the bundle of papers straight at his chest to stop him. 'I have a VO,' I persevered. 'I was told to wait by . . .' I crouched slightly, peered through the hatchway and saw the same officer I'd seen about half an hour before. 'I was told to wait by him,' I said, pointing to the officer who had done everything in his power to stop me from getting in. The man seemed to be grinning and turned away to hide his face. He too was eating something. Two other officers with him also seemed to be enjoying the joke at my expense.

'Come in, let's have a look. Who is it you're wanting to visit?' he asked.

'Downing – Stephen Downing,' I said, emphasising the second name.

The officer looked hard at the visiting order. 'It says twenty minutes. You should have been here at two o'clock.' He checked his watch.

'I was here well before two o'clock, as your colleague knows. I think you'll find the VO was stamped at the reception office before two.' I was getting angrier and angrier but I knew I had to keep my temper in check. If I upset them any further they would have a perfect excuse to refuse me admission.

'Come through, but you'll have to wait here. I'll check.' I was invited into a small courtyard sandwiched between the main gate and another heavy security gate about ten metres away.

The officer then disappeared into an office, lifted the phone, dialled a number, put his hand over the phone to make sure he couldn't be heard, put his pie down and turned his back. He was wearing a short dark top with the collar turned up. I could only hear snatches of the conversation but I heard both my name and Stephen's mentioned. I heard him say, 'Just a minute, I'll ask.' Then the officer turned and came back to where I was standing. 'The senior officer says can you come back tomorrow or Monday?'

'No, I certainly can't,' I said, burning with frustration. 'Look, I've come a hell of a long way, several hundred miles. The visit was booked in with your people. I've got a VO and that's been stamped as well. Do I take it you're refusing me admission? It will make a bloody good story for the nationals!'

The officer's face remained devoid of all expression. He turned and went back in. I heard him speak to the SO on the phone again, telling him I had come a long way and might make trouble. Eventually he put down the phone and walked slowly back. There was still no sign of any emotion or sympathy. 'Wait here, please,' I was told in no uncertain fashion.

'Can I see Mr Downing then, please?'

'Wait here.'

I must have waited another five minutes before I finally heard the keys in the other security door and the senior officer and two warders came through. 'Mr Hale? Come through, please. In here.' He pointed to the small office where the other warder had phoned from. 'Mr Hale. No papers. No notebooks. No tape recorders. No pens, no pencils, no rulers – nothing. Do you understand the terms?'

I was still holding the newspapers, books and gifts from Stephen's family and other well-wishers. 'What about these? It was agreed on the telephone on Tuesday that I could take them in,' I explained yet again.

'Nothing!' There was no further response.

'Surely the newspapers and books are OK?' I pleaded.

'They will have to be posted in at a later date. I'm very sorry.' One of the warders took the packages from me and I wondered what was going to happen next. It wasn't long before I found out.

'In here, please, sir. Do you agree to a strip search?'

I could hardly believe my ears. I was being treated like a terrorist. But I could see that if I wanted to visit Stephen I would have to agree to all their demands. Whether this was strict procedure or just a process of humiliation I wasn't sure. 'If necessary,' I replied. 'But why? What the hell is going on now?'

'We can consider your visit, sir, if you agree to be searched. Put your clothes on the chair. Shoes, keys, watch and coins in the tray. Down to your undies please, sir.' Reluctantly I began to undress and gave the officers their brief moment of triumph. Apart from the officer who had ordered me to strip, three others crowded into the doorway and sniggered. When I was down to my underpants and socks with my shirt completely undone and flapping, I was ordered to lift my arms while a warder ran his hands down my arms, legs and sides.

'Right, get dressed, sir. You will have an escorted visit. Nothing goes in or out. Hands on the table at all times. You will sit facing the prisoner and nothing is to be exchanged. Do you understand the terms?'

I dressed quickly. I felt cold as I threw on my clothes and headed for the door. My tie was still in my hand and I carried my jacket over one shoulder. I said nothing. But in the rush to get dressed I accidentally swept the warder's half-eaten meat pie on to the floor with my hand as I picked up my coins. As it fell I trod on it hard and deliberately, swivelling my heel over it to make sure it was well and truly flattened. 'Oops, sorry about that,' I said, trying to keep a straight face. It was a small but worthwhile victory. The look I got back from the fat warder was meant to terrify me. It didn't work.

Time was precious now. As I dashed outside I wondered just how much was left of it for my visit. 'How long have I got?' I asked the senior officer who was also trying not to laugh at the warder's predicament.

The senior officer glanced at his watch and then at the whingeing warder who had just lost his pie and looked for all the world as if he'd just lost a close relative. 'Half an hour probably. After you, sir,' he said, opening the other gate and still sniggering. We quickly moved through to a small exercise yard where there were a few prisoners doing odd jobs.

The officer opened the final door into the visiting room and the first person I saw was Stephen, patiently waiting for me. He looked calm and well. He was smiling and seemed pleased to see me. It was a defining moment – a moment that will stay with me all my life.

After all these months of phone calls and letters we were finally meeting face to face. On first impressions I thought Stephen was smaller than I had expected, with one of the gentlest faces I had ever seen. And this man had been in jail for over twenty years for a murder he hadn't committed. I felt emotion well up inside me as I moved forward to shake Stephen warmly by the hand, before we were both escorted to a specially allocated table. Then an officer who was sitting at another table called me over to him and explained the rules to me yet again.

As I agreed to the terms and walked back to the table where Stephen was sitting, I noticed three other officers were now positioned around it in a triangle about two paces away. They would obviously be able to hear every word of the conversation. There was quite a bit of noise in the room and a lot of other prisoners were seated at similar tables with visitors, but no one else had any warders supervising – and no one else was sitting opposite their visitors.

It was a very awkward atmosphere in which to conduct a civilised conversation, but I had to give it a go after all the trouble I had gone to. I first explained to Stephen the nerve-racking ordeal I had had to go through to get to see him. 'I feel quite thirsty. My throat's very dry,' I said. Then I noticed the WRVS refreshment counter in the far corner of the room and a few seconds later an enormous prisoner, who seemed to be on some kind of assistance duty, suddenly appeared at the table, towering over everyone. 'Tea, coffee, cold drinks, any food?' he asked.

'Yes, that sounds good,' I replied. But as soon as I'd said it I could feel a slight kick on the shin and I noticed Stephen had his mouth cupped by his hands, as if he was trying to whisper something to me. He was shaking his head slightly. I got the message. 'No, it's all right. I'll leave it till later,' I said.

The huge man muttered to himself, then moved away and started cleaning some of the empty tables and sweeping up round them. 'Why didn't you want me to order food and drink?' I asked Stephen. 'Is there something wrong?'

'That's old Billy. He's an odd one. He's in for poisoning,' Stephen whispered.

We laughed out loud. The three warders remained totally expressionless. I looked at the next table and there, lying on it, were the papers and books which I had brought for Stephen. Things were looking up. One of the warders must have relented and brought them in. 'Could I have those?' I asked one of the surly escorts.

'Have they been checked?' asked the warder nearest to the pile.

'I don't know,' said his colleague.

'Better have a run through them, then,' said the third warder.

One of them picked up the assortment of papers and held each page out in turn, shaking them and running some sort of small electronic scanning device across them to test for any traces of drugs. He went through each and every page of every newspaper, book and magazine. Finally he said, 'No, I don't think they've been approved. You'll have to post them in later.'

Stephen and I smiled at each other, amused by their sheer incompetence. As we began to feel more relaxed in each other's company I felt it was time to ask him about the terrible events of September 1973. But as soon as I broached the subject, one of the watching warders interrupted. 'No records. You must write nothing down.'

'How can I write anything down?' I asked. 'You took everything from me at reception, remember?' I couldn't resist adding, ' Or were you and your pals too busy enjoying the peep show?'

I was conscious that our time was limited and there was so much I wanted to talk about. I had to start somewhere, so I bit the bullet. 'Stephen, I've read everything very carefully that you've sent to me. And I want to ask you to talk a bit more about the confession you made. Can we start right at the beginning when you were in the cemetery?'

He sighed. It was obvious the memories were still quite painful for him despite the passage of time.

I continued, 'Did you, Stephen, at any time admit attacking the woman to anyone in the cemetery?'

'No. I only showed them where she was. I was permitted to continue working, at the request of one of the other workmen. I wasn't allowed to wash my hands, because they had blood on them from turning her over,' he replied.

'And did you volunteer to go with them to the police station?' I asked.

'Yes, they asked me to help with their enquiries and said they wanted to establish some facts about her visit to the cemetery. As I say, I'd already told PC Ball that I had found Wendy on the lower path.'

'And did you continue with the same story when you got to the police station?'

'Yes. For about eight hours I didn't falter in my answers. Upon arrival at the police station, I was taken upstairs to the interview room. I had lost all sense of time by then but guess it would be between 2.30 and 3p.m. I was again asked to relate my account of the story leading up to the first time that I saw Wendy Sewell – through to when the police arrived. I had to do this several times. They kept coming and going and would either sit or stand on either side of me so they could continually bombard me with questions. I suppose the objective behind it was to cause me to falter in my answers. But I never did, probably to their annoyance.'

'So what time did you confess to the attack?'

'I'd lost track of time. I guess I made an admission at around eleven o'clock.'

'Stephen. Why did you change your story and make the admission? I need to be sure.'

'I was cold, tired and hungry and in pain from what turned out to be an abscess at the base of the spine. Later on I had to have a four-hour operation for it at Walton prison hospital. I hoped that once I'd admitted it they would let me rest and either continue questioning me the next day, or find out who the real attacker was from Wendy Sewell or from their investigations.'

'So you agreed to let the police write your statement for you?'

'I've told you, I was ashamed of my poor spelling. It was abysmal. I used to hate it if I was called on to read a passage from a book when I was at school. I was really embarrassed by my failures. The police asked me to give an account, so I did. I was interrupted at intervals by a police officer in a suit – I think this might have been Younger, I don't remember – who prompted me by saying that such and such a thing sounded better, or it meant the same thing. I'll give you an example. I said "I watched her." He stopped me and asked, "You followed her with your eyes?" I said, "Yes." He said "OK, so you followed her. Go on." And this got written down as 'I followed her'. I did protest when that was read back to me, but they said it meant the same as watching her. I foolishly accepted this. It allowed them to manipulate my statement to their own advantage. So, yes, they did put words into my mouth and, yes, they did change my statement. I didn't sign or initial any of the alterations. I only signed it at the end.'

'In biro?'

'Yes.'

'And they wrote it in pencil?'

'Yes,' said Stephen with a wry smile.

I glanced at the warders. They appeared to have dropped their guard and seemed genuinely interested in what he was saying.

Stephen now seemed comfortable and was well into his stride when a bell sounded. Several visitors stood up to leave. 'Is that for us?' I asked, believing my half-hour-plus was now up.

'Not unless you want to leave, sir,' came the reply. I looked up. The three warders had been joined by another colleague in a dark-grey striped suit. There was some further whispering as they huddled together and I heard my name mentioned and something about the strip search and a crushed meat pie. One of them laughed.

The apparently senior officer, who had replied before, added, 'You can have another thirty minutes.'

Stephen and I shared some cool soft drinks and a Kit-Kat from the WRVS counter. I kept looking at my watch and was aware time was quickly running out. I pressed on. 'Let's talk about your boots, Stephen. Your mother seems to think you changed your boots at lunchtime when you went back home for a few minutes.'

Stephen replied, 'I was wearing my best dress boots when I left the cemetery. They are dark blue in colour, with a natural-coloured leather sole. They are about eight to ten inches in height with a black zip on the inside and black nylon lining. I had put them on in the morning by mistake and decided to change into my working boots for the afternoon.' Stephen gestured over his right shoulder, adding, 'My best boots are in my stored property locker here. My father asked the police a couple of weeks later if they wanted them for forensic testing. They said no. Yet if what they said was true and I attacked Wendy Sewell before I left the cemetery, I would have had blood on them. When I went back to the cemetery I was wearing my working boots. I had blood on *them* because I had them on when I found Wendy. *They* were the ones that went off for forensic testing.' He laughed, inferring that the police had checked the wrong boots. 'But,' he continued, becoming serious again, 'if I had attacked Wendy Sewell I would have had a considerable amount of blood not just on my footwear, but on my hands and clothing. And I didn't have that much.'

I was trying to recall the exact police claims and was frustrated that I had no notes with me. 'Can you tell me, Stephen, if you had recently used the pickaxe handle that was used to beat Wendy Sewell?' I asked.

He shrugged. 'All pickaxe handles look the same. I'm not able to say if I used that particular pickaxe handle. I told the police that I had used a pickaxe handle about three weeks previously, but I can't say if it was that one. It would, though, be possible to say if the handle used to hit Wendy came from the council store in the unconsecrated chapel because, if it did, it would have BUDC stamped on it – short for Bakewell Urban District Council,' he added.

'Did the police check to see if the weapon had come from there?'

'During the time I was there, no checks were carried out. From memory I think the council pick handles were checked later and tallied . . . none were missing. I think one of the workmen told my family this some time afterwards.'

The bell sounded just as Stephen finished speaking. It had been quite an ordeal for him – and me. The loudspeaker called for all visitors to leave the room immediately. I thanked Stephen for his co-operation and said we must keep in regular touch by letter, and I hoped to be able to see him again soon. In the meantime, I pledged to continue with my investigations and wished him well. We shook hands before he was finally ushered out of the room.

Outside, I was handed back my newspapers and articles. The officer who had 'lost' his meat pie gave me a final glare before I went through the gates and marched down the steep path and back towards town. This was to be one of many similar prison visits that I was to make to Stephen over the next few years.

When I got back to Matlock I checked with my informant who had given me all the leads on DNA and the murder weapon. Did it have a BUDC mark? The answer was No. So the chances were that it had *not* come from the council store. Then Ray told me that the private detective, Robert Ervin, had checked the same print with the council years ago. The council inventory had said there should be six handles in the store. A check was made and the number tallied. All six had the BUDC stamp.

Information was coming in thick and fast. In late February I sent in a further submission to the Home Office and police headquarters. It included the following points:

Forensics*:

- A blood sample which did not match Downing's or Wendy Sewell's blood group was found on the murder weapon. Whose blood was it?
- Although fingernail scrapings had been taken from Mrs Sewell, their existence was not disclosed on the list of forensic evidence at his trial, or to Stephen's Defence Counsel. In fact, they lay undisturbed in police vaults for twenty-two years and, when I first made enquiries about them, I was told they did not exist.
- The police took fingernail scrapings from Downing. There was nothing in them to connect him to Mrs Sewell.
- Stephen's fingerprints were not found on the murder weapon. I was also told, when I first made enquiries, that the murder weapon had been burned, and that fingerprints had not been taken from Downing.
- The accused said he had put on his best blue boots by mistake that morning and changed them when he went home at lunchtime because he knew his father would be annoyed with him for wearing his best boots to work. He was meant to have committed the attack before he went home for his break, yet it was the boots he returned in which had blood-stains on them. Police declined to check his best boots, even though Mr Downing senior offered them up for testing.
- If Downing had committed the attack as described, he would have had the opportunity to change his clothes and clean his hands before returning to the cemetery. Surely he would have done so?
- The Home Office's forensic expert did not attend the scene of crime.

* The first four forensic points originated with police information.

The scene of crime procedures:

- It was assumed that Downing had taken the murder weapon from the council store in the unconsecrated chapel. A check on the pickaxe handles in the council store would have revealed that all were clearly stamped BUDC (Bakewell Urban District Council), yet the murder weapon contained no such marking. Checks at the time showed that no pickaxe handles were missing from the store.

The new witness statements:

- One man, questioned at the time, has admitted that he and another man, also questioned, gave false alibis. He has now claimed to me that they were both, in fact, in the area of the cemetery that day. New statements from other witnesses corroborate his presence there. This man named a third man who was due to meet the pair at the cemetery.

- A woman has written anonymously claiming to have been in the cemetery that day and has named people present . . . including Wendy Sewell.

Other considerations:

- Home Office reports describe Downing as a 'model prisoner, always polite, co-operative', and that his behaviour is 'exemplary'. They state he has never admitted to the offence and the statements confirm: 'He has done twenty years in custody, I believe due to his continual denial of the offence. There is *no* evidence to show that he is a danger to the public. He still maintains he was wrongly convicted on the grounds of questionable evidence and panic-induced false admissions. He realises that his maintained denial of the offence has and continues to interfere with progress, yet he remains firm in his denial.'

- In March 1994 Stephen Downing was allowed a home visit to his family in Bakewell, Derbyshire (under supervision). The officer's report from Clive Tanner said, 'He coped very well and there were a lot of people there who knew him before and were coming up to him and greeting him. It came across as very strange to me, how in a small community, where I assume a murder only takes place possibly once every

100 years, when the offender returns he is warmly welcomed by a great deal of the local people. Maybe there is something in the point he is trying to make about *not* being guilty.'

I enclosed copies of the anonymous letters, extracts from Stephen's prison reports, the report concerning Stephen's home visit and an account of Syd Oulsnam's telephone conversation with me.

16

IN MARCH 1995 the *Matlock Mercury* newsroom received a call from a medium, Christine Smith, who lived in Chesterfield. She claimed to be in touch with Wendy Sewell's spirit and offered to help in our campaign. I was naturally interested in the call, but was highly sceptical of getting involved with a clairvoyant. Nevertheless I arranged to meet Christine at Bakewell cemetery.

'Just leave me alone for a few minutes,' she said when we arrived at the gates.

She was younger and more attractive than I had envisaged, with a trim figure. She was wearing a shortish tight skirt, black stockings and high heels – certainly not the old gypsy and shawl image complete with crystal ball and horse-drawn wagon that my reporters had conjured up. I remained where I was as she entered the cemetery and, without any prompting, began to trace the exact footsteps of the victim – footsteps which had been taken twenty-two years earlier.

Christine occasionally stopped, as though she was listening to something. When she came to the grave of Anthony Naylor on the bottom path, she waved me over. 'It's here. Or it's about here somewhere. I can feel it,' she said.

'What can you sense?' I asked.

'There's anger, confusion, surprise, shock and extreme pain. I can feel something tight round my throat. I'm choking. I can feel something pulling. The texture – it's a pair of tights, I think. Someone's behind me – it's another man! My head hurts. I can taste blood – dizziness . . . my head!' Christine exclaimed, her face contorted.

She seemed a little faint and frightened. 'I feel she has been betrayed. It's someone she knew and trusted. It's a wolf in sheep's clothing,' she added.

We were standing at the exact spot where Stephen had found Wendy, badly injured. Christine turned her back on Anthony Naylor's grave and pointed across the cemetery to a place some twenty yards distant. 'I'm sure she was found somewhere else,' she said.

She was looking straight at the tombstones in the middle of the cemetery, at the grave of Sarah Bradbury. It was true that, in the time it had taken Stephen to get help and return, Wendy *had* moved and was staggering about on the graves Christine was indicating. This had not been reported at the trial or since and I could not see how Christine could have known about it beforehand.

'You mentioned something around her neck. Something about tights?' I enquired and added, 'As far as I know she was attacked with a wooden shaft, not strangled.' The details of the attack were hardly confidential information and had been widely reported, yet Christine had introduced a completely new theory – the possibility of choking and strangulation.

'Yes, definitely tights, I could feel the texture,' Christine confirmed. 'She stripped and was then choked or strangled *before* being bludgeoned.'

'Stripped?' I repeated. 'You mean she had begun to undress herself?'

She nodded. This was another interesting new theory. It would suggest either Wendy had been forced to strip by a man who intended to sexually attack or rape her, or she had a pre-arranged assignation with a lover and was willingly undressing when she was attacked. Christine added that Wendy had kept all her secret thoughts and details of meetings in a diary.

After a few brief moments she said, 'Wendy can't pass to the other side until this is resolved.'

Christine had come up with several theories – strangulation with tights, two attackers, grabbed from behind, the fact that Wendy knew and was meeting one of the men who killed her and had begun to undress *herself*.

I remembered Ray Downing's description of Wendy on her final bus ride into work from Middleton-by-Youlgreave – she had been wearing tights underneath ankle socks. Ray had noticed this as she crossed her legs and her trousers rode up above one ankle. Yet I had seen no reference to tights in any of the police notes, trial notes or forensic reports I had managed to obtain, although I was sure they were on the scene of crime photographs I had seen. Apart from that, Wendy's purse, shopping basket, handbag and other personal possessions were never referred to . . . including a diary. Yet Ray had also noticed some of these objects during the morning bus journey. Again, I asked myself, had anyone checked her office, or Catcliff Woods? Had these possessions been found in the cemetery and not put on the list of scene of crime exhibits?

I thought back to the scene of crime photographs. I still could not get those horrific images of Wendy out of my head. Then it struck me. I wanted to double check something.

I waited until Christine had left, then popped over the road to the Downings' home to ask if I could have another look at the photographs. Yes, I was right! There seemed to be bruising on Wendy's *neck*. How could that have got there, unless from some form of strangulation? As I flicked through the photos I noticed the tights lying on the path, yet there was no sign of any of Wendy's personal items, such as the basket and the handbag Ray Downing had seen her carrying on the morning bus journey to work.

The following day I contacted the local police to give them details of Christine's walk around the cemetery. My enthusiasm did not appear to be reciprocated.

The missing possessions were troubling me. I had the official list of case exhibits from the Home Office. No mention of any personal effects there. I wondered if anything else existed. I made a phone call to one of my police informants. He soon came up with a few more detailed documents, listing items found at the scene of crime. Nothing I didn't know about . . . clothes, pick shaft . . . and then I saw a memo attached to the file. It stated that no personal items were found at the scene. I saw no reference to any search of the adjacent woods having been made. What had happened to Wendy's bags? What was in them? Were any of her personal items later found at her office? Had anyone looked?

As always, more questions than answers.

For now, Christine at least gave me another good splash in the

Mercury. 'BEYOND THE GRAVE CLUES' announced the headline that week. That will give some people something more to worry about, I thought.

17

IDECIDED TO MEET Stephen's lawyer, Simon Lacey, for a chat about appeal prospects and to find out the likelihood of his release on parole.

I knew Stephen had already enjoyed a successful home visit to Bakewell in March 1994 and had obtained occasional weekend leave to meet with his parents while they were on holiday in Weymouth, with all visits under escort. I knew any application for consideration of release via the appeal courts would have to be routed via the government's C3 department, which specifically dealt with claims of miscarriages of justice.

Simon Lacey was an amicable young man in his twenties. Solicitors from his Dorset firm represented many of the inmates at Dorchester on routine matters such as prisoner complaints and parole applications. It was probably seen as a way for young lawyers like Lacey to cut their teeth. He could not, however, give me much encouragement about tackling an appeal. On the contrary, he warned that my involvement could actually harm Stephen's chances of parole, even spoil his chance of release. I took his meaning. It was not uncommon for prisoners who rocked the boat to find their status within the system suddenly taking a nosedive. If they tried to beat the system, they had to be prepared for things getting a whole lot worse before they got better. I had to spell out this concern directly to Stephen and his parents.

My earliest contacts with the Home Office suggested the Stephen Downing file had been passed around like the proverbial hot potato for years. And years back, someone had found a dark and dusty hole in which to lose the file. I was still coming to terms with the apathy shown from the outset by both Derbyshire police and Home Office officials. They seemed to hold the firm belief that no one in prison is ever innocent. Denial of a serious offence was always considered just an excuse and meant the inmate was potentially more dangerous.

After talking with several nameless individuals, I began to wonder how many other Stephen Downings had been locked away and forgotten. To me, he was an ordinary Joe. He desperately needed someone who would take the time to listen to his claims and, more important, find someone prepared to stick his or her neck out and investigate the merits of his case. Although I fully supported his claims, I often wondered whether I was up to the task. The family had tried in vain for more than two decades to have their claims heard and even I soon began to wonder whether it needed someone else – with more authority than a local newspaper editor – to present Stephen's case and sustain this daunting task.

One of my first conversations with the Home Office in March, though, gave me that extra impetus to keep going. Some anonymous, ill-informed and pompous senior desk jockey in C3, the Criminal Cases Unit, kept telling me, 'Downing is in the Verne prison. He's been saying he's innocent for years. Nobody really cares, nobody's in the least bit interested in him. He's just one of many who continually say they're innocent,' he added sarcastically. 'They're all the same. I don't know why you bother. He's just a nobody.'

I could not believe my ears. I was furious and told him so. 'Look, first of all he's not at the Verne, he's been at Dorchester for several months. Secondly, there is new evidence to support his claims of innocence. And finally, *I* care. For more than twenty years he's been saying he's innocent. Does that not tell you something? He's a *somebody*. Everybody is a somebody. He has a mother, father, sister and friends, who also care.' I could almost hear myself on the soapbox.

The man finally lowered his tone. He obviously wasn't used to being spoken to like that and added drearily, '797501, Downing, Stephen, he *is* in the Verne. The records clearly show this.'

'Then your records are wrong,' I replied heatedly.

'I don't think so, sir,' he argued.

'Yes, I think you will find he is . . . sir.'

'I can tell you exactly where he is, where he's been since 1973, and how long he's stayed at each establishment. I have all his records to hand.'

'Then I suggest you get them updated pronto. I can assure you that he is in Dorchester prison.'

'No, sir, the Verne.'

'Dorchester,' I repeated.

'Why do you keep saying Dorchester, sir?'

'Because I went to see him last week. Your department and the prison service gave me the clearance. I can give you the visiting order reference number, time, date, etc. He is definitely in Dorchester prison. I even have the date of his transfer.'

He suddenly went very quiet. I could hear some mumbling, then shouting in the background. There seemed to be further raised voices. 'Well, thank you for the information. I'll make enquiries and if you are right we'll update the files.' He seemed disillusioned after our little chat.

I could not believe this typical, anonymous official. He sounded very 'public school', very self-important, but had constantly refused to give his name, saying it was 'section policy' not to give a name and that he did not want to get involved with any personal circumstances. I was not going to let him off the hook. 'What do you mean, "make enquiries and see if you're right"? Who did I see at Dorchester, then . . . *Mickey Mouse?*' I challenged.

'We'll make enquiries, sir.'

'Before you go,' I persisted, 'you claim to be very thorough with your records. Tell me, what was Mr Downing's sentence?' I asked.

'Oh, that's easy.' The note of confidence was creeping back into his voice. 'Mr Downing was convicted in February 1974 at Nottingham Crown Court. He was given a mandatory life sentence and ordered to be detained at the Queen's Pleasure.'

'And was there any recommendation of tariff given?'

'Yes, they recommended a minimum tariff of seventeen years.'

'Really, seventeen years? So, he should be out by now, then?'

He hesitated, realising he had been led into a trap. 'Seventeen years . . . mmm . . . hang on a minute . . . I'm sure it says seventeen years . . . that's strange.'

'Yes, you are quite correct. By rights he should have been out about five years ago. So why is he still inside?'

I could hear him shuffling papers and mumbling again. Then his composure returned. 'Of course, he's what we call an IDOM, "In Denial of Murder". If they don't admit to their crime they're pushed back down the queue.'

'But what if he's innocent? He's hardly likely to admit to something he didn't do. What if he never changes his plea?'

'Innocent!' he almost spat out the word. 'They're *all* innocent, aren't they? That's what keeps journalists like you in business.'

If he had not been miles away on the end of a phone, I am sure I would have given him a bloody nose. 'If you had read the file I sent, you would at least have some understanding of the case. He's been in jail for over twenty years for a crime he has always said he didn't commit . . . and jumped-up pen-pushers like you don't even know where he is. You make me sick! I'll report this conversation to your superiors at the Home Office and to my MP, Patrick McLoughlin, who's a junior minister.'

There followed a few seconds of silence.

'Will that be all, Mr Hale?'

'No. I want your assurance that the file will be updated and given your full consideration.'

'We'll look into the matter and make relevant enquiries. Thank you and good day.'

13 March 1995
HM Prison
7 North Square
Dorchester
Dorset

Dear Don

Thank you for your most recent letters and the books that accompanied them. I have read a few very good fantasy fiction and sci-fi novels. I think I would have to rate Tom Sharpe as perhaps the funniest writer I have ever come across and Terry Pratchett's Discworld novels as the most imaginative. I find the ones with the witches in to be his best. I have rather a soft spot for Magrat Garlick. The other two Nanny Ogg and Granny

Weatherwax consider her to be a 'wet hen'.

I have enclosed a free entry ticket for up to three children to the Ideal Home Exhibition. If you have no use for it you may be able to pass it on to someone else to use. I like to return a favour wherever possible.

What a pity we are having such wonderful weather. I hanker after the walks I used to be able to take at the Verne and now I'm stuck indoors and behind bars, though hopefully not for much longer.

Stephen Downing

Was I becoming paranoid? Each time I went out, whether on foot or by car, I thought I was being followed. Whenever I drove any distance in the car, suddenly another vehicle would appear, following close behind. I recalled trips across to our publishers at Chesterfield when I had felt I was being followed. There had certainly seemed to be one or two cars on my tail directly after leaving the office . . . sometimes late at night, when the blazing headlights always kept their constant distance. And on the return journey – sometimes into the early hours. It raised the spectre of my very own mobile stalker. Whether day or night, it kept happening. This seemed to go on for months, or did it? Were the threats finally hitting home? Was it affecting my judgement? And who would be following me, the cops or villains? Was there really any difference? Both sections appeared hostile. I regularly took the advice of the 'friendly' detective inspector to check under my car each time before moving off. Unexpected or strange parcels were opened very carefully. Trips to Chesterfield, Wirksworth, Ashbourne and visits to other witnesses were limited and kept strictly confidential. It was all done on a 'need to know' basis.

Only a few people were informed of my appointments. Interviews about the Downing case were only to be conducted by me and I kept asking staff if they too had heard any unusual clicks on their telephones either at home or work and ordered them to meet strangers in very public places or preferably in the office. There would be no night jobs or anything out of town without permission. I kept asking my wife Kath if she thought we were under surveillance and from whom. Then I kept talking myself out of it. After all, why should anyone want to check on my movements or want to listen in on my phone calls? Perhaps I really was just being paranoid. Visits in relation to the Downing case were normally made along major roads to avoid potential problems in isolated spots. However, living in a rural community meant it was very difficult for anyone to ignore country lanes.

It was during a prearranged visit to Ray Downing one Friday afternoon that I believed I was definitely being followed – again. A light-brown Ford Cosworth seemed to keep pace with my own car during the journey to Bakewell. It looked very similar to the car I thought had followed me the previous day, but I tried to convince myself it was just coincidence. As I watched the car in my rear-view mirror, it seemed to speed up or slow down in time with me. At one point I drove so slowly along by the Whitworth Hospital at Darley Dale that I even expected a bicycle to overtake me, but still the car retained its distance behind.

I looked hard to see who was driving. There were two men. Both had dark suits. The car looked clean and modern. I looked for the two-aerial give-away of the local plain-clothes plods, but couldn't quite see one. I pulled into the car park at the Happy Eater near Rowsley and went into the building. I looked again in the mirror as I turned and noticed the car go past. Yes, it was definitely two men. They both tried to stare straight ahead as the car moved slowly past. I noted the registration number. Not a local plate. About twenty minutes later I left, refreshed and relieved, ready to continue my journey. I looked about but couldn't see anyone. A couple of miles further on though, there was a car parked with its bonnet facing the road at ninety degrees and just set back slightly from a small clearing. After I passed, it pulled out and drove about 300 yards behind me. It was the same car. And just as I had begun to convince myself I was being paranoid.

Reaching Bakewell town centre, I deliberately ignored the sharp left turn up King Street towards the Downings' house and continued round the roundabout, taking a hard 360-degree turn and doing a full circuit. At the crown in the road I almost collided with the car that had been following me – and gazed directly into the faces of two very surprised individuals. Of course, I didn't recognise them. I continued up the hill and on to the estate towards the Downing family home. At the top of the rise, just past the cemetery, I noticed the car some distance behind me. One of the men seemed to be arguing with the other. I quickly drove down a small ginnel near the rear of the Downings' house and parked up. As I climbed out, I saw the car speed past and continue towards Lady Manners School, unaware of my sudden turn.

The following day, I spoke with one of my friendly police contacts and related the story. He said he would check out the registration number, but explained that he was a bit pushed at that moment. 'There's a bit of a flap on. Some southern lads are in town. Leave it with me and I'll get back.'

I doubted if the 'southern lads' had anything to do with my own small-time adventures but still wondered what was happening.

That night, at home, I received a phone call at about nine o'clock. The caller just said, 'Chelsea, ten minutes.' This was one of a number of prearranged call signs. The call had come from a local phone box. I decided to leave the car at home as the meeting place was only a short walk away.

It was dark and I turned off the kitchen lights before going out the back way and through the rear of All Saints Primary School. It wasn't the most direct route but it was protected from view and, as I cut across the back of the County Council car park, I realised that I couldn't be followed directly by a vehicle or by another person – unless both routes were being monitored. At the agreed point, I looked around. It was quiet and there seemed to be no one else about. I leant against the car park wall opposite the Edgefold social club and waited. A hand suddenly grabbed my shoulder. I almost jumped a mile. 'Bloody Hell! I've lost another two lives,' I declared.

'Sorry, mate. It's all a bit hush-hush at the minute. I couldn't take any risks. It's more than my job's worth to be seen talking with *you* at the moment.' My contact was a good local community bobby. He always had his ear to the ground and was very useful to me.

'Why, what's up? These London boys are not following me, are they?' I must have looked puzzled.

'No. At least, I don't think so. They say they're on to something completely different. A big drugs job out towards Clay Cross. But that car number, I think I know who it was. It's either special branch, MI5, or the "invisible men", a couple of guys working with CIB2, you know – the Complaints Investigation Bureau that doesn't exist? The car's registered to a special government departmental pool. I had to put the request down to an anonymous road traffic complaint but the inspector had me on the mat.

'These guys are Premier League. I can assure you it's worse than the Kremlin in there at the moment. The word is they are very interested in some of the people you are interested in. What is more, in your submission you mentioned some potential links with the Barbara Mayo case and the murder of Wendy Sewell.'

'Is there a connection?' I asked innocently. My sources so far were merely local gossips.

'Not that I'm aware. But there's something funny going on. Confidential files, new faces, London accents. I remember that Mayo murder and Scotland Yard. The girl was heading for Catterick and was found near Chesterfield,' the policeman reminisced.

'Well, I have found some potential connections between the Mayo and Sewell murders,' I replied, wanting to appear to know more than I actually did about this aspect, which in truth was little at this point.

He looked hard at me. 'That's what I mean. Be careful mate.'

'But are you saying there is a connection?' I asked again.

'I'm not saying anything. I simply don't know. But it was certainly high-profile at the time. And now there's a sudden revival of interest from HQ. One of my colleagues mentioned some ex-military connection. There seems to be a reluctance to reopen your man's file,' he added. 'If you claim a connection, watch your back.'

'So what about my two spooks?' I asked.

'I think you blew their cover.' He laughed. 'They're now working out of High Peak for the next few days. Two cocky cockneys, Hawkins and McBride. I don't think we'll see them back here. Must go, cheers!'

'Yes, OK, cheers. Many thanks.' I watched him disappear over to the far side of the car park and past the Lido swimming baths back into town. I turned the opposite way and walked back up the hill the long way round. It gave me a chance to think.

★

Almost from day one, the West Derbyshire Conservative MP, Patrick McLoughlin, supported my campaign to have Stephen Downing's case re-examined by the authorities. I provided him with updated reports and discussed new developments on a regular basis. At the time, Mr McLoughlin was also a junior cabinet minister. He shared my concern at the apparent apathy from the police and supported my original submission. He agreed to urge Derbyshire police to make a more positive and rapid response. With support from the MP and regular coverage in the national newspapers, television and radio, the case remained high-profile for some time. And C3, the Home Office Miscarriage Investigations Unit, became actively involved following my early submissions.

On 27 March 1995 I received a letter from the unit stating the grounds on which the Home Secretary could refer Stephen's case back to the Court of Appeal. It said,

> The Home Secretary would not normally consider it right to exercise this power of reference unless presented with new evidence, or a new consideration of substance that has not been before the courts and which appears to cast doubt on the safety of the conviction.
>
> We will be looking to see whether the representations disclose grounds on which it would be appropriate for the Home Secretary to take any action. It may be necessary to make further enquiries into the conviction. Although the enquiries will be carried out as quickly as possible, this may take a little more time.
>
> We understand that Derbyshire Constabulary are not actively looking at the allegations made in your case, but will do so if our consideration of the case reveals any matters that require further investigation.

It was around three weeks later in April that I became aware of being followed yet again. This was the occasion when a quarry-type lorry tried to ram me off the road as I drove along an isolated cross country route one night. I escaped then by the skin of my teeth, knowing it was probably the most serious attempt on my life to date. At least it made for yet another interesting trip up the stone steps to the local police station the following day.

July to December 1995

18

IT WAS ABOUT halfway through 1995 that Stephen Downing changed his lawyers and engaged solicitors Woollcombe Beer Watts at Newton Abbot in Devon. I was introduced to solicitor John Atkins. John was able, confident and always enthusiastic. Initially he helped convert my findings into an acceptable legal submission. Unlike Stephen's previous solicitor, he was keen to look at the possibility of an appeal. Several threats of legal action by his firm eventually persuaded Derbyshire Constabulary to release important paperwork and exhibits, including the murder weapon. I had already seen much of the paperwork from unofficial sources. Now John was able to study it in depth. He proved a tower of strength throughout my campaign, often giving countless hours of unpaid time to help the cause.

September 1995

As I looked through the shelves of our new 'Downing' filing system at the *Matlock Mercury*, now full of dusty old papers and folders, the name Robert Ervin kept appearing. Ervin's involvement was extremely interesting. He was the private detective who had worked with Stephen Downing's original lawyers. Ervin died about 1984. He spent many years on the Downing case, working on and off for the family for some ten years after Stephen's conviction.

Ervin was a former member of the Army's Special Investigative Unit. He was convinced throughout that Stephen was innocent of the murder of Wendy Sewell, and in 1980 helped to compile a new appeal proposal to William Whitelaw, the Home Secretary. He also contacted the former West Derbyshire MP Matthew Parris.

He produced medical evidence to confirm Stephen Downing's learning difficulties at the time of the murder, contained in psychological and psychiatric reports. He always felt that Stephen's naivety had not been fully explained in court.

Despite Ervin's optimistic and even euphoric mood when he talked to the *Mercury* in the summer of 1980, he was told about six weeks later that Home Secretary William Whitelaw could not see any fresh grounds for an appeal. I realised that I'd been following in Robert Ervin's footsteps. I knew it was vital that I find his missing documents and notes on the Downing case.

A long, tortuous and frustrating search took me from Ervin's widow on the outskirts of Chesterfield – who could give me no help – to the home of a former colleague of Ervin's, Bobby Vince, who lived near Sheffield. I found out he had also passed away, but neighbours told me his elderly sister was still alive and in Rotherham. Her name was Constance Riley. I realised she would be an old woman by now and, in any case, only had a tenuous link to Ervin. I also wondered if she would be of any help or know anything after all these years.

But then I thought about my own elderly parents, their fondness for reminiscing about the past, and their reluctance to throw anything out. This made my decision simple. I headed north for Rotherham.

I made good time, and pulled in at a newsagent's on the outskirts of town to ask for directions. The house was only a mile or so away. I found it within ten minutes and drew up outside. It was a large, detached Victorian property with a massive driveway and reminded me of the house our family doctor owned when I was a child. It even had an old concave brass bell push. As I pressed it I listened carefully and could hear a faint ringing somewhere inside.

'I'm coming! I'm coming!' piped an elderly lady's voice from high above. A well-dressed woman with half-rimmed spectacles and white hair tied neatly in a bun opened the door moments later.

'Would you be Constance Riley?' I asked. I pulled out my ID card and gave her a brief explanation for my visit.

'An editor,' she said, sounding very surprised, 'and a young one at that! Yes, I'm Connie. Come on in,' she continued, giving me a quizzical smile.

I followed her into her dark, imposing sitting room, and we sat on

an old velvet sofa. I told her about Stephen's case without mentioning any names, and about the work that her brother had done. 'This
could be vitally important,' I said. 'I'm trying to find any paperwork
your brother or Robert Ervin may have done on this case.'

'I think most things were thrown out when Ethel – that was
Bobby's wife – died. She never really recovered from the shock of
losing Bobby. She had cancer. I think Mr Ervin had problems too.
His heart, I think. He suffered a few heart attacks, retired – then
poof,' she declared. 'But some things did come here. Bobby was only
an amateur sleuth, though.'

I sat up in anticipation. 'What sort of things?' I asked.

'Some papers and files. Some old army stuff. Mostly junk. But you
don't like throwing things out, do you?'

'Indeed not, Connie. And where are they now?' I enquired.

She struggled to her feet again and waved her stick. 'In there. I'll
show you where it is.' She pushed me into another room. It was piled
high with all sorts of household rubbish. Papers, newspapers and old
photograph albums were everywhere. Connie led me over to the
sideboard. 'Here, this is Bobby's stuff. You have a look and I'll play
you some music. Any requests?'

'No, not really,' I said. I was now too engrossed in rummaging
through all the paperwork.

'Something from *Swan Lake*, I think,' came her voice from the
piano in the other room. I could just see her sitting on the stool and
I could hear her warming up. I moved one pile and then another, and
kept sneezing due to the dust. There were files full of old bills,
invoices, some yellowed newspaper cuttings and numerous letters to
and from the army. The rest all seemed to be official military papers
and old photographs.

Every now and again she would stop playing and shout through
to ask for my opinion of her performance. 'Wonderful – excellent!'
I shouted back. I was beginning to get a bit despondent when I
finally saw it. Sticking out from near the bottom of the pile was an
ancient dog-eared file marked 'Downing Appeal'. I just managed to
stop myself from shouting 'Eureka!' There were old papers – mainly
typed carbon copies. They were very faint and some I couldn't even
read. I could make out names and addresses, but the main body of

the documents had often faded so badly that the words were illegible.

As I looked around I found two other files on the case, and pulled them out. When I was sure there were no more, I returned to the sitting room.

'Have you found anything?' Connie asked.

'Yes, thanks, Connie. These papers could be very interesting. I wonder if I could borrow them for a while? I'll return them after photocopying them.'

She turned and gripped my hand between both of hers. 'I don't want them back. Keep them. Do what you will. I'm sure Bobby wouldn't mind. You were on the same side, after all. You've given me some company and I don't get much. And I've had a chance to show off my piano playing.'

'Wonderful, Connie,' I declared. 'I've really enjoyed your music and your company too. It was excellent. I'll be in touch.'

'You old smoothie. Now if I was about forty years younger . . .' She chuckled as she showed me to the door.

I finally opened the files from Constance Riley's house later the following day. Much of the paperwork I had already seen before. I was halfway through the second file before I spotted anything of note. This was a copy of Ervin's letter from 1979 to the South Yorkshire police asking for information on any other unsolved murders with a similar background. It was very faint and I could hardly make out the exact date. I found no sign of any reply.

Ervin's notes mentioned the Barbara Mayo murder case and he seemed to be querying whether there was a possible military connection. His notes contained the names of several soldiers. There were also references to the murder of a woman called Jackie Ansell-Lamb. Both women had been killed within a few months of each other in 1970. Barbara Mayo's body had been found in Derbyshire, that of Jackie Ansell-Lamb in neighbouring Cheshire.

I couldn't help wondering if Ervin had heard the same rumours as me – that five men from the Bakewell area had been questioned in connection with the Mayo killing, one being Mr Red, and a second, another associate of Wendy's. I kept trying to put the other two murders out of my head. I thought it was difficult enough trying to solve one puzzle without the complications of two others. Yet I kept pulling out old news cuttings about the search for the murderer of student Barbara Mayo around the Chesterfield area. One from 1970 ran as follows:

HAVE YOU SEEN THIS MAN OR THIS TYPE OF CAR?
If you have seen a man who looks like this driving a Morris 1000 estate car, the Mayo Murder team wants to hear from you.

Detective Chief Superintendent Charles Palmer of Scotland Yard told a press conference late on Wednesday, 'We are urgently requiring information about this car driven by a man aged between 25 and 30, of medium build, with mousy coloured hair brushed back with a quiff at the front, who was seen to give a lift to a girl closely resembling Barbara Mayo and dressed in very similar clothes.'

Witnesses say that the girl was picked up at about 4p.m. at Kimberley, Nottinghamshire and driven via Nuthall to junction 26 of the M1. The car was seen to travel north towards Chesterfield.

From witness descriptions a photo-fit likeness of the man police want to interview has been built up and humanised by an artist. It is perhaps significant that this road provides a cross-country link with the motorway where Jacqueline Ansell-Lamb, another young hitch-hiker, was found strangled last March near Knutsford.

Police throughout the present murder enquiries have constantly linked the two killings and detectives from the investigating Cheshire force have been here in Chesterfield to liaise fully with Chief Supt Palmer's murder squad.

On Monday further checks were carried out at Kimberley and on the M1 intersection. The Chief Supt declared, 'If I have to check every Morris Minor 1000 Traveller in the United Kingdom I will do so and, in fact, I have already started.'

The article was accompanied by the photo-fit picture of the man they wished to interview and a picture of the suspect's car. I was told by a former acquaintance of Mr Red's that, at the time of the Mayo murder, he drove a red Hillman estate. I looked at the photo-fit. The description I had been given of Mr Red from 1970 could have vaguely matched, though by no means in every detail.

As I continued to thumb my way through Ervin's old cuttings files, I noticed another reference to the Mayo case. It was the *Derbyshire Times* front page from Friday, 28 September 1973 – just two weeks after the murder of Wendy Sewell:

MAYO CASE STILL UNSOLVED. RETIRED CHIEF TO CONTINUE HUNT FOR KILLER

The detective who hunted the killer of Londoner Barbara Mayo for eleven months retired from Z Division of the Metropolitan Police at the weekend. But Chief Superintendent Charles Palmer vowed to his colleagues before he left: 'I'll still find the strangler.' The Chief Superintendent began his hunt for the killer three years ago when he was seconded to Derbyshire CID to lead the murder hunt – one of the costliest ever undertaken by the county force.

But eleven months and thousands of man-hours later, Chief Supt Palmer was taken off the case and returned to London. It was the first murder case in which he had failed to find the killer. Before he retired, he took photostat copies of the entire Mayo file and intends searching through them until he discovers the vital clue which might send the killer to jail.

I was certain that Ervin was drawing a connection between the murders of Wendy Sewell, Barbara Mayo and Jacqueline Ansell-Lamb.

There were plenty of old cuttings on the Downing case, too. Even more vital were copies of old police reports which mentioned that the attack was probably committed by *two* people, the one who had landed the fatal blows being right-handed. Stephen Downing was left-handed.

As I rummaged further, I found an extremely important document relating to the alleged threat made to Stephen in the cemetery when he found Wendy. It was a letter dated 22 February 1974 from Ervin to Stephen's solicitors.

It described how, during a visit Ray had made that day to his son, Stephen had told him about the mystery man who had threatened him shortly after he had found Wendy. He told his father exactly what the man had said and what he had been wearing, giving an almost identical account to the one he had given me a few weeks earlier.

Here was positive confirmation that Stephen's lawyers had been told of the threat made in the cemetery against his sister, a few days after he had been convicted. This backed up what Stephen had told me, although his reasons for keeping quiet up until then were not explained in Ervin's note. But another dust-coloured folder revealed advice from Stephen's counsel, Mr Dennis Barker QC, dated 5 March 1974. It showed that Mr Barker felt Stephen had left it too late to tell the story of the mystery man who made the threat. He expressed the opinion, 'Mr Dickenson [Stephen Downing's solicitor] saw Mr Downing on a number of occasions, on not one of which did Mr Downing make any mention of this happening. Nor did he to his father on any visit, nor to any of the psychiatrists, nor to myself or junior counsel in consultation. Moreover, he made no mention of it in the witness box, though he had ample opportunity to do so . . . In my opinion no Court of Appeal will allow this fresh "evidence" or explanation to be given on appeal – and even if they did, they would pay no attention to it.'

I conceded that Mr Barker was bound to give this advice in the circumstances, yet I could also fully understand *why* Stephen would have kept this information secret for five months. He and his younger sister, Christine, were extremely close and he felt protective towards her. He would have harboured deep fears for her safety, and felt a profound reluctance to put her at risk in any way by talking about the man who threatened him.

Mr Barker strongly advised against going for an appeal on several other grounds. Turning to Stephen's confession, he acknowledged that 'The Crown's case rested in large measure on oral admissions and a written statement made by the accused to the police.' He then, quite amazingly and totally wrongly in my opinion, repeated his assertion made at trial a month previously that there had been no impropriety on the part of the police in obtaining this confession.

'No objection could have been or was made to the admissibility of this evidence,' wrote Stephen's learned counsel. He then added, 'Mr Downing could not and did not, give any real reason why he made such admissions.'

'What?' I exclaimed out loud. Had Mr Barker forgotten about Stephen's complaints at trial, highlighted in Mr Justice Nield's summing up, that he was 'tired, hungry, my back hurt and I was only just able to keep awake'? Had Mr Barker forgotten, even though the judge reminded him and the rest of those in court, that Stephen said, 'Mr Younger put his hand on my shoulder twice to wake me up'? Had Mr Barker forgotten, even though the judge pointed it out, that Stephen said, 'I signed the written statement. It was untrue. I made it because they said they would question me all night if necessary and I did not realise Wendy was very badly hurt. My statement was read out to me. I was *told* to make it, that is the impression . . . it was not of my own free will'?

Had Mr Barker forgotten the judge's comments, 'The questioning had gone on at the station for eight or nine hours. As the hours wore by this young man became tired and you may have little hesitation in concluding that if a suspect is falling asleep and having to be shaken, it is no time to continue interrogation. That is bordering, you may think, on oppression if he is not given food and the rest of it . . . what was put, you see, there was this condition of tiredness . . . one officer had said, "Admit it. We know you've done it." Another said, "You will be questioned all night." Another said he would bet his wages he'd admit it . . . Those questions would seem to indicate the suggestion of some measure of impropriety'?

I continued reading Mr Barker's letter of advice against appeal. He acknowledged that the judge's summing up had been 'impeccable'. If he thought it so 'impeccable', I reasoned, why had he appeared to ignore it on this vital question of impropriety?

Finally, there was a reference to Mrs Beebe. Mr Barker said he had not called her to give evidence at the trial because 'her evidence would have been wholly inconclusive. All she could say was that she saw nobody in the cemetery as she walked along at about 1.12p.m. . . . and that she would have seen a person if he or she had been there. But the undoubted fact was that Wendy Sewell *was* there at that time.

The most that could be gleaned from Mrs Beebe's evidence would have been that she [Mrs Beebe] did not see her and this evidence would in no way have assisted Mr Downing.'

I had to concede the logic in that, but there was no reference to Mrs Beebe's children. *They* were the ones who had seen something which terrified them. *They* were the ones who had allegedly seen someone jumping over a wall out of the cemetery, someone with blood on them. I got the feeling that neither the police nor Stephen's defence team had ever got to the bottom of what the children saw.

Ervin had unearthed information about the running man and, like me, had been desperate to find out who he was and amazed that the police had failed to look into the sightings more closely. One of Ervin's memos, dated 1 January 1974, revealed how he had learnt 'a Peter Wheeler had heard that a man had been seen running from the direction of the cemetery by a Mrs Hadfield and that she had said a Mr Paling had also seen this man and that he had seen him leaning over a wall saying: "*God, what have I done!*" or words to that effect'.

So it appeared that, even though Mrs Hadfield had reported the running man to the police within days of the attack and the police had interviewed Mr Paling on the night of the attack, the Downings' private detective, working for Stephen's Defence team, had only just heard about these things through chance remarks among neighbours some three months later.

Ervin had subsequently obtained his own statements from Mrs Hadfield and Mr Paling. I found them both in the files of documents. They broadly fitted with Paling's account given to the police, Mrs Hadfield's account given to me and the evidence of both witnesses at trial.

However, on closer reading they contained some interesting new details.

When Ervin interviewed Mr Paling, this witness had queried the time at which he saw a man rushing up the road. His evidence given to the police and read out at trial, stated that it had been around 1.10pm . . . but George Paling told Ervin, 'It could have been nearer 1.30p.m.' and repeated his claim that 'the man was really exerting himself . . . he was definitely in a hell of a hurry'. This time difference was important. If the man seen by Paling was connected to the attack and the attack had been committed while Stephen Downing was away from the cemetery between 1.08 and 1.15–1.20, then it is likely the man *would* have been running away nearer 1.30 than 1.10.

There was also an interview between Ervin and Mrs Hadfield, which added a few more details to what she had told me. She mentioned the children who were playing 'having seen a man coming out of the cemetery'. This echoed what Mrs Beebe, and another witness on the estate, had told me. She had also given Ervin a slightly more detailed description of the running man's clothing, adding that he wore 'brown boots and a jeans-type jacket like those in the war, and a battle-dress-type belt'. She had not told me about his footwear, or the style of his denim jacket. She confirmed his fair hair, but added that it was 'wavy hair, more wavy than curly'.

And Mrs Hadfield had given Ervin a very enlightening description of what had happened when she went to report the man to the police. She said, 'The policeman, Ernie Charlesworth, said, "I don't think it's relevant. I think it's just somebody got caught in someone else's bed" – or words like that. Mr Charlesworth said, "I suppose you know we have someone for the murder" – something like that. I got the impression from the police that I was wasting their time.' That man Charlesworth yet again.

Another note caught my eye. It was simply a man's name ringed in biro. The name was Mr Red. Next to it was the query, 'Sheep sale, Shropshire?' Again Ervin's thought processes all those years ago were in tandem with mine. There may have been a sheep sale, but did this man actually go to it?

A number of scrawled and faded documents containing summaries of witness statements, gathered by Ervin, began to emerge from the dossier. It was proving to be a veritable treasure chest. As I read them, more pieces began to fall into the jigsaw.

22 September 1973. Mrs Gibson: Police called twice Friday night, but had gone out. Police called Saturday and took a statement (told not to say anything). Girl took – or told them – where incident occurred. Police did not call on day of attack or at any time until now.

Mrs Sheldon: Police called Friday night. Did not take a statement. Did not say they would return. Child asleep when police called so did not require showing where incident occurred. Police had not called on day of attack or until now.

Mrs Beebe: 'The police came around but the kids were asleep and they didn't even bother to take a statement. I was told later that the children had been taken out of school to show the police where they'd seen the lady on the graves. The police claimed this was impossible and the children couldn't have seen anything as she wasn't on the graves until the workmen were present. They claimed the victim Wendy Sewell had stood up and fell forward across the graves (this would have been 1.20p.m. at the earliest) and the children would have been back at school by then and therefore couldn't have seen anything.'

Mrs Beebe had gone on to tell Ervin of the threats she had received, echoing exactly what she had told me twenty-one years later.

There were many other jottings from Robert Ervin and copies of handwritten, anonymous notes referring to sightings of several children in the cemetery at lunch-time on the day of the attack. These notes claimed the children had been playing among the grave-stones when they had suddenly been frightened by something quite extraordinary and had fled in panic. Here was more proof that the police had been aware of the claims by children in the cemetery of seeing something, but had appeared to dismiss them as figments of childish imagination.

I was just getting to the final few pages of Ervin's file when suddenly my face lit up. I held out a rather emaciated and faded document. 'Look!' I shouted out loud, before I realised I was completely on my own and nobody could share in my exclamation of delight. It was part of the Prosecution's medical report on Wendy Sewell. It said, 'Mrs Sewell suffered several lacerations to the skull.' This much I had read in the trial summary, but the next phrase hit me like a sledgehammer: 'She was also found to have a broken shoulder following a violent struggle with her assailant.'

This latter point alone completely contradicted the Prosecution case.

They had eagerly accepted Downing's supposed confession claiming he had hit her twice on the back of the neck. He had made no mention of any struggle. I knew I had stumbled across a real gem.

After I had read through all Ervin's paperwork, I contacted Matlock police station to advise them of my findings. As I was talking, one of my reporters entered and caught my attention. He said there was an urgent call for me on the other line. Ironically, it was from another policeman, but this time a more friendly and communicative bobby. He claimed he had some vital news for me and asked for a meeting.

The following day I drove to Monsal Head, through Bakewell and Ashford, past Syd Oulsnam's house and high up to the hotel which stood in isolation at the edge of the ravine. It was here that I had arranged to meet my police contact. I arrived just before the appointed time of 2p.m. I went into the bar and bought two half-pints of best bitter, then took them outside to one of the pub benches overlooking the panoramic view.

At about ten past two I saw his car pull into the car park. Although off duty, he still looked like a copper as he strode across to meet me, dressed formally in a beige raincoat. 'Dave, lose the coat and loosen up. It's a wonder you're not wearing a helmet,' I advised. I gave him the half-pint of bitter, but he was obviously very nervous and kept looking around. 'Look, you're just having a quiet drink with an old friend,' I insisted. 'Relax.'

'But your face is on all the paperwork at the nick at the moment,' he replied. 'Your detective pal is just there to keep you sweet.' He was referring to the detective at Matlock whose slick, friendly approach was, I had to agree, somewhat more sophisticated than that of the regular county bobbies. He spoke in hushed tones just to make sure no one could overhear him.

'I know that,' I replied, 'but it works both ways. It's better to appear co-operative and all chummy, don't you think? Now, don't tell me you've dragged me all this way to tell me something I already know?'

'You know the Prosecution witness George Pearson has got a record? He's an ex-con — went to prison in 1966 just before the World Cup. He missed the final.' He gave the distinct impression that it was more of a crime to have missed the World Cup victory over Germany than to get sent down. 'He has a record for burglary and petty,' he continued, 'and he was at school with your Mr Red.'

We had a report about Mr Red back in 1973. Everything! Apparently Mr Red was questioned over the Barbara Mayo case in 1970, along with four other men from Bakewell, two of them associates of his. He was interrogated for two days at Chesterfield police station, but eventually they had to let him go. No forensics on him.' He added that Mr Red had also been pulled in for questioning over Wendy Sewell's murder. 'But he had a good alibi,' he said, 'his uncle. He claimed he was with him at a sheep sale somewhere near the Welsh border.'

This confirmed what I had already seen in the police reports from 1973, although these had suggested Mr Red had been given an alibi by *three* people – two uncles and another man. I had seen that of the third man – James Mellor. 'Were there any other witnesses to prove this sheep sale story?'

'Two others – just family, it seems. We had to let him go. There was some kind of further inquiry in 1979,' he added, 'but I don't know the details.' That was interesting. I filed the information away in my memory. 'Mind you,' he continued, 'you were right. Downing's prints were not on the murder weapon, but it looks as if there's a clear palm print.'

'And who does that belong to?' I asked with an air of innocence.

'Now there's your mystery. Could even have been one of our guys. It was a real cock-up!' I assumed he was referring to the fact that the forensic evidence may have been tainted by lax scene of crime procedures. I recalled that back in February, another informant had told me that all the exhibits, including the murder weapon, had probably been taken away from the scene in one large bag. The risk of cross-contamination was obvious.

Dave was still very nervous, stopping to look around again before continuing, 'The victim did put up a hell of a fight, though. Keep this to yourself for a few days to put me in the clear. It looked as if she had been kicked as well as beaten, most likely by someone wearing winkle pickers.' This confirmed what I had just discovered from Ervin's file – that Wendy had put up a violent struggle against her attacker.

Dave downed his drink in one and got up to leave.

'Thanks mate, much appreciated,' I shouted after his already retreating figure. I finished my own drink as I watched him walk across to his car and drive off.

That Wendy had 'put up a hell of a fight' was further confirmation of a struggle and again totally contradicted Stephen Downing's original confession on which his conviction was based.

Later that day I met up again with my Central TV friend, Alan Taylor, in a pub. Like me, he was annoyed about Ernie Charlesworth's claims that Stephen had been responsible for other childish pranks about three or four years earlier, when he was fourteen – pranks that someone else had already admitted to and been reprimanded for.

'This Charlesworth certainly had a lot to answer for. I only wish I could get him on the stand,' he grumbled, pulling out the documents I had given him. 'Look,' he emphasised. 'Stephen claims he was not cautioned, prior to making any statement. Naturally, if this is true, then any or all of the statements are worthless. They should *not* have been used in court.'

He ran through the timings, pointing out the anomalies. 'I've been researching the victim,' he went on. 'She was no angel. Fell out with her husband and fell in with everyone else, it seems. You know all about the stories that she had a baby about five years before the murder, numerous affairs, casual flings and, like you, I've also heard there was something funny going on over at that wool shop on Buxton Road. Anyway,' he continued, 'I went to see the man who everyone keeps saying was the father of her child, John Marshall. He tried to deny everything at first. Told him I'd already got the birth certificate and adoption papers and his name was on them. He was sweating a bit, then he admitted it.' Alan grinned. Both he and I knew he had no documents at all relating to Wendy Sewell's child. But his trick had worked. 'I've also been putting a bit of pressure on Syd Oulsnam. He's reluctant to talk to reporters ever since he phoned you. It seems George Pearson and Syd have reported you, me and Frank Curran to Bakewell police for harassment. They've apparently told the police that reporters keep hounding them.'

'Really!' I said. 'Well, I think I can live with that one. They've never been mentioned by name in the papers or on television. And in any case, it was Syd who phoned *me*. It will be interesting to see what they have told the police.'

'They're certainly worried,' Alan told me. 'Look what happened with Syd over that DNA article.'

Alan's mention of DNA reminded me that I should write to Stephen to ask if he would be prepared to take a DNA test. If he were willing to do so, I believed it would put even more pressure on the police to test others alleged to have been near the scene of crime that day. Despite Frank Curran's bold assertion in the *Star* seven months previously that police were about to carry out DNA tests on vital suspects and witnesses, nothing of the sort had, of course, ever happened.

'I'm following up on Mrs Hadfield's running man too,' he continued. 'I'm going to have a go with this guy Mr Blue next week.'

Some time later, Alan visited Mr Blue in his office at his place of work. Mr Blue had done very well for himself and held a very senior position within the organisation. Arriving unannounced, Alan later told me that Mr Blue was 'shaking like a leaf' at being confronted yet again with Mrs Hadfield's testimony. Following Alan's visit he took several weeks of sick leave from his job.

19

WHEN I'D FIRST made an appeal for information about the Downing case early in 1995, I was overwhelmed by the response from the public. It was as if people had been waiting for this very moment to be able to tell the truth. Many people had simply lost faith with the local police force.

When I'd first arrived in Matlock in 1985, Derbyshire police seemed to be the cause of much merriment in local pubs. Two years previously Chief Constable Alf Parrish had been suspended following a county council investigation into police finances and the 'unauthorised' spending of thousands of pounds on the refurbishment of his private office at force headquarters in Ripley. Seventeen months later the then Home Secretary Douglas Hurd, in an unprecedented move, retired him in 'the interests of efficiency' after a career in the police spanning more than thirty years.

The deteriorating state of the force over which the new Chief Constable, John Newing, presided at the turn of the decade was first highlighted by Geoffrey Dear, Her Majesty's Inspector of Constabulary, in his annual report for 1990. He concluded,

> The bureaucratic requirements of the county council and the police committee are a major obstacle to the efficient management of the force. The county council's corporate strategy does not permit any realistic growth in police spending in real terms. This has meant a virtual standstill in developing the constabulary and its resources for the last eight years. The innovative spirit so evident in other forces inspected is translated, at best, into cheerful apathy in Derbyshire.

Geoffrey Dear's criticisms prompted Chief Constable John Newing to admit in his own report of 1990 that community policing in Derbyshire was a 'myth.' Home Secretary Kenneth Baker joined in the condemnation. He described Mr Dear's damning report on the Derbyshire Constabulary as 'amongst the worst ever on any police force'.

By mid-1991 the situation, if anything, was even worse. Derbyshire police force found itself facing the loss of its certificate of efficiency and John Newing evidently felt frustrated at having, once again, to defend his force. He conceded, 'There is no doubt morale is worse now than it was twelve months ago. Morale is bound to be low. If the morale of this force is at the point it is alleged, then this report could be the thing that tips it over the brink.'

Newing insisted, however, that his force was not the worst in England. He put up a staunch defence of his officers and blamed Derbyshire's problems on lack of funds. 'We have the best officers in the country. It's about resources. On that matter Mr Dear and I are as one; the force is under-resourced. Our capability is stretched to the limit. We can't keep going on this way.'

In 1993 Geoffrey Dear refused to grant Derbyshire police a certificate of efficiency. The same thing happened the following two years. The third refusal of a certificate in March 1995 was accompanied by Home Office intervention.

Home Office minister David McLean stepped in to announce emergency funding, and on a visit to Matlock said, 'We have to remind ourselves of the past funding decisions. In a crucial period in the 1980s, when every other force was expanding, for whatever reason Derbyshire did not bid for more bobbies.'

This was the turbulent background against which journalists, like myself, had to conduct relations with the Derbyshire police. A force which held the dubious distinction, in the annals of policing history, of being the only one to lose its certificate of efficiency three times, in three consecutive years, was bound to be sensitive and defensive when approached by the press. Moreover, it was a record which the force was to hold for all time, as certificates of efficiency were scrapped shortly after Derbyshire completed its hat-trick of failures.

This may help to explain why Derbyshire Chief Constable John

Newing, and his assistant Don Dovaston, also proved formidable opposition to Stephen's lawyer, John Atkins, when he requested essential paperwork relating to the Downing case. Often it only arrived after repeated demands had been made.

Dovaston, in particular, proved a formidable opponent to defence barristers and at one time even threatened legal action following the publication of a story in the *Matlock Mercury* in September 1995 in which I accused Derbyshire police of 'dragging their feet' over reinvestigating the case. I said that, even though they had had my submissions since February, they had failed to act on new information I had provided.

It was to spark a bitter row with Dovaston who threatened legal action unless a full apology and retraction was given. It was almost a week before a letter arrived from him. He complained,

> I am concerned about several paragraphs within the article . . . [which] show the author's lack of understanding of this country's judicial system. The comments about Derbyshire Constabulary are reprehensible and libellous. I therefore request that, at the first opportunity, you issue a statement in the *Matlock Mercury* to correct the inaccuracies.
>
> The statement, in a format acceptable to this force, should retract the allegations and apologise to the chief constable and his officers. I have to inform you that if you fail to comply with my request or provide me with evidence in support of your claims, within the next seven days, I shall have no alternative but to seek redress through the Press Complaints Commission and the legal process.

I was blazing when the letter first arrived and was tempted to write back immediately stating, 'Bollocks!' I wondered again whether half of these faceless bureaucrats had actually bothered to read the mass of paperwork forwarded to their boss. I sent a copy of Dovaston's letter to the company lawyers, then phoned him to arrange an interview.

Dovaston completely refused to communicate with the paper.

I believed there was sufficient evidence to contradict most, if not all, the police claims. I had case notes, internal memos, copies of

confidential data, scene of crime reports, medical notes, copy statements and a host of fresh evidence. I wrote back to say that I had
evidence to confirm each and every one of the points raised and
challenged the police to contradict my claims, knowing it was
impossible. I added that the information I had published was both fair
and accurate and moreover was 'in the public interest' and 'fair
comment'.

Stephen's lawyers claimed the police action was yet another
desperate and badly planned exercise designed to suppress vital
defence documents – which would eventually backfire.

My own reports were not intended to form a witch hunt against
individual officers at the time of the murder or since. They were just
statements of fact. The police, though, and indeed successive bodies
of bureaucracy since, have tried to find – without much success – the
names of my special police informants. My feeling was that if the
authorities had told the truth in the first place there would have been
no need for informants.

The whole episode with Dovaston and his team became a farce.
They seemed determined to attack my fresh evidence and submissions, and refused to discuss any aspects of the case.

20

IT WAS DURING a very dull day in early November 1995 that I heard a faint knock on the back door of the *Mercury* office.

As I opened the door I was confronted by a very large woman in her early thirties who almost filled the doorway. She had a child's arm gripped in each hand and the two youngsters were almost lifted off their feet, both crying and whining by her side.

'Are you that Don Hale?' she asked.

'Yes,' I replied. 'How can I help you?'

'I've got some news for you about your murder case,' she said.

'Would you like to come inside?' I asked.

'No. A friend of mine wants to meet you urgently – and it's strictly private. You know what I mean? No cameras, no tapes.'

'Who is this friend, then? Where do they want to meet me? What information do they have?'

'Look, I don't know all the details,' she said, turning back to me. 'It's a woman though. The back of Somerfields supermarket, three o'clock tomorrow afternoon, OK?'

'Yes, fine,' I replied.

As I wandered along to the agreed meeting point the following day I looked at my watch. It was a couple of minutes before three.

I still thought it might be a hoax or a set-up. Then I was prodded hard in the side. A woman in her mid-fifties was staring hard at me. She looked like an ageing hippy and there seemed to be so many rings in her nose, ears and eyebrows that I wasn't sure whether to shake her hand or tie her to a post.

'So you're that editor bloke then?' she asked without looking at me.

'Yes, I'm Don Hale. I understand you might have some information.'

'I've got this friend who's keen to meet you up at Flash Dam. He has some very interesting news,' she explained.

Another meeting in another isolated spot. My thoughts drifted back to the lorry chase. She asked, 'Does the name Mr Red mean anything to you? And a sheep sale near Wales?'

'Tell me more.'

'Don't know a great deal. "Crabby" he calls himself. Used to be a nurse. Seems to know about your case, something from the early Seventies. He says he's prepared to meet you if you're interested.'

'How much?' I asked.

'No money. He's bad with AIDS. Money isn't his thing. Take a few cans of lager if you must. He's just trying to survive,' she said, grabbing all her bags.

'OK, I'll be there,' I agreed.

Reaching the dam the next day at half past two, I parked on the road. It was only a short walk to the old public entranceway up a steep grassy bank. The area had been deserted for years. It had once been a popular boating and leisure attraction in private grounds but had now become overgrown and derelict.

As I approached I could see a man sitting on the bank throwing stones into the water. There seemed to be nobody else about. It was a very quiet and isolated spot. 'Crabby?' I enquired.

The man didn't even turn his head to acknowledge my presence, and remained seated and continued to throw stones. 'The newspaper man,' he finally said.

'Your friend said you had some information?'

The man remained quiet. Perhaps he was having second thoughts. The place was more overgrown than I first realised and the sunlight danced upon the stagnant water. Crabby looked as if he'd been living rough for some time. He was in his late fifties with short-cropped hair. He was unshaven. He wore a badly torn grey jacket and a red and white checked T-shirt with grubby jeans and old boots. He seemed painfully thin and his cheeks were hollowed. He had a ring in each ear lobe. I could hear him wheezing. He didn't appear to have any baggage with him. I offered one of the cans of lager I had brought with me. He snatched it without even looking at the label. He pulled open the top and drank half the contents down in one. 'You know Bakewell?' he asked.

'Reasonably well,' I replied.

The man rose to his feet and, as he pushed himself up, I could see his legs were extremely thin. 'Well, that Wendy Sewell murder that's been in the papers again. I know who did it.'

'Really,' I said, trying hard not to sound too surprised or optimistic. After all, wasn't this the reason for the visit? 'And just what do you know, then?' I enquired.

'I know it wasn't that lad that got caught.'

He now had my attention. 'And have you any proof?' I asked hopefully. I kept turning round to make sure no one else was likely to appear. The man still looked as if he could handle himself in a fight and I wanted to be on guard – just in case.

As he stood up straight, he crushed the can and flung it into the shallow water. He seemed quite tall now, about six feet. He still didn't look at me, walked a few yards along the bank, then sat down again. He grabbed another can and began to gulp down its contents eagerly.

'I didn't always look like this,' he explained. 'I had a good job once as a medic in a nursing home near Sheffield. It was also a sort of hospice for the terminally ill. Got AIDS though, didn't I, not from the patients but through my own stupid fault. Must have been a contaminated needle. Who knows? Who cares? Full-blown AIDS though. It's only a matter of time. Perhaps a few weeks, or months? Anyway, I've only got a limited time left on this earth like many of the poor buggers I once cared for.'

He suddenly seemed even more despondent and picked up a few more small stones to throw into the water. I was determined to try to get him to talk more. 'Would you make a statement?' I asked.

'No flaming statements. Anyway, I won't be around long enough for it to make any difference.'

'Your friend thought it could help get this Downing out of jail,' I said.

'Perhaps it will. That's for you to tell. I know Dolly – the woman you spoke to – from the road. She lost her son. I think he would have been about the same age as your man. Poor sod! Twenty-two bloody years inside for someone else. It was only when Dolly showed me an old cutting that I put two and two together and realised it was connected with one of my former patients. Dolly wanted me to talk to you.

'I worked at this hospice place for about six years. We used to get all sorts. The wealthy and the poor. Money can't buy you health. And even if they'd had money – they always seemed to want to return to their roots at the final hours. I used to work nights, mainly. Had visions of being a rock star but it wasn't to be. I used to nick a few things – drugs like. Soft stuff, mainly, but then I got hooked. They'd turn a blind eye as no one wanted to work this "graveyard" shift. This would be about early Seventies. I would look after the old sods who had cancer. Put one or two out of their misery. They begged me,' he explained, as if asking for sympathy or absolution.

'The reason I've come today is this. This patient was a farmer from north Derbyshire. He seemed OK, but quickly deteriorated. Cancer of the liver. Very advanced. He was odd at first, kept himself to himself and didn't have many visitors. Gradually, though, he began to talk and open up. The pain was terrible. He'd have a variety of drugs but found difficulty in sleeping at night. He'd talk to me and then ramble on for hours about all sorts. He'd mention dates, times, places, names. Rubbish mostly, but then he kept shouting something about a murder. He shouted it out several times one night and I had to call for assistance to help calm him down. He mentioned a Wendy, then Mr Red, then murder again. Had her head smashed in or something. He sounded so guilty of something. At first, I thought perhaps he'd done it.

'The next day, when he'd settled down, I asked him about it and he wanted to know what he'd actually said. Later his nephew, a tall young man, visited and I could see him talking with him and they were pointing towards me. The following night the same thing happened and then I thought he'd probably read somewhere about a murder. He got wound up again when I quizzed him, but later when the drugs took hold he became more lucid. When he was in a state he would shout out, "No, I won't tell lies. Stop it. It was murder!"

269

Certainly, whoever he had been talking about had threatened him – made his life a misery. He still seemed terrified of this person, whoever it was.

'His only visitors seemed to be the nephew and a woman I assumed to be his daughter. She didn't come very often and seemed to travel some distance. The lad came every two or three days. I often over-heard them talking. He would stay for an hour or so and sometimes he would read to him before he fell asleep. I think he kept going on about sheep. It's so many years that I can't remember all the details now. I kept trying to talk with the nephew after his visits, and about a week later the old man suddenly grabbed my arm and told me to sit down. It was in the early hours and he was restless. I bribed him a bit. I said, "You tell me about this murder and I'll give you something to help you relax." He was going to get it anyway, but I couldn't give it for about an hour.

'Anyway he finally explained that in 1973 he had been asked to lie for a relative. He'd gone to a sheep sale somewhere on the Welsh borders with a couple of friends. He only mentioned a name once. Gave me a funny look after that. Anyway, when the group returned from the visit, this man Mr Red was sitting waiting for them. He was in a right old state. He threatened them and forced them to agree to give him an alibi. He said the man had a vicious temper and reluctantly they all agreed. They had been told the excuse that Mr Red had knocked an old lady over in his Land Rover. It was all rubbish but he said he'd been drunk. The uncle said it was the same day as the Bakewell murder in 1973 – but they only heard about that later, when the girl had died. He knew the victim was Mr Red's girlfriend.'

During much of the time Crabby was telling his tale I sat down on the bank next to him. Crabby stayed crouched, with his knees pulled up to his chest. He continually picked up stones and skimmed them across the surface of the water while he gathered his thoughts again. He was now on his third can. He continued, and there was a lot of emotion in his voice.

'It was only a month or so later when the old man died. It was sudden but peaceful. The next day the young nephew came and collected his things and arranged for the funeral. He gave me a knowing wink and said he would put things right. He gave me a tenner for looking after his uncle.'

I'd had no proof up till now that Mr Red had asked anyone, let alone threatened them, to give him an alibi, although the rumour mill in Bakewell had started churning out stories along these lines once my investigations had begun to gather pace. But here at least was direct testimony that a conversation *had* taken place, in which it was said that Mr Red had made these threats and had *not* gone to the Welsh–Shropshire border to a sheep sale on the day of the murder. The problem, though, was that it was hearsay evidence. The farmer was already dead and my informant hadn't long to live. Crabby refused to give a written statement. He didn't want his own relatives to get involved or to be threatened afterwards. He refused to go to court or to become a witness. Although his tale was extremely interesting, I wondered if it would be of any use.

I asked him if the old farmer had ever given any indication as to why the girl had been murdered. He thought long and hard and tried his best to remember. All he could think of was that she had become some sort of liability. He said she had refused to keep her mouth shut over something important. He kept repeating she had some information that could have buried Mr Red. He kept saying others were involved.

I stretched my arms to relieve the stiffness in my joints and began to thank Crabby for his time and trouble.

'Hey, where are you going? You've not heard the rest yet,' he said.

'The rest?' I asked with some astonishment. 'What else can there be?'

'Your murder case may be linked to two others. And the ironic thing is, I believe I know who was responsible for these too. It's the same man. The relative of the dying man.'

'You must be joking,' I replied.

Crabby stood up and wandered about the bank. He seemed relieved to have got the story off his chest. He explained, 'The man had told his nephew. The nephew wanted to go to the police and believed Mr Red was responsible for the Sewell murder. The old man wouldn't let him until he'd passed away. He told him it was his decision after that. He was still wary of attacks on his family if he spoke out. At other times during his ramblings I had heard him say something about someone picking up girls on the A1 and giving them a good time – and a good slapping. Now I can't really be certain if he was talking about Mr Red, or this other mate of his at the time. He mentioned another man, Mr Orange. The farmer said he was the one who had actually finished Wendy off. Pole-axed her. High as a bloody kite.'

Mr Orange! The last time I had heard *that* name was when Syd Oulsnam had phoned me back in February. He was the man Mr Red and Oulsnam had, according to Syd, arranged to meet up by the cemetery on 12 September 1973.

Crabby continued with the farmer's dying testimony. 'On other occasions he said Mr Red said something to the effect that the police couldn't or wouldn't catch Wendy's murderer. He had boasted that he was too clever. Said he had a "friendly" copper. He and this other guy were both allegedly at the cemetery in 1973. His mate was apparently much younger but a bit handy – if you know what I mean. Keeps alive by doing a few odd jobs. Has a regular contact overseas. Lives by his wits.'

Crabby's description of Mr Orange broadly fitted everything I had been told about him.

Crabby took another long hard swig from his can. 'These were all my notes about the conversations,' he said, pointing to some papers. 'Not much else to do during these long nights. The farmer was always restless. I patched things together from his better times and from endless hours of sitting and nursing him.'

Crabby gulped down the last of the four cans and rolled a cigarette. He had hardly looked at me at any time during the meeting but now he wanted to emphasise some points and he kept waving his finger at me. He was getting a little tipsy. He spat on the ground. He was wheezing heavily but seemed determined to continue. He ran his hands over his face, then back over the top of his head. He began shaking as he went on with his explanation: 'This other man Mr Orange was supposedly strong and well built like Mr Red. He was in his late twenties, very fit and had the look of an ex-boxer. He had lightish hair and quiff.'

As soon as Crabby mentioned it, I remembered the reference to a quiff in some old newspaper cuttings I'd found in Ervin's notes. Police were supposedly looking for a man with a quiff in 1970 after the Barbara Mayo murder. Then I thought of the reference to Wendy being kicked by winkle pickers, which one of my police informants had come out with recently. The 'Teddy Boy' hairstyle and footwear could fit together, I reasoned.

Crabby got to his feet again and relieved himself in the tall grass of the high banking, but he kept talking. He was now sweating. He took a small bottle from the inside pocket of his jacket, and took another good long swig before continuing.

'The old farmer was in a right state. Mr Red had apparently taken great pleasure in explaining every last detail to him over and over again. Just what he did to that poor girl – he enjoyed seeing the old man squirm in disgust.'

Crabby seemed to know the story backwards. He had probably told it many times before. He stretched his arms. We had been talking for about an hour. It was getting quite cold. He turned and stared at me for the first time. His eyes were watering and he kept sniffing.

I thanked him, and told him his uncanny recollection of events could prove invaluable – although I was still uncertain as to whether it was just an elaborate hoax.

21

ON 29 NOVEMBER 1995 I received a severe knock-back. The Home Office sent its initial response to my submissions of January and February. It was addressed to MP Patrick McLoughlin and had been sent by Timothy Kirkhope MP, the Parliamentary Under Secretary of State. It said,

> I have looked very carefully at what you, Mr Downing senior and Mr Hale have said about Stephen Downing's case and the various documents which have been submitted to us.
>
> I have to say at the outset, that I have not found anything in these representations that provides grounds for the Home Secretary to refer the case.
>
> As you will appreciate, the points raised in the representations have been considered, or could have been considered, by the Courts already.
>
> I am sorry, for I know this will be a disappointment to you and Mr Downing's family.

I was devastated. After more than a year's hard slog, all seemed to have come to nothing.

I have reproduced below some of Mr Kirkhope's responses which I felt were totally wrong, or missed the point. In brackets are the replies made by Stephen Downing to these responses. Mine are added at the end.

RE: THE CONFESSION BEING OBTAINED BY OPPRESSION
'Following examination of his clothing, which was heavily bloodstained, he was again questioned and finally admitted that he had assaulted Mrs Sewell.

He did so about 10.45p.m. He made a detailed statement under caution about the attack and his movements shortly afterwards at 11.10–11.30p.m.'

(I would not say that my clothing was all that heavily soiled, save at the knees where I had knelt down. I was *not* cautioned and it was put to me that I *had* to make a statement. Even though I had asked for a solicitor, I was told that I did not need one by DI Younger. It was about 03.00 when I was taken to Buxton HQ for the night.)

'There is no evidence to suggest that he was questioned continually.'
(By the same token there is none to say that I wasn't. In point of fact it was carried out in relay with the longest gap being about five minutes between one group leaving and the next arriving.)

'He drew attention to the blood-stained pickaxe handle lying on the path, 25 feet away which he said he had been using earlier in the day. At 6p.m. . . . he told DI Younger that, contrary to what he had said earlier to the police, he had last used the pickaxe handle three weeks previously.'
(I did not make any mention of the pickaxe handle. I was later *asked* about it by senior police when they arrived at the scene . . . It may be worth noting that he refers to my use of *the* pick axe handle three weeks before . . . and not *a* pickaxe handle. . . . There is a difference.)

'Mr Downing retracted his confession at trial.'
(I did not retract my confession at trial, but 13 days from my date of arrest and some five months *before* the trial.)

'He agreed on cross-examination, that "he was not starved" in the police station.'
(I was not 'starved' . . . but at the same time I was only given a single sandwich and a small lukewarm tea. I did not receive anything further until I was given some breakfast at Buxton HQ, which would have been about 08.00 hours the next day.)

'Although Mr Downing's counsel at trial cross-examined the police about their conduct during the various interviews of Mr Downing, he also told the court that they, i.e. Mr Downing's Defence team, were not suggesting that there had been any impropriety on the part of the police.'
(I clearly believe that oppression was much in evidence by the continual relay of teams of interrogators and the shaking of me to keep me awake.)

I added:

'The blood-stains to his clothing can in no way be described as "heavy". It was apparently more than seven hours before the investigating officer, DI Robin Younger, noticed them.

'In the prosecution's own notes, there is confusion over the time he was cautioned. It is also strange that, if the police thought he was guilty, why was he denied the aid of a solicitor, parent or guardian for this period of extensive interviews?

'It is curious, to say the least, that Downing should have confessed to PC Ernest Charlesworth. He was the officer who allegedly was determined to "catch this little pervert" and made several completely unsubstantiated allegations about Downing when he was just fourteen years old. Charlesworth was also the same officer who repeated similar claims to the victim's husband, David Sewell, within days of Downing's arrest, claiming he had been "under suspicion for years".

'PC Charlesworth was also mentioned as being "uncooperative and disinterested" by several witnesses with potential and vital evidence at the time of the Sewell murder inquiry.'

Re: Mr Downing's admission statement was written for him in pencil and that, because he had a low IQ, he would have had difficulty in either reading or understanding it, or the seriousness of the situation

'I note from a psychiatric report commissioned by his solicitors pre-trial on his mental state that he was not suffering from any mental disorder, that he was fit to plead, understood the charges and appreciated the likely consequences if found guilty.

'There is nothing moreover in the Judge's summing up or at trial to suggest that Mr Downing failed to understand what was happening in court, or to appreciate the seriousness of the charges brought against him.'

(If I am acknowledged as having a low IQ at the time of the trial, then it must also be accepted that I would not be aware of the full potential of the proceedings and eventual consequences.)

'It would have been perfectly proper – and indeed normal practice – for the police to write down Mr Downing's statement and that he signed it in several places as being true.'

(I did not read the written statement. It was read to me, with the explanation that various extracts would read better the way it had been worded by them. I accepted what was told to me without realising the need to clarify the points.)

I added:

'Although his low IQ was known, it was not made clear in court until *after* the jury had reached their verdict. It may well have affected their decision if they had been made aware of all these details beforehand. Would a naive youth with the reading age of an eleven-year-old really have known how crucial this statement was likely to become?'

RE: THE ADMISSIONS MADE BY MR DOWNING IN HIS STATEMENT
ARE INCONSISTENT WITH THE PATHOLOGIST'S REPORT

'To support this contention, the representations point to Mr Downing's statement in which he says he hit Mrs Sewell twice when in fact she received, in the Crown pathologist's view, some seven or eight blows in a frenzied attack to the head – her head was cut in ten places; and to the evidence given by several witnesses at the trial who thought his manner at the time when he left the cemetery was "cool and calm", which would have been inconsistent with having just committed a frenzied attack.

'It is clear from the summing-up that the discrepancies were fully explored at trial. Mr Downing's demeanour on exiting the cemetery at 1.08p.m. and on reporting the finding of the body were also before the jury.

(I only admitted to the attack so that I could be left alone. As for the number of blows, I just picked a figure at random.

Witnesses who saw me say I was cool and calm, which would hardly be the case had I recently committed a frenzied attack.)

I added:

'Within a few days, it was clearly known that she had been hit seven or eight times in a frenzied attack. Why was Downing not questioned again over this anomaly in his confession statement?'

RE: THE SCRAPINGS TAKEN FROM UNDER MRS SEWELL'S
FINGERNAILS SHOW NO LINK WITH MR DOWNING

'There is no mention in the summing up or in the other papers of any

fingernail scrapings having been taken from Mrs Sewell. But it seems to have been common ground at trial that she was hit from behind, that she fell forward on to her side and then on to her face and that, although she had attempted to rise, and indeed managed to move some distance from the path where she was attacked, she did not put up a struggle against her assailant. It would not be surprising, therefore, if fingernail scrapings taken failed to reveal any trace of contact with her attacker.'

I commented:

'I have reason to believe that Mrs Sewell's fingernail scrapings *were* taken. Why were these not shown on the trial list of exhibits? And if they were *not* taken from the victim, then *why* not, as it was clear she had suffered from a very violent attack?'

'The Prosecution's own medical report on the case, whose contents were not fully revealed at trial, states "Mrs Sewell suffered several lacerations to the skull . . . she was also found to have a broken shoulder following a violent struggle with her assailant."'

RE: MR DOWNING'S FINGERPRINTS WERE *NOT* FOUND ON THE PICKAXE HANDLE

'It appears that the pickaxe handle was heavily smeared with blood but there is no mention in the summing-up at trial, or elsewhere in our papers, of fingerprints, whether Mr Downing's or anyone else's, being found on it. It is clear from the summing-up, however, that the jury heard a good deal of evidence about whether or not Mr Downing was wearing gloves that day.

'I appreciate that Mr Downing's father would like to make further enquiries in relation to the lack of fingerprints and fingernail scrapings. But it is difficult to see what the results of these could add, in view of the above, to what is — and was — already known and before the jury.

'Certainly, I do not myself think it is necessary to pursue these enquiries. If however, he wishes, in the light of this letter, to pursue these points, then I would suggest that he contact the chief constable in Derbyshire direct. The decision as to whether or not he will release the material in question is for him, assuming of course it still exists.'

(The lack of fingerprints and nail scrapings show the lack of evidence on which a conviction was allowed to be sought. This failing shows the amateurish working of the police. I like the nice tactic at the end where he says it is a matter for the chief constable to release the material, assuming it still exists. I should like to raise the question of how much evidence has been destroyed since the onset of this investigation!

Although I did have a pair of gloves with me which I carried in the back pocket of my jeans, I did not wear them that day. Had I done so, within the throes of executing the attack I am sure that there would have been a great deal more blood on them than there is. It should also be remembered that the spots of blood are so small that they can only be seen under a microscope and identified as blood by means of chemical analysis.

I had a great deal of blood on the palms of my hands, which I pointed out to Ball and asked if I could wash them. He said no as it would be needed for forensic evidence. Had I carried out the attack, I could simply have washed my hands and disposed of the pickaxe handle either by burning it, or hiding it until a more convenient time for disposal. I could also have gone home and changed my clothing at the same time I changed my boots.)

I added:
'There was no mention of the taking of any fingerprints from the murder weapon in the forensic report. Surely, if the prints were taken, they would have been documented by the authorities and used by the prosecution – if Downing's were involved?

'Why, therefore, were prints not taken when it was known the murder weapon was heavily smeared with blood? Despite protestations from the police that Downing was wearing gloves, in statements taken on the night of the attack, the same statements they used to convict him, it clearly states his gloves remained in his back pockets.

'It has also been told to me that the weapon contained a clear palm print and possibly other fingerprints together with hairs, fibres and a third blood sample. Was it ever established who they belonged to – especially if not Downing?'

RE: THE TINY BLOOD-STAINS FOUND ON MR DOWNING'S CLOTHING, AND THE HEAVIER SMEARS ON HIS TROUSERS, ARE CONSISTENT WITH HIS HAVING TURNED MRS SEWELL OVER AND

WITH HER SUBSEQUENTLY SHAKING HER HEAD ABOUT

'It is clear from the summing up that the question of whether these stains could have been acquired by Mr Downing as a result of his kneeling down beside Mrs Sewell, turning her over, and then pushing himself backwards and upwards on her sitting up and shaking her head about, was fully explored at trial. And it was of course a matter for the jury to decide.'

(As Wendy Sewell had shoulder-length hair, this would have flared out releasing various size droplets of blood. It is safe to apply basic scientific logic that centrifugal force would have carried the smaller droplets, further assisted by the whipping action of her hair. This logic can be demonstrated by inverting a mophead and spinning it from left to right.)

'I note the suggestion in the representations that Mr Downing changed his boots between leaving the cemetery at 1.08p.m. and returning at 1.20p.m. and that any blood stains found on them after 1.20p.m. must therefore have resulted from his touching Mrs Sewell's body after he found her. But I note that he appears not to have made mention of this at trial, or an appeal.'

(I am almost certain that it was mentioned at the trial that I had changed my boots on returning home. However, the reason it was not raised at the appeal was that they first had to hear the evidence of Jayne Atkins. Had *that* been declared admissible, the evidence about my boots . . . and other new evidence . . . would have been heard.)

I added:

'The explanation of blood-staining has been well documented in the original submission and clearly explains about the violent shaking of her head. It should also be made perfectly clear that much of the blood-staining to Downing's knees contained coagulated blood, which implied that he had knelt in blood that had been there for some considerable time – and not therefore directly after such a ferocious attack.'

RE: MR DOWNING HAD INSUFFICIENT TIME TO CARRY OUT THE ATTACK ON MRS SEWELL IF, AS THE POLICE ALLEGE, IT OCCURRED BEFORE 1.08P.M.

'I have looked very carefully at the suggestion that Mrs Sewell may have entered the cemetery at a later time than 12.50p.m. and at the note Mr Hale made of the undated conversation with George Pearson's former lover. But I

wonder what real weight can be given to her recollections of what her ex-lover may have told her "many years" after the event?'

(I don't know if Mr Kirkhope is in any way qualified to question this person's state of mind as to what she may or may not be able to recollect. The events of that day are as fresh in most people's memory today as if it were the day it occurred. People have not been allowed to forget it, with the constant reminders from my family and others who have joined forces. An event as dramatic as this in a normally quiet and peaceful little town will be talked about and remembered for many years afterwards.)

'George Pearson saw and spoke with her on the Butts, he thought about 12.50p.m., and finally Charlie Carman, who was standing near the kiosk outside the cemetery gates, saw Mrs Sewell through the holes in the fence making her way down the back path inside the cemetery at about 12.50p.m. Downing was seen leaving at 1.08p.m. Ultimately, it was a matter for the jury to decide whether the attack could have been carried out in the 18 minutes in which Mrs Sewell and Mr Downing were both in the cemetery and, indeed, whether Mr Downing was responsible for attacking her.'

(Mr Carman was *not* standing by the kiosk, he was walking towards the Butts on his way back to work. I passed him and we spoke.)

RE: THE ATTACK TOOK PLACE *AFTER* MR DOWNING LEFT THE CEMETERY

'The representations draw on the recollections of Jayne Atkins, who stated that she saw Mrs Sewell in the cemetery with her arms round an unknown man just before she saw Mr Downing leaving the cemetery at 1.08 . . . . I note, however, that the Court of Appeal concluded that her evidence was "not credible". She had had numerous opportunities in which to tell her mother or social worker for example what had happened; she was frightened of neither. She had not however done so, although the events of that day were discussed many times by her family and in her presence.'

(I don't know why Jayne Atkins did not choose to vouchsafe her knowledge of the man seen with Wendy. While she may not be frightened of her mother or social worker, this does not dispel the prospect of her being disbelieved or having mistrust in either. After all, soon afterwards she was in a foster home.)

I added:

'In relation to Jayne Atkins and her evidence at appeal, she came from a very disturbed background; she thought Stephen must have committed the attack at another time and much later that day; conversations with her family confirm they were all frightened after the attack; and later, when Jayne finally agreed to give evidence, the family were threatened and warned off. Eventually, they had to move home.

'At the appeal, it was said police officers believed Jayne's account but said it must have been another day. It was her first day at school and she was wearing her new school uniform. She had heard the 1p.m. news headlines and then went to look for her dog. She confirmed seeing Stephen leave and saw Wendy with another man. She still remains frightened by what she saw.'

RE: MRS SEWELL'S CHARACTER

'I note all that is said in representations about Mrs Sewell's character; her having had male friends when she and her husband parted and that this may have continued after their reconciliation. But the information provided is at best speculative; as is the suggestion that one of her male friends might have attacked her.

'There is no evidence that there was anyone else in the cemetery other than Mr Downing when Mrs Sewell was attacked. And, although the Judge clearly reminded the jury to consider the defence's suggestion that because there were holes in the fence someone could have entered, attacked Mrs Sewell and left unseen, before reaching their verdict – they were clearly not persuaded by it.'
(I would say there are grounds to warrant a closer look at Wendy Sewell's male friends. Jealousy may have been one reason for her demise. Why did she leave her office in such a hurry?)

I added:

'Mrs Sewell's character *was*, in my opinion, of prime importance to the case. She was not merely the housewife portrayed by the Prosecution. She allegedly had a number of associations with prominent characters in and around Bakewell. Her friends admitted her promiscuity. She even had a child with another man. Admittedly she was not on trial, but her background and associations could have been confirmed. Information concerning several associations and her background were mentioned within the Home Office Summary. And, allegedly, two of her male associates were also questioned about another unsolved local murder some three years before the attack on Mrs Sewell.'

RE: THE SUGGESTION THAT IF GEORGE PEARSON, MR RED, SYD OULSNAM AND MR BLUE WERE INTERVIEWED THEY COULD PROVE DOWNING INNOCENT

'Having considered the representations, and in particular the contents of the anonymous letter, I regret to say that I do not think there is anything in these points, or indeed any of the others, which provides a basis for further useful inquiry. Since none of these people were in the cemetery at the material time, or in the case of one person in particular even near it, it is difficult to see what, if anything, they could contribute some 22 years after the event.'

(I am convinced that formally interviewing Pearson, Mr Red, Oulsnam and Mr Blue would make a world of difference and shed a considerable amount of light on the doubt that has been cast against me.)

I added:

'One of the most interesting aspects of this case (to which you have *not* responded) involved the alleged identification of certain individuals. Three of them have allegedly given false information and a fourth has never been interviewed.

'The details of the blood-stained man seen running away are well documented. The young man was said to be running "like a bat out of hell", towards Lady Manners School. Why, when a witness, Mrs Hadfield, went to the police station and saw PC Charlesworth with her evidence, was her claim dismissed? All the reports were on file. Why were these claims not investigated?

'In conversation with me, Oulsnam has admitted taking Mr Red to the cemetery on 12 September 1973 some time before 1p.m. In this case, Mr Red and Oulsnam have both given false statements to the police in the past.

'According to a new witness, George Pearson gave misleading information to the police about timings and his whereabouts on the day in question.

'According to the statement of Wendy Sewell's boss, John Osmaston, Mrs Sewell had a male visitor to her office, who spoke in an "abrupt" manner to her shortly before she left for a "breath of air". The visitor has never been traced.'

Tim Kirkhope's initial knockback and eagerness to gloss over much of my submission claims, was to be the first of many similar disappointments over the next few years.

1996

22

1 January 1996
HM Prison, 7 North Square, Dorchester, Dorset

Dear Don,

First I should like to wish you, your family, and all at the *Mercury* a very Happy New Year.

I should also like to say thank you for your Christmas card and good wishes for the season. I hope that you had a most enjoyable Christmas. I'm sorry to say that it was pretty mundane in here, but then I guess that is only to be expected from a prison such as this. The victuals were down on last year's offering. I had a cheese omelette with the traditional trimmings.

By and large the wing was fairly quiet as numbers were down. However, this was anything but the case on New Year's Eve when from around 20.30 hours until about 01.30 hours, it was just a constant barrage of riotous noise. Hardly a minute went by without someone shouting and/or banging on their cell door.

I and one or two others, and no doubt staff also, are looking forward to returning to a 'normal' regime, and with it comes the anxiety for me of waiting for the outcome of the Parole Board's recommendations and whether or not the Secretary of State will agree to their decision. I have been wished all the very best by a number of staff for a favourable result from the Parole Board. They also expressed a hope that I am released this year.

Thank you for the calendar of events for the past year highlighted in the last edition of the *Mercury*. I live in hope that it will not be long before you are able to publish an exclusive ahead of any story another paper may print!

Before I close I would like to say a special thank you to you for all the support and hard work you have put into fighting the case on behalf of my family and myself.

I hope that you are keeping well, and that the year ahead will be a good one for you.'

Stephen Downing

In January 1996 I finally learned that Stephen was to have his case reviewed thanks to the new evidence I had submitted. Patrick McLoughlin and myself were to go to London to meet Home Office Minister Timothy Kirkhope later in the month. Things were moving ahead on several fronts. But my optimism was to prove premature.

A letter arrived from Ann Widdecombe, the new Minister of State at the Home Office. She said more psychological and psychiatric reports would be needed to assist with the latest parole review, and she confirmed that any transfer to an open prison would require approval from a minister.

Not too unexpectedly, a letter soon followed from the Lifer Group at HM Prison Service, confirming, 'On the evidence available to the panel, the Parole Board considered implausible Mr Downing's protestations of innocence in respect of the offence, which had a sexual motive. The panel noted that throughout his sentence Mr Downing has, as a result of his protestations of innocence, undertaken no work directly related to the offence.' Attached were copies of reports from Home Office Psychiatrist Dr Rowton-Lee, who commented,

Staff who knew Downing best took the view that his behaviour inside in recent years has been impeccable. He was a hard-working man, choosing his companions carefully. He behaved and presented himself in such a way that movement to open conditions seemed to be appropriate after 21 years imprisonment. I too took this view.

However, one problem remained, which was denial of the offence after initially admitting it. My view, nonetheless, was that he should progress to Category D conditions for a continuing assessment of his safety for release. He has continued at interview to present well, and it was difficult to fit this man with the profile of somebody who behaved in such a way.

Julia Long, psychologist at HMP Verne, added to a growing list of experienced staff unable or unwilling to accept his claims of innocence. Her report, written in September 1995, also acknowledged Stephen's excellent patterns of behaviour, but she remained concerned simply because of the denial aspect:

> Downing has attracted a number of favourable reports indicating he is a model prisoner, as evidenced by his behaviour on the wing and observation of his interaction with both staff and inmates. On each of our earlier interviews he was courteous and co-operative, and always punctual.
>
> However, his continued denial rendered fruitless any attempt at offence-focused work. In addition, his seemingly over-confident and dismissive attitude towards his offence, combined with almost continual allusions to potential future litigation, could be seen within the context of attempting to subtly manipulate and control the process.
>
> In the light of lack of any offence-focused work and his persistent denial, it is my considered opinion that Downing is not an acceptable risk for release at this time.

My heart sank as I realised that the stumbling block was always going to remain Stephen's supposed mental state of being 'in denial of murder' – an affront to the British legal system. Admit it and, with good behaviour, you could be out in ten years. Deny it and the key is thrown away. The idea that there are innocent men and women serving time in British prisons who want to clear their names – well, the authorities refuse to admit that option. If they're in prison they must be guilty.

So the status quo remained – Stephen had by now served almost twenty-three years, six years over his recommended tariff. If he had lied and said he was guilty, he could have walked free at least six years ago. But since he consistently maintained his innocence he had to stay in jail. This was the disgraceful legal anomaly which was addressed by Ed Fitzgerald QC when he took up Stephen's case in early 1996. He had expressed an interest since the early days and, as one of the country's foremost human rights lawyers, he was an ideal man for the job.

Ed is no stranger to controversy. He was instrumental in getting Derek Bentley's posthumous appeal granted and currently represents Myra Hindley, Jon Venables – one of the two boys who murdered James Bulger – and various IRA prisoners. He is the nephew of the late Lord Longford.

Ed decided to go straight to the European Court of Human Rights. This legal challenge to the British government was to prove an expensive, hard-fought, bloody and often bitter battle. But it had to be done in order to make the government aware of the preposterous anomalies within the system.

At Stephen's trial, the judge had ordered him to be detained 'at Her Majesty's Pleasure', a sentence applicable only to juveniles, with a recommended tariff of seventeen years. Only the Home Secretary had it within his or her power to decide when the release date should be. The Home Secretary maintained that this procedure for releasing juvenile murderers had been in place since 1908 and had worked well.

Ed Fitzgerald and barrister Kate Marcus obtained a legal ruling for two other prisoners at the European Court of Human Rights in Strasbourg, which challenged the Home Secretary's power in this respect. Stephen Downing's case became the first to test the European Court ruling in the British Courts. But this legal argument over Stephen's human rights was to drag on for a further four years.

The government, after much stalling, was eventually to be forced into a remarkable climbdown. It was a personal humiliation for Home Secretary Jack Straw, who had consistently appealed against all European rulings in this case.

A principle had been established, and this unprecedented European victory was to prove one of the major turning points of the campaign. It meant the government had to permit Stephen Downing, and every other prisoner in the UK who had served time beyond their recommended tariff, the basic human right to have an oral hearing with the Parole Board. It applied to prisoners, like Stephen, who had been 'in denial of murder'. The European Court had ruled that an independent court-like body or judge should take over the Home Secretary's power, which had been in place in England and Wales since 1908.

The European case attracted the attention of the national press, but had no bearing on Stephen's appeal against conviction.

Throughout 1996, Stephen's legal team were also fighting the British government on a second front, for which they were heavily reliant on me and my colleagues at the *Mercury* for information and updates. I believed the most probable escape route, other than a rope ladder, was via the Court of Appeal. It was through the *British* courts that his lawyers were fighting to prove Stephen's original conviction unsafe.

Stephen's solicitor, John Atkins, travelled to Derbyshire to view the scene of crime and to meet Stephen's family for the first time. He stayed at our house in Matlock. Later he wrote to me with an outline of his views and those of Ed Fitzgerald and Kate Marcus, whom he had visited at their Doughty Street chambers in London:

As you may be aware, Stephen Downing's case is, in our opinion, broadly unsafe for two main factors.

Firstly he gave a confession under conditions which today would simply not be allowed as a matter of law. No one, let alone a seventeen-year-old with a reading age of eleven, would be allowed to sit for nine hours under police questioning without having the opportunity of legal representation or indeed an adult friend present. In Stephen's case, this simply did not happen.

We have, therefore, a confession to a police officer, not the detective officers doing the questioning, but the uniformed officer standing at the door. This in itself is rather odd, and it seems, further, that the officer's account of what he said does not tally with the actual time that he would have had to say it. The nearest analogy is the quart in a pint pot.

The second strand of Stephen Downing's appeal rests on the rather unpleasant subject of blood-staining. I have made it clear that my own view is that Downing's Prosecutor's forensic evidence is flawed in the extreme. We are told, for example, that there were slight splashes on Downing's shirt with heavier staining on the knees and toes of his boots.

The fact of the matter is this – Wendy Sewell's head was crushed by blows from a pickaxe handle. The person wielding that pickaxe handle would, by the account of the ambulance-man superintendant at the time, have been covered in blood pouring rather than dripping from the end of this instrument.

Additionally we are told that Stephen Downing found Wendy Sewell's body on the footpath in Bakewell cemetery, and this is accepted as fact because of blood-stains found at the scene. He runs away to get help from Wilf, the gatekeeper, and on his return the body has moved some 20 yards over extremely rough and difficult terrain for an able-bodied person, let alone someone whose brains have just been severely hammered.

There was no blood in the intervening space between where she ended up, where there is blood, and on the path, where there is also blood. It is my opinion, therefore, that someone must have helped Wendy Sewell to move that distance, and the reasons for this would be to try to conceal this ferocious and appalling attack. This is only my opinion, therefore expert opinion is essential in order to establish what I am saying is correct.'

I ran a story in the *Mercury* describing how the opinion of scientific experts would be needed to help to free Stephen. Quite unsolicited, many of our readers offered money. One, who wanted to remain anonymous, promised £50,000.

I told John about this remarkable generosity but, though he was amazed and very grateful, he was confident our application for funds from the Legal Aid Board would be successful. He was right. Stephen won funding of £13,000 to fight his case for appeal. It ensured that some of the country's top forensic experts would assess the scientific evidence, and the way it had been presented at Stephen's trial.

At about this time Sam Fay became ill and had to attend hospital for tests. His appearances at the office became less frequent and eventually I had to bring in Marcus Edwards – a schoolboy from Wirksworth – to join the team as a part-time reporter.

Sam still made the odd visit to the office and also took an occasional trip out to watch his beloved Matlock Town, but he was becoming weaker and weaker. He tried to retain an interest in Stephen's case but his concentration was waning. He needed all his strength to fight his own battle.

Shortly afterwards he was admitted to the Whitworth Hospital in Darley Dale on a semi-permanent basis. Then came a further blow. Jackie announced she was looking for pastures new. She had her heart set on a move to Raymond's News Agency in Derby – at this rate there would soon be nobody left but me and Norman.

During this period Stephen continued to be much preoccupied with his imminent move to another jail. Some of his supporters had suggested that Nottingham might be preferable, because it would be relatively close for his family to visit. Stephen's primary concern, however, was his progress through the system to more open prison conditions, which he felt he would not enjoy at Nottingham as it is classified as a Category B prison. The following letter, which I received on this matter, also highlights his efforts to gain an education.

I was always full of admiration for Stephen's stoicism in the face of bureaucracy which would have been enough to grind down a saint. In my dealings with the Home Office I had often felt like screaming. Stephen always remained calm and tried to make the best of things, doggedly striving to improve his learning and his lifestyle within the cruel confines of his world. I could not begin to imagine what private horrors the state had imposed on him during his years of imprisonment, but his letters to me were always composed and understated.

> HM Prison,
> Dartmoor, Yelverton, Devon
> 14 October 1996

Dear Don,

As much as I appreciate all that everyone is trying to do for me, the mere mention of any other establishment is likely to have the Allocations Unit considering it as a possibility. I have already had to write, pleading with them to send me to Littlehey, rather than anywhere else.

It is true that I would be closer to home if I was at Nottingham, but that is a Category B prison and would be a step backwards for me in terms of progression through the system.

The reason I feel so strongly about Littlehey is that they offer education seven days per week and part of the curriculum includes law and chemistry, which I would like to study. I know of no other prison which offers those.

It is the only prison in the country granted a licence to manufacture Braille typewriters. Also on offer is the chance to go camping at weekends. This I would never get at Nottingham or anywhere else. I have mentioned it to my family and they are happy to travel there every fortnight.

At the end of the day I am the one stuck behind bars, so I want my incarceration to be as comfortable as possible.

Stephen Downing

Yet towards the end of the year, continual knock-backs from the parole board had got to Stephen. I had not known him quite so low since we had met.

HM Prison
Dartmoor, Yelverton, Devon
2 November 1996

Dear Don,

I am appreciative of Mr McLoughlin's concern for my welfare. I am wondering if I might be able to call on his assistance to help me obtain a transfer before Christmas. With only a few weeks left my chances seem rather slim, hence the need for all the help I can get.

This will be my fifth Christmas without a visit from my family. While this may be considered just for me, it is grossly unfair for my family to be treated in this way. It is supposed to be the policy of the prison service to promote family ties. I should hardly call this promoting such a policy. I will be writing to John [Atkins] to see if he can assist.

If it wasn't for my family I would withdraw any attempts at an appeal, parole, etc and say 'You've kept me this long, you can keep me for the rest of my life,' and I'd not bother to conform in any way.

I'm sorry to feel so despondent, but you get that way when the Home Office is not content with just having its pound of flesh.

Stephen Downing

1997

23

THE CAMPAIGN WAS given a boost at the start of the New Year. A renowned scientific expert was highly critical of the way forensic evidence had been presented at Stephen's trial, and the conclusions that had been drawn from it.

Russell Stockdale, a partner at Berkshire-based Forensic Access – independent scientific consultants to the legal profession – examined in detail the blood-stained clothing, shoes, personal items and murder weapon, the latter having eventually been released by Derbyshire Constabulary from its 'Black Museum'. He said the evidence available had broadly backed Stephen's own version of events, that he found Wendy, turned her over, and got splashed with blood as she shook her head; and *not* that of the Prosecution, which claimed certain blood-staining to Stephen's clothes could only have come from him attacking Wendy Sewell.

Welcome though his report was, I found it ironic that he had reached the same conclusions as Mr G. E. Moss, the forensics expert who had written a report at the request of Stephen Downing's defence team in January 1974. The same basic information, currently being paid for out of a £13,000 Legal Aid purse, had been available for use in Stephen's defence at his trial twenty-three years previously.

In addition, with modern developments in forensic science, it was possible to show that the tiny blood spots found on Stephen's clothes could also have resulted from Mrs Sewell's exhalations as she lay mortally wounded.

Mr Stockdale attacked Norman Lee, the Home Office forensic expert at the time, for not even attending the scene of crime. He went on scathingly,

The scene of the incident was *not* examined and recorded sufficiently to determine how and where the attack began and ended. In particular, it is *not* clear whether all the blows were struck whilst Mrs Sewell was on the path or whether, after initial blows there, she was pursued in among the graves where she was later discovered.

Accounts of the scene are scant to say the least, with no detailed descriptions among the papers I have seen of blood-staining there, or any reference to searches for blood having been made.

A second report soon arrived by a specialist in photographic analysis, Geoffrey Oxlee, a founder member of the Society of Expert Witnesses and an imagery analyst for over forty years. The murder scene was photographed by Derbyshire police soon after the attack, and it was this photographic evidence that Mr Oxlee had been asked to examine. He concluded:

If the photography I examined is all that was taken, the scene of crime imagery after the body was removed is unsatisfactory and unprofessional.

I am very surprised that colour photography was not used. The use of colour photography in these circumstances is extremely important. Black and white imagery fails to identify staining due to blood, especially over the key grassy areas over which Wendy Sewell apparently travelled from the point of the attack on the path to the place at the graveside of Sarah Bradbury where she lay mortally wounded.

It is probable that the artefacts were numbered with chalk and photographed after the general scene of crime pictures had been taken. Considering the reported extent of the injuries to Wendy Sewell there appears to be a relatively small amount of blood on the clothing photographed. Of course there are many explanations for this, including that the clothing was taken off *before* the injuries were made. There are stains on the trousers, probably caused by blood but the boob tube and the plimsolls appear to have no blood-stains.

It is very strange that the police appear not to have taken pictures of the blood-stained trail which, given the extent of her injuries, Wendy Sewell must have left if she moved *unaided* over the distance. I can see no clear evidence of blood in the grass along the route. If there was a trail of blood, why not record that evidence? I can only assume there was no trail of blood!

He went on to question whether someone else could have moved Wendy to the gravestones in the middle of the cemetery. 'Did Downing have time to batter her, sexually assault her and move her? If he did not move her, how did she get there? How did police examine this seeming anomaly?'

How and when Wendy got from the path where she was attacked, over to the graves in the middle of the cemetery, has never been explained, either at trial or since.

My own inexpert opinion is that she probably *did* move herself. She was seen to be thrashing about and trying to stand up, so maybe had the strength left to crawl? I always thought it significant that she had moved in the direction of the workmen's store. Had she seen them arrive in their van and tried to move towards a source of help? Surely if someone had been trying to temporarily conceal her whilst they made their getaway, they would have simply thrown her over the wall into the woods right next to where she lay?

Mr Oxlee's report had at least pointed out the 'unsatisfactory' forensic investigation and recording of crime imagery surrounding this issue, which no one ever got to the bottom of. He also suggested that Wendy's clothing may have been taken off before she was attacked, again contradicting Stephen's account in his confession statement. I was thankful that the experts' reports not only matched my initial findings but added further credence to Stephen's claims of innocence. His conviction was looking more unsafe by the minute.

Lawyer John Atkins was also delighted with the findings of the reports, and decided the time was now right to seek counsel's opinion with a view to seeking leave to appeal. He hoped this could be approved as early as March.

Then came the inevitable news – the news I had been dreading. In early February Sam Fay died. His family had told us to expect the worst but nevertheless it was still a major shock.

I had worked with Sam since my arrival in 1985. I knew he was disappointed not to have been given the editor's chair himself but he was already at retirement age and there was a need for modernisation, a task which could only be undertaken by a younger man.

Sam had been an institution in the Derbyshire Dales with more than fifty years service behind him in local journalism and a distinguished army career. I had successfully put his name forward for an MBE. Ironically Sam's final days were spent at Whitworth Hospital, the local care unit, which together we had campaigned to save about ten years before.

The funeral service at St Joseph's on Bank Road was packed to capacity. It seemed the whole town wanted to pay their last respects to a much-loved friend. I knew that as well as a friend he was an irreplaceable colleague, whose support I would desperately miss during the final years of the fight to free Stephen.

By this time Jackie had left to join the agency. She was replaced by Marcus whenever he could get along after school or during holidays. He was soon as enthusiastic about the Downing campaign as the rest of us, but I still desperately missed Sam.

In the spring of 1997 C3, the Home Office department dealing with Stephen's case and other alleged miscarriages of justice, was disbanded. It was replaced by a shiny new department, the Criminal Cases Review Commission, or CCRC, based in Birmingham. The new body was set up following the recommendations of a Royal Commission on Criminal Justice. It was felt that the old system for investigating suspected miscarriages of justice had failed, following a series of high-profile cases such as the Birmingham Six.

In March 1997, Stephen's was one of the first cases due to be considered by the new authority. He was quickly allocated a case file reference number 0059/97 and I received a polite note to confirm that, after nearly four years of hard slog, the Home Office had simply run out of time to re-examine his case.

My initial concern was that, after over three years of negotiation and submissions with the Home Office and C3, we were suddenly back to square one. Would the mass of paperwork eventually find its way to Birmingham? Would this new body study my work again from scratch?

The commissioner appointed was Barry Capon CBE, a man I came to know well over not weeks, not months, but years of correspondence. He had retired in 1996 as chief executive to Norfolk County Council, a post he had held since 1973. He was clerk to the Norfolk Police Authority for over twenty years and had been clerk to the Norfolk Magistrates Court Committee and secretary to the Norfolk Probation Committee, giving him a wide understanding of the judicial system. He had been awarded his CBE in 1992. The first thing I learned about Mr Capon was that he appeared to be in no hurry.

When I started to deal with the new commission I soon realised I was embarking on another soul-destroying, long-drawn-out and frustrating journey, re-submitting files and documents that had been systematically checked and re-checked countless times before. Despite umpteen assurances from the CCRC that Stephen Downing's case would be treated with some urgency, its advancement seemed only to attract one speed: dead slow.

The need to go through the same things yet again with different people increased my workload to an unprecedented level. This was coupled with severe problems with my parents in Manchester. My wife Kath and I travelled north most weekends to help with shopping, gardening and odd jobs for both sets of parents. My mother had been in deteriorating health for years.

Often she didn't remember who I was. She was suffering from Alzheimer's disease and had problems eating and drinking. She spent time in hospital and often, when she came home, she was unable to look after herself or my father, who had his own serious medical problems, which included Parkinson's disease. They were a tremendous couple, always friendly and supportive, and always there when I needed them. Their constant downhill slide was a bitter blow, and made me very depressed.

There seemed no relief from the pressures of the day job, the stress of dealing with Stephen's problems, and the ever-present personal problems. Kath was particularly brilliant during this time and continually tried to keep my spirits high, encouraging me to continue battling against adversity. It was a time when it seemed the whole world was about to fall on my shoulders. But day after day, week after week and month after month Kath refused to let me give up – she never lost her temper with me and she was always optimistic.

<h1 style="text-align:center">24</h1>

Summer 1997

A much-needed bonus came during the summer of 1997 when I received a phone call out of the blue from one of the directors of the *Mercury's* parent company. He told me that a new witness might be willing to come forward to add further support to Stephen's claims – a retired detective who had served nearly thirty years on the force and had been based at Bakewell. It appeared that my colleague had met the man – who I will call Rodney Jones – at a funeral and he thought that the graveyard location plus the fact Rodney had met a man from the Mercury Group had finally pricked his conscience. The former detective had told my colleague he had been reading about the progress of the case. He had had something on his conscience for many years about the Wendy Sewell murder, and felt the time had now come to talk about it.

I picked up the office phone to dial the number I had been given, then immediately put it down again. I wondered if it could be a trick. Why should an ex-detective suddenly want to offer confidential information after more than twenty years of silence – to a journalist? I sat back and thought about the situation for a few moments then picked up the receiver again. What the hell? I thought. I've nothing to lose. I dialled the number and after a few short rings Jones answered. When I told him who I was he immediately started to sound rather nervous, even panicky. He refused to talk on the phone but, after some persuasion, agreed to meet me the following day at my office at 11a.m.

He arrived right on time and gave the false name we had agreed during the call the previous day. He seemed obsessed with not being seen coming into the *Mercury* offices, although he had parked his large blue Volvo right outside. I ushered him straight through to my private office. Jones entered, looking like one of those 1930s American private eyes with his coat collar turned up and a distinctly shifty look in his eyes.

'You're not to record this,' he said immediately.

'No, nothing will be recorded,' I reassured him, 'but it would be helpful if I could take some notes.'

'No notes,' snapped Jones. 'Let's just talk things through first.'

Jones had only recently retired from the force and was terrified of losing his pension if he talked to the press. He was also concerned about breaching the Official Secrets Act. I did my best to calm him down, gave him a cup of hot coffee – three sugars as requested – and agreed a special code to preserve his anonymity on future visits.

I studied the man very carefully. He was sweating before the interview even started. I set about trying to coax out of him the reason for his visit, all the time attempting to conceal my excitement that I might at last be nearing a breakthrough.

'I joined the force in 1962,' Jones explained, 'but I left a few years later when I became disenchanted. I became a publican, but soon realised that police work was in my blood and returned to join the old Derby and County force at Buxton about November 1971. I was in CID there for about five years, then I moved to Matlock, then Clay Cross. Later I was transferred to the police house near Taddington, then finally I moved to Bakewell.

'Towards the end of 1979 I was working late in CID at Bakewell police station, when I was asked to see someone who apparently wanted a word in private.

'This person, whose name was Steven Martin, was a young man who owned a florist's shop near Ripley. He said he lived with his father near the shop. He made mention of his uncle who was related to Mr Red and lived at a farm over towards Tideswell. The uncle was said to have bred fighting cocks.

'The uncle had confided in Steven Martin and told him that Mr Red and another man had forced him to give them an alibi stating that he had been with them on that day in 1973. He wanted people to tell lies for him so there would be no connection with the murder.'

Jones paused for a breather. He was looking round all the time. He kept saying he hoped no one else from the office had seen him. I still wasn't quite sure whether he was genuine, a crank, or even a police spy determined to find out more about my progress on the case.

When he mentioned the uncle/nephew relationship, it immediately brought back to me Crabby's comments at Flash Dam two years previously. Crabby had mentioned a young man who had often visited his dying uncle in the hospice where Crabby worked. Jones said the uncle had been a farmer from Tideswell, a village to the north of Bakewell about halfway to Buxton. Crabby had mentioned the uncle came from the same general direction, although he hadn't been as specific. Neither location was far from where Mr Red lived, nor from Chelmorton where another man who gave Mr Red an alibi lived. It seemed Jones and Crabby were talking about the same group of people.

At last, I thought, some missing pieces of the jigsaw were finally turning up.

As Jones continued he also confirmed what I had known for years: Wendy Sewell had been Mr Red's girlfriend.

'The uncle was sworn to secrecy by Mr Red, but he was dying and he felt he had to tell his nephew, Steven Martin,' continued Jones. 'When his uncle died just a couple of weeks later, Martin felt he had to tell the police. He thought something should be done. That was the reason he came to the police station – he told me the whole story.'

Jones now seemed upset and I thought I saw a tear in his eye. 'Steven Martin had always thought Mr Red had been to a sheep sale,' he went on. 'He was devastated when he found out the truth.'

'I can't remember if Steven told me the names of the other people who corroborated the alibi at the time. They were responsible people, though. They were farmers who had gone to buy sheep, all relatives of Mr Red. I think their statements were checked. Martin was in his mid-twenties at the time. I saw him again several times and even went to his house a couple of times.

'I applied for a copy of the Prosecution file on the Sewell murder, and it arrived within a couple of days. I took it home to read and study.

'I got myself thoroughly acquainted with the facts. There was a disputed witness statement by a man from Buxton.' I assumed Jones must have been referring to the uncle from Tideswell, or maybe the man from Chelmorton. Both places were near Buxton.

'I was really worried by now. There were major flaws in this case,' he continued. 'I noticed about a dozen false statements from officers who did not exist. They were neither signed nor dated. There were other statements from officers who clearly had not taken the details. I queried one particular statement taken by an officer, which had his name and number on it. When I checked it with him, he denied any knowledge of it. He said it was all rubbish. He said not only hadn't he signed it, but he hadn't written it.

'He's an inspector now. He was too scared to do anything about it then. He told me to leave well alone and that they'd obviously made a mistake. It was no mistake though. It was part of the cover up.'

This was very alarming – Jones seemed to be saying that certain statements had been fabricated.

'Then things took a surprising turn,' he continued. 'I had a visit from a detective superintendent from Buxton, Tom Naylor. He barged right into the office and pushed me against the wall. He had his arm locked against my throat. I was almost choking. He said he hoped I didn't think I was going to get Stephen Downing out of jail. He said the shit would certainly hit the fan if I did and he said the press had better not get a whiff of what was happening! I later found out that the lads at Buxton called him "Creeping Jesus". He would suddenly appear behind them without them hearing his approach. He told me that I had to interview Mr Red with a detective sergeant, and *then* interview other witnesses. I said I didn't go along with that, but I was told in no uncertain manner that that was the way I had to play it.

'Mr Red came down to the station at Bakewell with his solicitor at about 7p.m. a few nights later. As instructed, I interviewed him with a detective sergeant. Mr Red was wetting himself. He was soaked in sweat and shaking like a leaf. He was shaking so much that he couldn't even light a cigarette. He constantly denied ever knowing the Sewell woman. He said he wasn't even sure he'd gone to the sheep sale and couldn't remember the details. But he did say there were about four people who went there by car, who he named.

'I was unhappy about interviewing suspects, *then* witnesses. I decided to refer to the fact that this request had been made by Naylor when I wrote my report. I put it in the last paragraph.

'I realised that the normal procedure would be to pull everyone in *at the same time*, and interview them separately, so that suspects and witnesses did not have time to compare notes and get their stories "straight".'

Jones's note in his report had not gone down well. 'Within a day or so I was given one of the biggest rollickings of my life by another officer at Buxton,' he said. 'He told me there had been no need to put these comments on my report. I thought my future was on the line. But I heard nothing more. I saw Steven Martin again later and he was not happy with the outcome.'

I remembered Crabby's comments on Mr Red's 'friendly' copper, and another of my informants claiming a high-ranking super-intendent had supported Mr Red's alibi. I wondered if he could have been referring to 'Creeping Jesus', Tom Naylor?

'I gave a two- or three-page report to the divisional commander,' continued Jones, 'but again I heard nothing more. I retired in 1990 and I've been wanting to get this off my chest for a while. I think your Downing man is innocent.'

I thanked Jones for his information. He wanted an assurance as to whether he could give this information to the authorities without losing his pension. I didn't know, and I didn't want to be accused of tainting a witness. I suggested Jones should contact an independent solicitor for advice. He left the office, saying he would be in touch again.

Meanwhile I made enquiries about Detective Superintendent Tom Naylor. One of my informants passed me a letter written by Naylor to Force headquarters on 1 February 1982. He explained that he had interviewed Ray Downing in September 1981, in response to a letter received by the chief constable from Ray.

Naylor wrote:

Mr Downing gave a long history of the case and his reasons for believing that his son was innocent. A great many of the matters he raised had been dealt with in the initial inquiry. His main points were . . . that he considered that Mr Red, a former associate of the deceased . . . may have been responsible for the murder.

Where possible, having regard to the length of time which has lapsed since the murder, I have found an answer to each of the points Mr Downing senior has raised. Mr Red was eliminated from the inquiry in the initial stages of the investigation.

On Saturday 30 January 1982, I saw Mr Downing at Matlock Police Station. I discussed the various matters he had raised and advised him of the outcome.

So it appeared Naylor had totally eliminated Mr Red from the inquiry in 1982, with no mention of his being re-interviewed in 1979, nor of the claims that his alibis for the day of the murder had been drawn into question at that time. This information could have proved vital to Stephen Downing's chances of an appeal in 1980. It appeared it had been suppressed. His defence team were never made aware that any such interviews or claims of broken alibis had occurred.

True to his word, Rodney Jones returned to the office several days later. He once again entered in a cloak and dagger manner through the back door, using his agreed assumed name. As soon as he was alone with me the words started to spill out.

'When Steven Martin told the police what he knew, he couldn't believe how uninterested they were. He had spoken to Naylor who had virtually told him to go away. After this final effort he just seemed to disappear.'

I found this sudden disappearance strange. Where had Martin gone? Jones did not know. He said he used to live in Ripley, a small town between Derby and Nottingham and, ironically, home to Derbyshire police HQ. He had mysteriously vanished not long after giving his statement.

'Nothing was ever heard from him again,' said Jones. 'So nothing happened. There was total silence from the police side. Martin's statement was filed away too. Without the lad it was impossible to progress.'

'So the police just let Mr Red off the hook?' I asked.

'That's why I came to you,' said Jones. 'I thought you would know what to do.'

'It's a bit late,' I said. 'It's from 1980 – will you at least give me a written statement?'

'No, no – definitely not!' said Rodney.

'Well if you won't give it to me, give it to Downing's solicitor or someone else. Even the Commissioner for Oaths,' I urged.

'And my pension? What about my pension? It's a lot to risk.'

I felt two emotions simultaneously. Sorry for a brave man who thought he was risking everything, and anger that he wouldn't put things in writing. In the end anger and frustration triumphed over sympathy. 'Then why bother coming to me if you haven't got the guts?' I demanded.

'I'll think about it. I'll be in touch,' replied Jones, as he left the office.

The following day Jones phoned me and agreed to visit a solicitor in London to discuss the position with his pension and the Official Secrets Act. After that meeting he was reassured enough to give a statement directly to the Criminal Cases Review Commission.

The file containing Jones's allegations from 1979 was only produced by the police following a marathon legal struggle, and High Court demands from Stephen's Defence team. Finally the police had to give in and corroborate all this crucial information – but at a price. John Atkins said the police made him agree that all the evidence relating to Rodney Jones's interrogation of Mr Red, which the police had at first denied existed, could not be shown to me or discussed with me.

John was furious. I told him not to worry. I had spoken with Jones on about five occasions, and knew the probable contents of the file. As long as Jones's statements became part of the defence evidence, I didn't mind.

25

IN THE SUMMER of 1997 I was asked by the Home Office to clarify what I knew about possible links between the murder of Wendy Sewell and two other unsolved murder cases from 1970 – those of Barbara Mayo and Jackie Ansell-Lamb. These latter two brutal murders were linked by the police. Ansell-Lamb was found face down and half naked in Macclesfield, Cheshire, just a few months before Mayo was found sexually assaulted and strangled near Junction 29 of the M1 in Derbyshire in the autumn of 1970.

As I trawled through the old newspaper cuttings, and Robert Ervin's notes on the Mayo murder, I noticed that Barbara Mayo and Wendy Sewell were strikingly similar in appearance. They were both young, attractive women with long, dark hair. Both had been battered about the head and had had their handbags and personal effects stolen.

One of the most remarkable coincidences seemed to be that at least five men from the Bakewell area were allegedly interviewed over the Barbara Mayo murder. I had heard these rumours for years from Bakewell residents, and had also been told the same thing by a police contact.

They debated that Mr Red had been one of the men questioned. Police had been looking for a fair-haired man driving a Morris Minor Traveller. I was told by a close associate of his that Mr Red, who was blond, had owned a red Hillman estate in 1970, and wondered if the similarity between the two makes of vehicles had contributed to his being pulled in by the police. Another close male friend of Wendy's had also been questioned about the Mayo murder.

I mentioned that Mayo and Ansell-Lamb had both been strangled. Although the post-mortem made no mention of Wendy being strangled, I told of the testimony of the medium who had raised the matter of strangulation with tights. Although I realised this would be regarded as unreliable, I had seen mortuary photographs of Wendy Sewell and there did appear to be bruising to her neck. I also questioned the apparent disappearance of her tights.

I drew another parallel – all personal effects had been taken from Mayo and Ansell-Lamb. None of Wendy Sewell's personal effects were ever traced. All the victims were found half-naked, face down and attracted many anonymous letters.

My report was despatched as requested and, just a few weeks later, almost three years after my first submission to Derbyshire Chief Constable John Newing, the county force suddenly organised a press conference to announce they were reopening the Barbara Mayo murder case after nearly thirty years. More surprisingly, the officer taking the press conference and banging the drum for police efficiency, was my old friend Don Dovaston.

Their first press release on the subject stated, 'Detectives who have continued the investigation into the murder of Barbara Mayo for the past 27 years are to disclose a major new development in their hunt for the person responsible.'

A few days later came the main press conference. The press release issued after that conference revealed,

A scientific breakthrough has meant that a DNA sample has been obtained from clothing worn by the victim at the scene.

At a press conference today the man leading the investigation, Assistant Chief Constable Don Dovaston, said: 'The police never forget, and our files in relation to this murder have not closed. During twenty-seven years someone must have shown signs that others will have picked up on. I am appealing to these people to come forward and speak to us.'

I could not believe my luck. I thought maybe I had misjudged some senior officers. Perhaps they *had* at last taken note of my suggestions that there were links between the Sewell and Mayo cases. I expected a call from the police incident room asking me for further talks, and waited for another press conference to say they were now looking into possible connections with the murder of Wendy Sewell. Perhaps

Stephen would be released sooner than I anticipated. But nothing happened.

As that week's *Mercury* deadline was fast approaching, and I had still had no word from the police, I decided to take the initiative. The front page of the *Mercury* of 25 September 1997 appeared with the strap line: 'Bakewell murder links to Mayo case', with the main front-page story devoted to the similarities in both crimes. Under the headline FINGERPRINTS OF A KILLER, appeared pictures of Barbara Mayo and Wendy Sewell. Side by side, the physical resemblance was striking.

As the paper hit the streets, I made a call to the police incident room and outlined my lead story for that week. I got through to a senior officer who seemed genuinely surprised to hear of a possible Sewell connection, and said I might hear from them again. He added, though, that I should not hold my breath.

Several more days passed before my long-awaited call from the Mayo incident room came. 'Are you available for an interview?' I was asked.

'Yes, perhaps tomorrow afternoon or Friday?'

'No, I mean now,' came the curt reply.

'Well, yes, I suppose so,' I said, taken aback by this sudden urgency.

'Wait where you are, then. We'll be there in twenty minutes.'

Sure enough, less than half an hour later two detectives arrived at the *Mercury* offices. They had driven the ten miles or so across the moors from Chesterfield. They looked more like undertakers than policemen, dressed in identical dark suits. Fortunately, I had kept some of the files on the Downing case at the office and gladly showed the ones with Mayo links to my unexpected visitors.

I also showed them copies of my recent submissions to the Home Office, local MP Patrick McLoughlin, and the Criminal Cases Review Commission, all of which highlighted possible connections between the Mayo and Sewell murders. They seemed astounded, and told me categorically that the first they had heard of any potential links was when my front-page article had appeared that week.

They spent about an hour going over my files. When they came to the name of Mr Red, and the other close associate of Wendy's, their jaws dropped. Although I had always named all possible suspects and anyone connected with the victim in my official submissions, I had been very careful never to mention any names in my press reports. Up till this moment, the two officers had been unaware that Mr Red and this other man had been questioned over the Wendy Sewell murder.

'Why do these names surprise you so much?' I asked.

They explained that Mr Red was one of the men from Bakewell questioned over the Barbara Mayo murder – something which I had been told by a police contact over two years previously – and that they were shocked to find he had connections with Wendy Sewell.

'In my book to be interviewed over one murder is unusual, but to be interviewed over two, that is too much of a coincidence,' said one of the officers.

I explained that I had first given the basic information they now had in front of them to the chief constable's office back in January 1995. Assistant Chief Constable Don Dovaston, the man now leading the reopened Mayo investigation, must have been well aware of it. Moreover, I had sent a revised document about the links between these murders within the last few weeks to the Home Office at its specific request.

Eventually the detectives took photocopies of the relevant paperwork with them and drove off.

Later that day I received a phone call from Central Television's newsroom. They had read the front page of the *Mercury* and wanted to know if there were any updates on the Downing case worth running in their evening news bulletin. I told them two detectives had just visited me from the Mayo murder investigation unit and that they had taken away documents which referred to links to the murder of Wendy Sewell.

Two hours later a producer from Central got back to me and said the police had denied visiting me, and had added they had no intention of doing so. I could hardly believe my ears. I went over the details of the visit again, and said it had taken place in the reception office of the *Mercury* with witnesses.

The producer basically called me a liar, and put down the phone.

I asked my colleagues at the *Mercury* if I had been dreaming. I was so annoyed I picked up the phone and redialled the same senior producer in Central's Nottingham newsroom. He said he was satisfied with the statement from Derbyshire police and there was really nothing more to say. Unfortunately my old friend Alan Taylor, who had been such a supporter of my campaign to free Stephen Downing, had left Central Television by this time and no one else there ever really took up the case with as much enthusiasm.

This latest conversation terminated any further discussion with Central Television for some time – until Nick Kehoe, one of their reporters, dropped in months later to see if he could do a filmed update on the case. I handed him a copy of the entry in the *Mercury* visitors book from October 1997 which showed the names, ranks and details of my police visitors.

More than three years after the reinvestigation of the Mayo killing opened with such a flourish, it was wound down, after spending a fortune in man-hours and fruitless searches throughout the world, combined with hundreds of interviews and the meticulous re-examination of DNA evidence.

The killer of Barbara Mayo – and perhaps many others – remains at large.

There have never been any official statements from Derbyshire police on the connections between the murders of Wendy Sewell and Barbara Mayo, despite, alledgedly, at least two close associates of Wendy's having been questioned about the Mayo case three years before Wendy was murdered.

1998

26

HM Prison
Littlehey
Perry
Huntingdon
Cambs PE18 OSR
1 January 1998

Dear Don,

Can I wish you and your family a very happy New Year.

As from this Saturday I will be able to function as a listener affiliated to the Samaritans. John Atkins is pleased that I have been selected for training and sees it as a good thing as it can be put forward at my next parole review if I do not get my appeal.

As you rightly say this year looks like it could be an interesting one all round.

I was pleased to read that John Atkins and Paul Taylor should have their legal submission ready for the CCRC by the third week of this month. I hope that it will be met with very little opposition.

Thank you again for all that you have done for me. Perhaps this year you will see your efforts rewarded.

Yours sincerely,

Stephen

It was a cold dark night and I had only been home from work for an hour or so when the phone rang for the umpteenth time. It was nearly eight o'clock. I had just finished my evening meal.

Kath answered it. 'Don, it's a man who won't give his name. Says he must speak to you urgently about the Downing case.' She looked at me as if to say, shall I tell him to phone you at the office tomorrow?

I grabbed the receiver. 'It's OK, Kath, I'll talk to him.' I knew it could have been a crank but I wondered how he managed to get my home number. We had been ex-directory for quite some time. We had already been forced to change our number due to threatening calls at all hours of the day and night. Kath stood next to me with a frown on her face.

'Don Hale, Can I help you?'

He had a gruff, deep voice and sounded very cautious at first. 'Are you Don Hale from the *Matlock Mercury*?'

'Yes, I am. How did you get my number?'

'A friend of a friend,' he replied. 'We have a mutual interest. Some people responsible for the Sewell murder are customers at my business in Bakewell.'

He had definitely grabbed my attention. 'What people, and what's your business?'

'Look, I can't talk on the phone. Can you meet me tonight in about an hour?'

I was a little suspicious.

Kath looked even more worried. 'You can't go out again tonight,' she said into my other ear. 'It could be a trap. Where does he want to meet you?'

Gently, I pushed her away, asked the caller to wait, and held the receiver at arm's length with my hand over the mouthpiece. 'Kath, he wants to meet at 9p.m. at the Hurt Arms at Ambergate.'

I knew the pub in question. It was on the A6 going towards Derby, about five miles beyond Matlock. It seemed a reasonable spot to meet.

Kath was shaking her head. 'Tell him no,' she said. 'He can come to the office.'

I covered the receiver again. 'He says he can't see me tomorrow. And I can't go to Bakewell. He doesn't want to be seen with me. He claims to have some information about suspects in the Sewell murder.' I smiled back at her. She knew how stubborn and determined I could be over this case.

'Yes, I'll see you at 9p.m. How will I know you?' I asked the caller, and repeated his reply out loud. 'Tall, grey-haired, late fifties, light–

coloured overcoat. Standing by the main bar. OK, see you then.'

I put the phone down and Kath gave me one of her glares. 'You're stupid!' she said. 'You've only just got home and now you're dropping everything to meet an anonymous stranger. Why?'

I looked at her, tried to appear relaxed, and smiled again. I could give no clear explanation and there was no logical reason for going out again in the dark to another secret meeting. But I was beginning to find this investigation totally addictive. I had become obsessed with following up new leads.

It was only about a twenty-minute drive to the Hurt Arms. There was very little traffic and I arrived ten minutes early, bought a Coke and took a seat just inside the main door. Three men came in within a minute of each other. Each was on his own and looked about the place. Two of them roughly matched the description I had been given. I stood up and wandered across to the bar. I figured whichever one it was would recognise me and make the first move. I almost approached one man who was leaning on the bar, and kept glancing casually towards the main door. Then another man quickly entered and ordered a drink. He wore a light-coloured overcoat. He immediately walked up to me and asked if I was Don Hale. He shook my hand and offered to buy me a drink before I ushered him towards my seat by the window.

He was tall and thickset. He had a gravelled-looking face and short, spiky white hair. He continually looked about, trying to see if anyone was watching. After some prompting he gave me his name, then said I couldn't tell a soul. He said he had business premises in Bakewell town centre.

Then he immediately came to the point. He said that Mr Orange had attacked Wendy Sewell in Bakewell cemetery. He believed Mr Blue was somehow involved. Both had lived in the same area.

Soon other familiar names came into the conversation – Syd Oulsnam, Mr Red and George Pearson. The businessman claimed he had overheard some of these men talking to each other at his premises over a fairly long period. As the case had developed over the years, he said the conversations had become more nervous and intense. He knew Mr Blue had moved away some years back, and confirmed that the lad had been much younger than the others. We agreed to meet again a week later at the same place.

The following day I ran Mr Orange's name past Ray Downing. To my surprise he told me Mr Orange had become a 'friend' of the Downing family immediately after the murder. Ray said he seemed to take an avid interest in the family's claims of Stephen's innocence, and often asked if they thought the case would be reopened. Of course, at the time the family were oblivious to any suggestion that he might have been involved in the murder.

The businessman and I had a second meeting, then a third, but still he was being evasive and cautious. He claimed his livelihood and reputation were at stake if it became known he was talking to me. I wondered if his claims were part of an elaborate plot to apportion blame. There were still many pieces of the complex jigsaw missing. Many permutations rattled about in my head. Most of the key players knew each other in some way, and most had been pals at about the time of the murder. My informant said a friend of his had heard Mr Orange boasting that he had 'finished Wendy off'.

In such a small rural community it was difficult to make rapid progress when so many people were interrelated, close friends or neighbours. Despite several meetings, I still wasn't quite sure from what he was saying whether the attacker had acted with another man following a drinking binge, or had been hired by somebody else to kill Wendy Sewell. The message I was getting from the businessman, though, was clear – two people were involved, and Wendy had become something of a liability.

After talking with him, I became convinced others had known Stephen would be in the cemetery at the time of the attack. He was an obvious fall guy: a young lad with learning difficulties who would almost certainly find the victim and be blamed. In the relatively remote location of the cemetery, there would be few witnesses to support his claims of innocence.

This time I was determined to track down the elusive Mr Orange.

1999

27

Mr Orange had disappeared from the area for a while around 1996, coincidentally at the same time that Stephen's case began to gain national publicity. Now, I heard, he was back doing odd jobs, and sometimes seen out in the area's pubs at night. Ironically, he would often phone Ray Downing just before closing time to book a taxi ride back home. Ray and Mr Orange always chatted in the car and discussed Stephen's case. I think Ray used to add the extra mile, indicating something special was coming up, just to test Mr Orange's reaction. Like me, he had heard the rumours. I asked Ray if, the next time he drove Mr Orange home, he would try to get him to phone me, or agree to meet me somewhere. I tried to imagine what must have been going through Mr Orange's mind, if the rumours were true. Had he been drawn to the Downing family because he was worried that Stephen might know too much?

Eventually Mr Orange sent a message via Ray that he would talk to me at a club in Bakewell. I went there with Marcus. We travelled to the club at the agreed time. I bought the drinks and we waited. It was like being in a fish bowl. My face was known and I felt as if everyone were watching me.

After ten minutes or so, I asked if Mr Orange had been in. The barman said we had just missed him – he had moved on. We drank up and headed for the nearest pub. Again, there was no sign of him and once more we were told he had just left, we ended up at a third pub.

I had never met Mr Orange before and, as we scanned the many customers in the lounge, I noticed someone vaguely fitting the description I had been given, standing by the bar talking with a couple. I walked over, bought some more drinks and eased into a conversation with him to make sure I had the right man. When it became obvious it was Mr Orange, I asked him to join us at a table in the corner. He smiled and walked across with us.

In many ways he was nothing like the picture painted by Ray. Physically the characteristics were the same, a fairly fit-looking guy in his early to mid-fifties, tall and wiry, fairish and going a bit grey, but he was dressed very smartly.

I began to gain his confidence, talking in general terms about the Downing case. He was fairly non-committal at first, telling me that Ray had said this, that or the other. I then asked him how long he had known the family. He seemed a bit surprised at that particular question.

'I met the Downings shortly after the murder,' he explained. 'Can't quite remember how it came about but I saw Ray and Nita about town and Ray kept us informed of what was happening to his lad in prison.'

I looked back at him to gauge his reaction. 'You became friendly with the Downings after this murder, didn't you?' I asked.

He took a swig of his pint and stared back. 'Not particularly,' he replied. 'Just wanted to know what was what. Ray used to tell everyone about Steve.'

I quizzed him about his life in those days. He said he often became drunk and disorderly. 'I was a pain in the arse,' he admitted. 'The police were always picking me up. I kept coming back to Bakewell during the early Seventies, then going away again.'

'Spent time in the glasshouse, didn't you?' I queried.

Again he looked slightly surprised. 'About eighteen months. Always in trouble with drink.'

'And now? Are you a reformed character? What made you go off the rails in the first place?' I was keen to know what might have affected his behaviour during his early days in town.

'I get by. I do what I want to do,' he said. 'Do a few jobs, live on my own.' He drank down the rest of his pint in one and immediately started to sip the pint I had bought him. 'I work alone and live alone,' he said. There was little expression on his face.

I tried to ask him about 12 September 1973. I wanted to know what he had been up to that day.

'Don't know. Can't remember now.'

'Were you questioned over the Sewell murder?'

'Don't think so. No reason. I wasn't about then. Anyway, the police said it was open and shut. Downing had confessed.'

'If you can't remember, how do you know where you were?'

He shrugged his shoulders. 'I was away at around that time, like I told you.'

'Did you know the victim?'

'I think everyone knew Wendy. I'd seen her about. But I didn't *know* her – if you get what I mean?'

I caught the drift of his insinuation. I told him certain details of my own investigations, deliberately mentioning George Pearson, Syd Oulsnam and Mr Red.

I looked at him as I mentioned each name. He stared into his pint and took another sip, this time a little more nervously. He admitted he'd worked with both Mr Red and Oulsnam.

'And Pearson?'

'I know George. Everyone knows George.' He said Pearson 'used to be a bit of a lad with the ladies' and had done time.

I mentioned some of the new evidence which shot holes in the timings, forensic evidence and the confession given by Stephen. He seemed to show more interest. He was still drinking fairly rapidly. I noticed more of a flicker when I mentioned forensics. I thought I would lay it on a bit thicker. 'The forensics are strong,' I told him. 'Syd asked me about DNA a few years ago. It's amazing what the police can find out from DNA. Of course, they didn't have this technology in 1973. If there were hairs, fibres, blood samples or a palm print, it could identify the killer,' I emphasised.

He started talking about Pearson again. I paused to see where he might be taking this conversation – but he suddenly went silent.

'Syd told me he was parked near the cemetery that day,' I teased.

'Did he?'

'Did you know Syd at that time?'

'Probably. I knew of him.'

'I thought you worked with him and Mr Red?'

'I've worked for a lot of people. Take what I can when I can.'

'But you have worked for them both?'

'Yes. On and off.'

He then mentioned that Pearson knew Mr Red years ago. They had been at school together. I thought it strange that he should keep deflecting the conversation back to George Pearson.

I asked him if he would talk to the police or CCRC if they asked, and he agreed, adding, 'Nothing I can tell them really.'

I dropped the bombshell. 'Some people think you did it. They say you finished her off.'

He hardly moved. There was no immediate reply. Then there was a slight shift in his position as he grabbed at his pint. 'No. No way,' he replied calmly.

'I gather someone has been to the police to say they've heard you say in the pub that you hit her. That you finished her off.'

'No.'

'Have you ever said that?'

'No.'

'It's a strange thing for a friend of yours to say, then – claiming you've said you finished her off.'

'Who said this?' he asked.

'Can't say. But he knows you. Why would he say it?'

'Don't know.'

'Did you say it for a joke?'

'No. I've never said that!' he insisted.

'So you would talk with the police and authorities and confirm that?'

'Yes.'

'And what about DNA? Would you go for a test if necessary?'

'Yes, I suppose so – but I never said that.'

He was plainly puzzled as to who might have talked to me, but quickly changed the subject. We chatted for a couple of minutes about trivial things. I could tell he was anxious to go. He checked the time. He had a lift booked. He swigged down the rest of the pint, said his goodbyes and left.

Marcus and I followed after a few seconds. I could see Ray's taxi outside. Mr Orange was in the front seat talking animatedly to him. I waved to them both, then Ray drove off with Mr Orange into the darkness.

★

Progress with the CCRC seemed to grind to a halt in the middle of 1999 – more than two years after they had accepted my files and submissions for consideration, and I had been given an understanding they would be dealt with quickly. This was extremely frustrating and resulted in Patrick McLoughlin, Stephen's MP, raising the matter in the House of Commons. He asked the Leader of the House, Margaret Beckett, if the Home Secretary could make a statement on the progress of the Criminal Cases Review Commission. Mrs Beckett replied,

> The Hon gentleman will know that we inherited long delays in many parts of the criminal justice system. That is a source of concern to the Government, as it rightly is to the public, and we are trying to take steps to diminish those delays.
>
> That applies, too, to the Criminal Cases Review Commission. Ministers are aware of and are concerned about the delays, and we are considering what can be done to ease the position.

More than fifteen months later, Patrick and I were still asking the same questions. Again we faced a blank response from the commissioner.

At that time the visits to my parents' home in Manchester increased. My mother and father were both having severe health problems. The 120-mile-plus round trip at the end of a long hard week was affecting my own health.

My mother was eventually taken back into hospital for more tests, as she found great difficulty in eating. I hoped she would soon recover and regain her strength. It was not to be, however, and following a brief spell in North Manchester Hospital, she died suddenly.

Completely out of the blue Steven Martin made contact with Stephen Downing, nearly four years after my clandestine meeting with Crabby, who had first mentioned the elusive 'nephew' figure. It was now two years since Rodney Jones had told me that Steven Martin had first raised questions about Mr Red's alibi back in 1979, and that he had vanished shortly afterwards.

Martin claimed he hadn't realised that he had appeared on a missing persons list, as he had been travelling the world and had only returned to Britain in 1999. He was happy to confirm many of the details given to me by Jones. He gave a statement in support of Stephen that same year and wrote to him in prison. Steven Martin's letter contained the following words:

> I have recently been approached by the Criminal Cases Review Commission who I'm sure you are aware are reviewing your case. I gave some information 22 years ago.
>
> I wasn't aware that it related to your case until a Police Inspector came to visit me. He impressed on me at the time how convinced he was that you have been serving time for someone else's offence.

More and more people were now starting to believe these final words.

2000

28

MY TRIPS TO Manchester continued. Most weekends were now engaged in visiting my father who resided in a care home in south Manchester. His health fluctuated. Whenever possible, I would take him out in a wheelchair to Wythenshawe Park or Platt Fields. I spent time with him in the home reading or updating him on developments. He never really got over the loss of my mother and one day I received a call from my brother to say he had died suddenly. It was one of the saddest days of my life. Within twelve months I had not only lost both parents, but two of my best friends and most ardent supporters. The loss occurred just a few days after my last visit, when he had looked so much better and, according to staff at the home, had even joined in with another resident's birthday party the night before and had a little dance. The shock of losing my father hit me hard.

Apparently from spring through to summer, CCRC Commissioner Barry Capon had been claiming to many media outlets, but not to me, that the Downing decision would be taken in June, July, August, then September. The commissioner may have thought it was easy to string along a local newspaper, but now the nationals had started to take an interest and they weren't going to be fobbed off that easily. The pressure was on.

Mr Capon had also told Patrick McLoughlin and the BBC that he would not be looking into the possibility that others might be responsible, as that aspect of the case did not fall within his remit.

Why then, I and several other journalists repeatedly asked, was he now looking into that precise aspect and interviewing suspects and their associates? I had discovered that this new and unexpected area of investigation was taking place, which intrigued and pleased me and Stephen's supporters. For more than five years I had given the authorities clear evidence that others *were* responsible – I had named names and provided new statements which cast doubt on the alibis of key individuals.

I was less than pleased, however, at Mr Capon's apparent failure on occasion to grasp critical pieces of evidence.

Syd Oulsnam claimed to Mr Capon that he had never spoken to me. Mr Capon queried this with me, even though I had sent details of all my phone calls and meetings with Oulsnam to C3, and subsequently to the CCRC. I asked, if I had never spoken to Syd, why then had Oulsnam allegedly reported me to the police in 1995 for harassment, even though *he* had actually phoned *me*?

Then I received a phone call in which Mr Capon challenged the fact that Wendy Sewell had had a child. That had not been mentioned in the court, he said. In fact, he persisted, it had been specifically mentioned that the Sewells had no children. I explained that I had made that very point in 1995. She did have a child, but it was out of wedlock. The father of the child was not David Sewell, but a local man named John Marshall with whom she had had an affair. Moreover, he had admitted to a colleague of mine that he *was* the father of Wendy's child. Mr Capon remained unconvinced and asked me to produce a birth certificate.

One Bakewell woman of around Wendy's age told me she had been in the same local maternity hospital, long since closed down, a few weeks after Wendy. She had often enquired of Wendy's mother, whom she regularly bumped into in Bakewell, as to how her daughter's pregnancy was progressing. Their babies had been delivered by the same midwife. She could practically tell me the child's birthday.

A quick check through the hospital and Register Office records soon produced the birth certificate. It stated: Registration District: Bakewell. Date and Place of Birth: 3 September 1968, Darley Hall, Matlock. Name: Thomas. Sex: Boy. Mother: Wendy Sewell, formerly Crawshaw, of Brooklands, Wyedale Crescent, Bakewell. Registered: 16 September 1968. There was no mention of the father.

I sent the birth certificate to Barry Capon. I also sent a letter in which I pointed out: 'It has been a long hard road to present evidence in the Stephen Downing case. As you may recall, I first forwarded information in January 1995 to Derbyshire police and the Home Office. C3 later took control of matters and, as far as I know, all the relevant paperwork was forwarded to your offices with the first batch of cases in April 1997. Now here we are some three and a half years later, and you are still looking for vital information.'

A major cause for concern became evident when I received an unexpected call from Syd Oulsnam. I had not spoken to him for five years, since he phoned me in a panic about DNA evidence. When he called he said he had received a letter from Barry Capon stating I had given evidence against him.

In my dealings with the Home Office, and subsequently the CCRC, I had always assumed, and indeed been assured of, anonymity and confidentiality. Now it appeared my evidence had been leaked to an associate of a potential suspect. It beggared belief!

I hastily arranged to meet Oulsnam in a pub car park where, he said, we could talk 'man to man'. I again took along Marcus Edwards, just in case there was any funny business. Syd was sitting waiting in his van. I told Marcus to sit tight and made sure he had his mobile phone with him. As I got out of my car, Syd beckoned for me to come across to join him in his van. As I opened the passenger-side door, it activated his alarm system. WARNING! THIS VEHICLE IS ALARMED! it roared repeatedly, until Syd, swearing under his breath, leant over and flipped a switch. What a start to a hush–hush meeting, I thought.

I tried to get new information out of Oulsnam. He admitted once again that he had been in his van, parked on the wasteland at Burton Edge near the cemetery, on 12 September 1973. But now he had changed his story from 1995: he said he had been alone, not with Mr Red. Ever since his 1995 phone call to me, Syd had told police he had never even been near the cemetery that day, let alone given Mr Red a lift there.

When I asked him if Wendy was Mr Red's girlfriend, he replied, 'No, that was all finished a couple of years before.' In fact, up till now both Mr Red and Oulsnam had always told the police that the pair had never had a relationship.

He confirmed that Mr Red had been 'interviewed several times about this murder'. He also told me that he had copied the letter from the CCRC and given the other copy to Mr Red. Thanks, Barry Capon, I thought to myself.

Oulsnam then made a rather odd comment, out of the blue, about George Pearson. He told me that Pearson and Mr Red had been at school together. I could not help wondering if he was trying to deflect some blame, possibly partly under instruction.

Sure enough, the letter from the CCRC Oulsnam then produced spelt out my evidence against him chapter and verse.

The following day I complained to my union, the National Union of Journalists. The union was horrified by the possible consequences of Barry Capon's action in blowing my cover.

The commissioner had been made aware of previous threats to my life, yet here he was, writing to all and sundry explaining I had given evidence against them – even supplying them with copies of my statements. On 25 August I wrote a letter to Barry Capon setting out my concerns. In it, I expressed fears for my personal safety:

> Your actions may well have put my life, and those of my fellow journalists, at risk. You have also given potential suspects an opportunity to know in advance about the allegations, and to prepare statements accordingly.
>
> It was my understanding that any information given to your office would remain confidential. My anonymity is essential. I am concerned that you may have identified me to some very violent people. You must be aware that I survived two hit and run attempts in 1995, and received a number of threatening calls during the early days of this investigation.

The issue of confidentiality had been a vital one ever since I started this investigation. Barry Capon himself had written to me on several occasions demanding to know my confidential sources, and appeared particularly annoyed that I always protected my informants within the police force. He wrote: 'I appreciate and understand why you are reluctant to reveal your sources within the police force. However, I wonder if you would be able to speak to each of the officers concerned and tell them that we are making enquiries and ask them if they are willing to contact me. Their approaches will be treated in confidence. When you have done that could you please tell me and let me know how many officers you have spoken to.'

This continual implication that I was obstructing the CCRC's investigation was coupled with a warning from the police that I was not helping myself or Stephen's case by failing to reveal the names of my informants. For good luck they usually dropped in the claim that my obstruction could warrant a two-year stretch. That, of course, was like a red rag to a bull and it only made me even more determined to get to the truth.

The case was attracting unprecedented publicity, not just nationally, but internationally. One of the most astute reports appeared in *The Times Saturday Magazine*, written by Kirsty Lang who had made a Channel 4 News item. I was mentioned as a cross between Inspector Morse and Miss Marple, and the story took up the 'Bakewell Tart' tag that had been associated with this case for some time. The final paragraph left a thought-provoking message: 'If Stephen Downing is released, Bakewell will bring out the bunting for him. But the townspeople must also share some of the guilt. It was their silence, and reluctance to rock the boat, that contributed to his long imprisonment.'

A few weeks later, I received confirmation that the CCRC would decide on 13 November whether to refer Stephen's case to the Court of Appeal.

During a busy summer that had rapidly extended into autumn, then winter, news teams arrived from across the UK and from abroad, preparing items to coincide with the expected D-Day – when the CCRC promised that the Board of Commissioners were meeting to decide Stephen's fate. I was relieved that the media cavalry had finally arrived. But my main thought was that it was a pity they had not come some six years earlier. I still felt like the wagon master. They had been placed in a circle – but all the ammunition was used up.

13 November 2000, was one of the longest days that I have ever known. And once again, it was to bring disappointment.

I made several calls to the CCRC's press office in Birmingham. My phone never stopped ringing with other media enquiries – everyone desperate to know the result. The decision was imminent. However, after several more painstaking hours, I was finally informed the decision would not be announced until the following day – as the CCRC claimed they needed to advise the victim's relatives first.

Throughout this lengthy process the CCRC had shown little or no thought for the feelings of the accused or his representatives – and conveniently used this 'victim's relatives' shield as an excuse for further delays.

The time for the revised decision was eventually announced. It would be 3p.m. the following day. Could we believe them? Surely they couldn't deceive the world's media again?

On 14 November, a host of camper-type vans with satellite dishes and the latest hi-tech equipment lined Firs Parade in Matlock adjacent to the new *Mercury* offices. The phone almost melted with continuous enquiries. Between 2 and 3p.m. Sky News arrived, then the BBC and ITN. All the main players were camped in our small, first-floor editorial office. I had no idea how the announcement would be made. All I could do was sit and wait. I tried hard to tell the reception staff not to put through any unnecessary calls as I was waiting for probably the most important call of my life.

The office had a rather eerie feeling. No one could concentrate. Talk was strained. It felt like the clock had stopped. 2.30 came, 2.40. And still nothing. No news. Who was going to tell me the decision? I fully expected the commissioner himself, Barry Capon, would make contact. I felt he at least owed me that after all my years of hard work.

Stephen was waiting at Littlehey, packed and ready – just in case they let him go straight away. I doubted that, as I was convinced he would still need a bail hearing – unless the Home Secretary used some of his magic to allow a release under parole conditions.

At two minutes to 3p.m. my phone rang. It was Patrick McLoughlin. 'Have you heard the decision?' he enquired.

'No Patrick. They said I would be notified by 3p.m. – probably by fax. I have told the girls to keep the line free.' I was hoping he wouldn't block the line in case the commissioner was trying to get through and, at first, hadn't realised he already knew the decision.

'You've done it!' he replied. 'Downing's case is to be referred to the Court of Appeal. Go to the fax and you should have the official press release any moment.'

He may have said something else. I can't remember. My mind suddenly went blank. I had been sitting at my cramped desk in the corner of the room. All the cameras had recorded the call and my reaction. I suddenly felt emotionally drained. All my years of hard work had finally proved successful. It was not the end of the matter – far from it – but it was an important milestone that many had doubted would ever happen. I felt my determination had been fully justified.

I told the TV crews of the conversation and my immediate feelings, then dashed downstairs to grab the fax as it came off the machine. There was a tear in my eye as I read the official statement.

It was dated 14 November 2000 and was a copy of the fax sent to the MP at 2.32p.m. that day with specific instructions. It stated:

> Commission refers conviction of Stephen Leslie Downing to Court of Appeal. The Criminal Cases Review Commission has referred the conviction of Mr Stephen Leslie Downing to the Court of Appeal.
>
> Mr Downing was convicted on 15 February 1974, at Nottingham Crown Court of the murder of Mrs Wendy Sewell. He was sentenced to be detained at Her Majesty's Pleasure.
>
> His appeal against conviction was dismissed by the Court of Appeal on 25 October 1974. Mr Downing applied to the Home Office for a review of his conviction. His application was transferred to the Criminal Cases Review Commission for consideration after 31 March 1997, when it assumed responsibility for the review of suspected miscarriages of justice.

On Wednesday 15 November 2000, the day after the decision, practically every national newspaper in Britain ran the news of Stephen Downing's referral story on their front pages – with many more continuing for days afterwards until the Sunday papers came out, and it all began again.

Derbyshire police, for once, had very little to say. Eventually they issued a press statement: 'The Derbyshire Constabulary has co-operated with the CCRC during their inquiry. This co-operation will continue during the appeal hearing.' A police spokesman said the force would have to consider reopening the murder case if the appeal found Stephen was *not* responsible for Wendy Sewell's murder. He added, 'We can't discuss evidence in public, although others can. It's all subject to the appeal.'

29

THE NEWS SPREAD like wildfire. I was bombarded with interview requests from places I'd never even heard of.

The *Media Guardian* of 20 November gave a typical account of life in the small *Matlock Mercury* office during this hectic time: 'In the cramped newsroom, a converted record shop storeroom, editor Don Hale's phone rings every few seconds. *The Times* is clamouring to speak to him, as is the *Express*, the *Mail on Sunday*, then Dutch TV wants a word. Yesterday he appeared on American lunchtime news bulletins. He tries to deal with everyone calmly and politely, agreeing to meet the journalists who want to interview him. For six years, Hale has waged a lonely and occasionally dangerous crusade to reverse the conviction of Stephen Downing, a seventeen-year-old gardener with learning difficulties.'

Most people continually asked the same impossible question: when would Stephen Downing be released?

On 16 November I received a letter from a cousin of Wendy Sewell's who was living in Ontario, Canada.

Dear Mr Hale,

Wendy Sewell was my cousin. I did not know of your campaign over so many years. I very much admire your tenacity.

I also have tremendous admiration for Stephen's mother, father and sister, for the continued faith they showed in their son and brother. No one can take away the hurt and pain that Stephen and his family have suffered. No amount of compensation will change that, no words from a Prime Minister, or even a Queen will erase the horrors Stephen has gone through or give him back his life. I expect that knowing people like you are supporting him for so many years and, perhaps, hopefully seeing the real culprits brought to justice will provide some measure of comfort

At the time of Wendy's death I just accepted what we were told not knowing the background to the case. I was fortunate to have had a couple of pints with Wendy not long before she was killed. I know we would have continued to be good friends had she lived. Wendy has no brothers or sisters to defend her. It really saddened and angered me to read through the articles and find no words of sympathy, solace or remembrance for another victim of this tragedy, the main one – Wendy Sewell – who was beaten to death. The memory I have of Wendy Sewell is of a young fun-loving cousin. She was my mum's brother's daughter and her parents loved her and were proud of her, just the same as Stephen's parents.

My anger is raised when I read 'The Bakewell Tart', a 'Semi-prostitute', 'numerous affairs and blackmail'. Even if she was the person Bakewell wishes to portray her as, she did not deserve to be beaten to death, to lie waiting for an ambulance for forty minutes, and to have those responsible free for all this time. She could have been saved!!

My anger is directed at those who have known for so many years who was responsible and said nothing. How can they sleep peacefully? I am sure that at the time of the murder there were several of Bakewell's good citizens saying, 'Oh, she got what she deserved.' No she did not. No one deserves to be beaten to death or to be called a 'Bakewell Tart' etc.

Come on, Bakewell, where is your north country kindness and generosity? Maybe if some of the brave men of Bakewell had kept their belts done up this tragedy would never have happened.

Yours sincerely,

Malcolm Beynon.

*

I began to be annoyed at the prison's attitude. At Littlehey they were preparing Stephen for release, building up his hopes and ensuring he had his bags packed, when in truth I felt they probably knew he would have to remain a prisoner for some considerable time. I believed it was all part of the deliberate torturous process. Prisons were a psychological test of strength. It soon became clear that Stephen might not even be considered for release until after Christmas unless the media pressure was increased.

Eventually the terms of bail were confirmed to the Downing family. They had to try to raise £5000 surety. It seemed another ridiculous and unnecessary move. There was still confusion at the police station as they attempted to hand the money across – only to be told they just needed a bond guarantee.

A date was finally set for the bail hearing. It would be in the High Court in London on 15 December. I thought that at least Stephen would be home for Christmas. His very first Christmas at home with his family in Bakewell for twenty-eight years.

Once again he was packed and ready to go, his belongings of nearly three decades stuffed into black bin liners and whatever cardboard boxes could be found.

The first sign of trouble came at the court building when some BBC reporters told me that it was a closed hearing. It seemed the press would not be allowed in court. I was furious. I burst through the door to the court and approached counsel. They shrugged their shoulders. It seemed nothing could be done. I had other ideas. There had been a notice posted outside court confirming it was an open hearing. The CPS and High Court officials had confirmed the same thing the day before. I thought that if it was listed as open, then it should remain open and marched towards the bench with the paperwork screwed up in my hand.

I asked the judge what was happening. This manner of confrontation was no doubt unheard of, but I needed to know directly the reasons for the U-turn. Stephen's legal team, flapped and tried to push me out. I explained that I had been described as Stephen's 'legal friend' and said that I, at least, should be allowed to remain. At that stage I was really angry. My patience was being stretched to the limit. 'This is totally unacceptable,' I said to the judge. I waved my paperwork at him. 'This court should not be closed to the press.'

I rarely lost my temper, but these people, who were all earning an absolute fortune from Stephen's misfortune, needed a damn good shake up.

The judge listened. 'Give me a few minutes, Mr Hale. I wish to consult with counsel.'

I stormed out of court. The world's press was outside in the corridor asking question after question.

An usher finally appeared and called me forward. As I entered the High Court again, an official said it would be all right for the media to come in. There was a buzz of excitement and anticipation as dozens of reporters packed the gallery and the tiny press bench. It was an old-fashioned court with small microphones hanging precariously from the tall decorative ceilings. Every creak of the door or movement on the benches made it virtually impossible to hear the proceedings.

Edward Fitzgerald QC eloquently outlined the main arguments for the Defence and was on his feet for about twenty minutes. I thought he had done a magnificent job in presenting a brief summary of my campaign submission. There was a hush, then another buzz and another hush. As the Crown Prosecutor, Julian Bevan QC, rose to his feet, you could have heard a pin drop.

Reporters were poised to note his every word. What he finally said will continue to amaze me for the rest of my days. He made reference to key parts of Mr Fitzgerald's claims, but then said he had only had the paperwork for about ten days and had not had time to read it. He also explained that he was about to go on holiday – that day – and would be unable to form an opinion as to whether the CPS should oppose bail. There was a stunned silence. Everyone looked at each other in disbelief. What did he say? We all sat and waited for the judge to lash out. Not read the paperwork! Hadn't realised the urgency, with Christmas looming and twenty-eight years in jail. He was in a rush to go on holiday that day? It all seemed so incredible. Had the world gone completely mad? Surely this could have been sorted out much earlier without the need for everyone to attend court. No wonder they didn't want the press inside. We all waited for the judge to throw the book at the QC in his crumpled pinstriped suit – but to everyone's surprise he agreed that if Mr Bevan had not had time to read the paperwork and form an opinion, they must take the view of opposing bail. Mr Bevan was given another month to study the file and the application was refused. End of story.

I borrowed somebody's phone and tried to call my wife and the Downings. Both lines were busy. I could hardly breathe. It was like trying to walk against a football crowd. Questions were fired at me from all directions.

I was told more of the press were waiting outside and was led along the packed corridors to face the madding crowd. As I approached the main door and looked out, there seemed to be hundreds of TV cameras, gantry lights and press cameras. It was dazzling. I found it hard to believe they were all waiting for me and glanced back to see if anyone else was coming. They waved me forward and the barrage of questions started again.

I challenged the government to act quickly. I hoped that Mr Blair and his family, and the QC on his holiday island, would remember Stephen Downing while they enjoyed Christmas with their families.

I said they would be enjoying the life of luxury, while poor Stephen would be eating cold turkey on a plastic tray on his own!

The message hit home and my comments were screened throughout the world.

Patrick McLoughlin had just spoken and seemed as furious as I was. He was determined to find out what had gone wrong. He stormed off towards Parliament with a pledge that he would raise the matter at Prime Minister's Questions. It was debated, and Prime Minister Blair said he shared the MP's concern.

Various TV news teams dragged me one way and then the other to give five-minute briefings. I was tired after standing about for several hours on a small traffic island opposite the main court building where the interviews were taking place. It was also very cold. I had just finished the first round of interviews when the BBC, ITV and others came back for lunchtime updates and I did several live face-to-face interviews. Their broadcasts kept going live to the bleak scene at Littlehey Prison in Cambridgeshire, where another media pack had been waiting hopefully to see Stephen Downing released.

I returned home to Matlock mentally and physically shattered. I had had a long, hard day in which I had done around fifty TV and radio interviews at various locations across London. I did not feel like getting up the next morning and preparing another edition of the *Mercury*.

Meanwhile, as Stephen Downing faced up to his twenty-eighth Christmas behind bars for a murder he never committed, the lawyer who opposed his freedom on bail was preparing to celebrate the festive season in the warmth of an African sun. Julian Bevan QC was tracked down by the press to his chambers in the Temple after the unsuccessful bail hearing. He told them, 'I am flying out tonight to Kenya. My son is getting married. I have been going for some time.' He said he had been unable to take in all the details of the case in time for the early-morning hearing, and retorted, 'Have you tried to read *War and Peace*? You couldn't have assimilated all the information. It's nine inches high. If a brief is three pages, not a problem. It's not three pages – it's probably three hundred pages.'

A spokesman for the Crown Prosecution Service gave the official explanation, 'A letter addressed to Mr Bevan *was* sent to his chambers when he was in court, and it was not opened by his clerk. It wasn't until 4.30p.m. the next day that he received a call from the Defence asking to discuss the bail application. He said, "What bail application?" and was told there was to be one at 9.15 the next morning. It was not his fault. Everyone deserves a holiday.'

The pantomime season had well and truly started.

Stephen was absolutely shattered. His bags were still packed. The prison staff had told him to get ready for release and now here he was, preparing to spend another night, and God knows how many more, at Littlehey prison in Cambridgeshire. 'My family and I are used to setbacks,' he told me, 'but it's heartbreaking. I'll be thinking of them at Christmas and I'm sure they'll be thinking of me.' He had no complaints against his own legal team. 'They put up a very good case,' he said.

The strain on the faces of Ray and Juanita was plain to see. The following weekend, as they had every other weekend for the past twenty-seven years, they filled their old car with petrol and drove for nearly three hours to visit their son in prison. In a rare outburst Ray exclaimed to me, 'Stephen has been locked up for a crime he didn't commit for twenty-seven years. We've put up with an awful lot over the years, but now we want to know when all this is going to end. We just want to bring him home. I'm sixty-eight now. I can't keep driving hundreds of miles to visit him every fortnight. It's hard to take after all these years, but we just have to try to remain positive. We can't wait to see Stephen. We've so much to discuss, and so many plans to make, but I never thought I'd be seeing him across a table in those prison visiting rooms again. I thought we'd be back in Bakewell in our own family home.'

For several weeks following the referral and particularly the failed bail hearing, I was asked to participate in numerous television programmes. I recall Jeremy Bowen on BBC *Breakfast News* first suggesting my name as a possible Journalist of the Year. The idea seemed ludicrous to me. Out of the blue, I was then contacted by Granada Television in Manchester who asked if I was available to attend the *What the Papers Say* TV awards in London just before Christmas. Prizes would to be presented by MP and former Tory minister Ann Widdecombe.

The invitation seemed ironic, for the prospect of meeting Ann Widdecombe again seemed almost too much to bear. I felt that she and her Tory cronies had, through Home Office channels, shown little or no real interest in Downing's case for years.

I travelled down to London with Kath and most of my editorial colleagues from the *Mercury*. I honestly believed I was there just for the ride. All soon changed however, as they came to the final award, Journalist of the Year. I could see the television cameras moving round towards me as host Clive Anderson read out the nomination. There were copies of the *Matlock Mercury* and my stories on the large screen. My name and reports appeared on his autocue. It was an unbelievable feeling as the media attention suddenly focused on my work and my marathon campaign.

It seemed to take for ever for him to read out some of the dedications. He said, 'Don Hale waged a lonely and dangerous crusade – without the backing of a Fleet Street organisation.' Eventually, he announced that I was the 2000 Journalist of the Year.

I suddenly felt quite shaky. I can only compare it with Matlock Town winning the FA Cup at Wembley. Unbelievable!

Next I heard from the *Observer*. I had been nominated as one of the candidates from a readers' poll as their possible Man of the Year. The list of nominations was incredible: Film director Sam Mendes, ex-Presidents Nelson Mandela, Bill Clinton, and President George W. Bush, actor Michael Caine, Olympic rowing champion Steve Redgrave, Nicholas Serota, Tim Smith, George Dubya and a host of other household names. Just to have my name included within such a prestigious gathering was honour enough, but actually to win was unbelievable. The features editor said that I had gained a landslide victory and had been selected as the top man for 2000.

Again, it all seemed totally unreal. After all, Stephen was still in jail. Despite all my hopes and efforts for a festive pardon for him, the Christmas deadline came and went.

> 8 December 2000
> HM Prison Littlehey,
> Perry,
> Huntingdon,
> Cambs PE18 OSR

Dear Don,

This is just a personal note of thanks for all the support you have given me and my family over the last twelve months, and at times when you have put aside your own problems.

I don't know who would have devoted so much time to a campaign as you have, and I should like to extend my note of gratitude to your long-suffering family for their understanding.

I hope that we have at last come to the end of what has seemed a never-ending journey.

I would like you and your family to enjoy the best Christmas you have ever had, and I hope the coming New Year holds lots of joy and happiness.

With warmest best wishes

Stephen Downing.

2001

30

JUANITA TOLD ME how excited she was at the prospect of having Stephen home, and how unreal it seemed after all these years of campaigning. 'Officially he is still a prisoner, and we can't take anything in to him, not even a present or some new clothes to come out in. He has telephoned to tell us that he's fine, but he's in prison and he can't find out what's going on. I can't imagine how it feels for him. He's had his bags packed and ready for weeks, and he's desperate to come home.'

She told me how, until a few weeks ago, Stephen's only civilian clothes were an out-of-date shirt and tie, and a pale-blue Seventies suit with flared trousers and wide lapels. which he had worn to his trial. 'When he first believed that at last he was going to be released, he tried the suit on. Of course' – she chuckled – 'it didn't fit him! He was a lad of seventeen when he went into prison. He's a man of forty-four now.' She said Stephen had since bought some new clothes out of a mail order catalogue, and had them ready for the day when he walked through the gates of Littlehey to taste freedom again.

But she also knew that his adjustment to the world of the twenty-first century would be far more complex than merely buying a new wardrobe of clothes.'I know there will be a lot to discuss,' she said. This serious-minded woman had obviously given much thought to the difficulties which might lie ahead, and mulled them over in her mind before sharing her conclusions. It was a trait I had often observed in Stephen. 'We don't know what is going to happen,' she said. 'We know that he wants to come back here to Bakewell, and then perhaps visit all the people who helped him and wrote to him in prison. But deep down I know that the problems are going to start when the initial euphoria and all the fuss and attention die down. He has been in prison for all his adult life. He has never had a bank account, never driven a car. He has never even had a proper girlfriend.

'We'll have a small party for all the people who helped him, and then we've got to try to help him begin to get on with the rest of his life. Stephen is very level-headed. He has never shown us any signs of bitterness at what society has done to him. He hasn't got an aggressive bone in his body, but we know he has a difficult time ahead. We fought and fought for twenty-seven years to prove that Stephen could never have murdered Wendy Sewell. Our next fight will be to help Stephen make his way in the adult world.'

Stephen's childhood friend, Richard Brailsford, was enjoying phenomenal success with collecting signatures for a new petition, and making plans for a New Year march and rally in Bakewell. We arranged with Bakewell police that we would assemble at the town's Showground, hold a brief rally and march through the town. It was a good turnout considering the atrocious weather and I was surprised that many participants had travelled a long way to take part – the furthest arriving from Norway.

In total some 14,500 new signatures were received and, within a few days, I travelled to number 10 Downing Street with Richard and his family to present the petition to the Prime Minister's office.

The date of Wednesday 7 February was announced for the new bail hearing. I was sure the date had been brought forward due to continued pressure from Stephen's supporters. Yet I remained apprehensive about the outcome. Surely the government couldn't be so cruel again? I had spoken with Stephen and, indeed, visited him again at Littlehey. I felt that, deep down, he believed something was truly about to happen this time.

At the High Court the barristers sought me out. Edward Fitzgerald QC asked if I would approach the bench again to insist on press and public access. This time both Mr Fitzgerald and the Crown Prosecutor, Julian Bevan QC, wanted the press present. Mr Bevan in particular hoped to make a comment about the media attacking him last time and following him to Kenya. Events had certainly worked in my favour and, although the judge asked counsel for their opinion concerning press coverage, he quickly bowed to the media's demand.

Ed Fitzgerald stated almost within his first sentence that he understood the Crown was *not* opposing bail. This meant Stephen had to be released – and released immediately. After such a long drawn-out campaign, the news hit me like a sledgehammer. The QC rambled on, setting out the case. I was only half listening. My mind was miles away with Stephen in Littlehey, wondering how soon he would hear the news. The media pack was rude and noisy. After Fitzgerald had uttered those first few memorable words, there was a mad scramble as journalists and their runners dashed from the benches to call in with the news. As at the last High Court hearing several months before, I could hardly hear another word as the door continuously slammed open and shut.

Mr Fitzgerald reminded the court that, at the earlier hearing, he had argued there was 'an overwhelming case' that the confession evidence should never have been considered by the jury at Downing's trial. The arguments were by now familiar to everyone. Applying either the standards of today, or those of the time, Downing's confession should have been excluded from the trial.

It wasn't until this moment that I learnt two key police officers from 1973, Johnson and Younger, had already given supporting evidence in the case during 2000. These officers had confirmed many of my own claims from 1994 and 1995 – that Downing felt intimidated during interrogation, that he was shaken to keep him awake, that there was a sweepstake in the police station that night that someone would extract a confession from him and, most important of all, that he *was* denied his basic rights. By now Ernie Charlesworth had died. I would have been interested to know what he would have had to say about all this.

The other main plank of the Prosecution case had concerned blood-stains found on his clothes after the killing. His explanation that he had come upon the scene to find Mrs Sewell severely injured was disbelieved by the jury. But Mr Fitzgerald said expert evidence about the blood-stains given at trial had been 'greatly undermined' by the new report of a top forensic scientist. New techniques had been developed over the near thirty years since the killing, and there was now evidence that blood spots found on Downing's clothes may have resulted from Mrs Sewell's exhalations as she lay dying.

Mr Fitzgerald argued that it was only Downing's refusal to admit his guilt that had kept him in prison for so long. He was a category C – low risk – prisoner at Littlehey Prison, Cambridgeshire.

QC Bevan confirmed the application would *not* be contested. Although acting for the Crown, he was heavily critical of the Derbyshire police and their actions from 1973. He conceded, 'I am happy to accept in this case there is a very real possibility that the rights he was entitled to were never brought to his attention. All the indications are they were not. Applying present-day standards, the Crown recognises that a failure to inform a prisoner in custody of his rights would be regarded as a serious breach, as, of course, would a failure to caution a suspect at the appropriate moment.'

It was now up the judge.

And then the dramatic moment came when Mr Justice Pitchford ended Stephen Downing's near three decades of incarceration by announcing he was to be released on bail pending appeal.

I left the court, almost swept along by a mob of journalists. Trying to gain a quiet moment of reflection was impossible. There was a tear in my eye and many congratulatory handshakes and pats on the back from friends I had encountered in the business over the years.

I was glad that I had had a dress rehearsal for meeting the press in December. Facing the pack didn't seem quite so daunting this time. MP Patrick McLoughlin addressed the crowd first, then I said a few words, followed by the victim's husband David Sewell – who still seemed bitter about the campaign and unwilling publicly to concede that the police might have got the wrong man all those years ago. 'It was five months from his arrest to his trial and, in that time, his Defence team was unable to come up with evidence to prove his innocence,' he insisted.

The Prime Minister celebrated the news of Downing's bail success during his Questions in the House. He complimented my tireless campaign and praised the dedication of the Downing family over the past twenty-seven years.

I was still talking on air in the BBC TV studios late in the after-noon, when Stephen finally walked out of prison. It was an emotional moment, and both the presenter and I stopped and watched the proceedings at Littlehey on the TV screen with a lump in the throat. The great doors slid open and Stephen stepped into the glare of the sunlight and spotlights for the first time in all those years.

He walked out alone, quietly and with dignity. There was no shouting or punching the air. He looked smart in his £45 navy-blue suit from Kays catalogue, and a purple tie. It reminded me of the time I had watched on television as Nelson Mandela walked out of jail. He and Stephen had spent exactly the same number of years, unjustly, behind bars. He managed to say a few brief words before being whizzed away to a secret location, prior to returning to Bakewell to meet his family.

The crowd of journalists at the prison was almost as great as that in London. The pack then moved on to Derbyshire in preparation for besieging the family home. I was committed to giving constant interviews until late evening. Channel 4 gave me a limo-ride home when they realised I was planning to catch the last train.

I was too tired to see Stephen that night and, in any case, it was too late. I am sure he was exhausted from the trauma of the day. I had spoken to him by telephone during my journey home up the M1, and rang again when I got back to Matlock.

On Thursday 8 February, the nationals were again full of the Downing case and reports of his freedom. All carried front-page pictures and stories. There were photographs of Stephen leaving prison and of me at the High Court with a celebratory fist in the air.

The next morning I visited Stephen at his home. I had been to that house so many times, but it came as a shock to walk in and see Stephen sitting there at the kitchen table grinning. We exchanged warm greetings. This was the moment for which I had worked for seven years.

'FREE AT LAST AFTER 27 YEARS OF HELL' claimed the *Daily Express*. 'Gardener jailed at 17 for girl's graveyard killing is released. Editor who saved forgotten inmate from dying in jail.' The *Daily Mail* said: 'WHY DID IT TAKE 27 YEARS? He was jailed as a teenager. Yesterday, this man walked free because of a glaring hole in the Crown case. Someone else did the killing. Police must find out who.'

'TWO MILLION POUNDS FOR 27 LOST YEARS' stated the *Sun*. 'Huge compensation awaits man wrongly jailed for the Bakewell Tart murder. Don Hale led the long campaign for his release.'

The *Guardian* said: 'FREEDOM FOR STEPHEN. Don Hale is the editor and long-time campaigner for Stephen Downing who was released from prison.'

The *Star*, the first national paper to take up Stephen's cause, said: 'WALKING FREE AFTER 27 YEARS – Murder case Downing wins justice fight.'

The *Daily Mirror* agreed and carried my own exclusive story: 'MY DANGER BATTLE FOR THE TRUTH'.

The Times gave a detailed account headlined: 'DOWNING GOES HOME TO UNCERTAIN FUTURE'.

While the *Independent* stated, 'ERROR THAT STARED LAWYERS IN THE FACE FOR 27 YEARS'. Like many, the paper pointed out that Stephen Downing had been badly let down by the legal system. 'Although forensic science and the dogged work of a local journalist have thrown up a whole raft of inconsistencies in his conviction, it was procedural travesty that gave him his liberty. A glaring error that had been staring lawyers in the face for more than 25 years.'

All thoughtful analyses of the case agreed there had been serious breaches of the Judges Rules on interrogation which would have rendered his confession – the main plank of the Prosecution case – inadmissible. Astonishingly, they were never used in court by Stephen Downing's original Defence counsel, Dennis Barker QC, so his statement, which he had already retracted, was read to the jury. As Mr Bevan QC had pointed out in court, 'This point has lain dormant for 25 years and has been obvious to any criminal lawyer and has been completely missed.'

The issues debated in court were of course, at this point, academic to Stephen Downing.

31

IN A SMALL hamlet deep in the Derbyshire countryside, the news of Stephen Downing's release was stirring poignant and painful memories for a man who was indelibly linked to Wendy. David Sewell was the husband who had sat by her hospital bed, holding her hand, speaking gently to her as she lay there battered and unconscious, her life ebbing away.

In the three decades since then he has kept his own counsel, wounded by the lewd gossip and suggestive comments surrounding his former wife's behaviour, deeply hurt, perhaps humiliated, by the headlines over the past eight years.

'I was away all day at work and she was stuck in Bakewell,' he explained to a colleague of mine from one of the nationals. 'She got temporary secretarial work. With me being away all day, and she being the sort of outgoing person she was, she made lots of friends . . . friends of both sexes. Some of the people she was associating with, I didn't feel were good for her. She was troubled in her own mind, and unsettled. There was quite a social life going on in Bakewell and she was mixing with people her own age who weren't a good influence on her. One or two of the girls, the same age as her, had husbands who were earning substantially more than me and they could swan around enjoying themselves all the time. I think her head was turned.

'I told her quite forcefully that I wasn't happy with the situation. I don't think she was having affairs, but I felt her behaviour was not appropriate for a married woman. I said my piece, and she defended her position. I told her if she wanted to do what she wanted, she would have to do it elsewhere. I can never be certain she wasn't having affairs, but I think I would have known. Whether she was pregnant or not before she left home, I can't be certain. But I don't think she was. I knew very little about the child – I don't to this day know what sex it was – but I knew who the father was. He was a businessman in the town and from an influential family. He was single and she could have gone to live with him, but whether she got short shrift from him . . . I'll never know. Then she contacted me and said she wanted to come back. We were apart for about a year, and in the meantime she had had this baby, but I have no idea exactly when the child was born. It was of no interest to me. We met again. She said that she would have liked me to adopt her child. I could not do that. I said I understood and respected the fact that there is a very close bond between mother and baby, but made it clear that if she wanted to keep the baby she wasn't coming back to me. If she wanted to come back, then she would have to make other arrangements for the child. I didn't want anything to do with the baby.'

This uncompromising attitude forced Wendy to make a decision. She gave little Thomas up for adoption, and returned to David. 'It was entirely her decision,' he says.

How happy were those last few years of Wendy's life?

David continues, 'It was a new start but, after what had happened, I no longer wanted any children. The situation wasn't easy for either of us, and there was a lot of pressure on us both, but we were trying. She had given up her only child and it seemed she wouldn't have any more – it might have helped us both if we had had a family – who knows?'

At about this time, Wendy was still working part-time as a secretary for the local Magistrates clerk. David said she opened a shop in Bakewell selling domestic furnishings. 'I think it was to fill a bit of a void in her life. She wasn't happy in herself, I think she was unfulfilled.'

In fact, people close to Mr Red have told me that Wendy and he were business partners in the shop, and that he could often be seen on the premises.

Three years after the Sewells got back together, they moved to the old farmhouse in Middleton.

'When I bought my first Bugatti,' reminisces David, 'I remember Wendy saying, "You've got your vintage car, now I want my vintage house!" We bought this house for £7100 and set to work renovating it. We did an awful lot of work on it, and made it into our home.'

It was from this home that Wendy set off on 12 September 1973, catching the bus driven by Ray Downing into Bakewell.

'I remember the day the assault happened,' David recalls. 'As usual we had breakfast together in the kitchen here. I kissed her and said goodbye.'

The next David heard of his wife was when the police telephoned him at his office at British Rail in Derby, where he was by then working as an engineer. He dashed back to Bakewell and, despite the fact that he had been twenty miles away when the attack happened, found himself in the cell next to Stephen Downing being grilled, he was made to feel, as a potential suspect. 'I wasn't free to go. I was helping with enquiries. I always felt my treatment that day was inappropriate. I only had a cup of tea and a biscuit, before I was allowed to leave early the following morning.'

With Wendy's mother, he travelled directly to Chesterfield Royal Hospital where his wife had still not regained consciousness. 'I went back again the next day, and in the afternoon she died as I held her hand. She didn't speak to me once – I was devastated.'

Now, all these years later, David Sewell believes DNA should be brought into play 'to sort the whole thing out once and for all'. But he still questions, 'If there were other people there, why didn't they come forward at the time?'

It remains to be seen if David Sewell's stance will change when he studies the new evidence and circumstances surrounding the case, as the town of Bakewell has slowly begun to give up its secrets.

Even he admits, 'Downing has been behind bars for twenty-seven years. If he had admitted what he did, he would have been freed long ago. I think it is a very strange law indeed that kept him in jail simply because he wouldn't admit he did it.'

He continues to insist that Wendy did *not* have a lovers' meeting in the cemetery that day. 'She was in the graveyard for an entirely innocent reason. Her mother had said she wanted finally to put a headstone on her husband's grave. She said she wanted a shiny black one. Wendy said she would go and get some ideas from the graveyard. People will say, no doubt, that there is no smoke without fire, but it's just not true that she was having a string of affairs. It is impossible to slander a dead person, apparently. If it wasn't, I would have taken action some time ago to stop these lies about her. I was with her at the time and I'm sure I would have known if she had been having all these affairs that are being suggested. She was no more than a normal woman of her time.'

Eleven years after Wendy's murder, David Sewell remarried. He and his wife Jennifer still live at Wendy's 'vintage house' in Middleton-by-Youlgreave. Nothing has been hidden between them. She listens as he continues to defend his former wife against the 'vicious and unfounded stories being peddled around'.

His new wife knows, too, the epitaph David Sewell put on Wendy's gravestone: 'May you find happiness in Heaven.'

Following Stephen's release many national newspaper reporters tried to talk to the men I had been chasing for years, the five who had all been named by witnesses as being near the scene: Mr Red, Syd Oulsnam, George Pearson, Mr Orange and Mr Blue. They did not have much luck. Nick Pryer of the *Mail on Sunday*, however, managed to speak with Mr Blue, who, to the best of my knowledge, had never been interviewed by the police.

Now in his mid-forties and highly successful in his chosen career, and living in a different part of the country.

He denies any knowledge of the Wendy Sewell murder, and says he was definitely not in the cemetery on the day Wendy was attacked, despite being named by Mrs Louisa Hadfield as the blood-stained man seen running away from the direction of the scene of crime. 'I was only vaguely aware of the murder at the time. It did not really have any impact on me at all,' he said.

I didn't know Stephen Downing. I moved away from Bakewell. The next thing I heard about the murder was about five years ago when Don Hale telephoned me and said I was supposed to have been seen running away from the scene.

I told him at the time that I had nothing to do with it. There is nothing that marks that day out from the rest of my life at the time. I remember nothing about the Wendy Sewell murder. I wasn't there. I know nothing about it. I can't give any accurate account of my movements on that day because it was just another day twenty-seven years ago.

I was never interviewed by the police at the time, and have never been interviewed since, although I have spoken to Don Hale on two occasions and also to a local television reporter once. I was amazed when Don contacted me the first time, and I told him everything I know – which is absolutely nothing.

I do not know why I have been identified. The people who say they saw me there were definitely mistaken. I am not particularly happy that my name is being bandied around in connection with the murder, but there is nothing I can do about it. I know nothing about it.

More recently, when two of my colleagues approached Mr Red to ask him if he would talk about this case, and to inform him that his name kept cropping up in connection with it, he replied, 'Docs it? I don't want to talk about it, I'll just have to leave it at that.' before shutting the door.

Most newspapers were now claiming that Stephen was likely to receive anything from £1 million to £8 million in compensation. All claimed their own inside sources and each time another publication seemed to add the odd £1 million or so to the estimate.

There was mass speculation from the nationals that the case was going to be, or indeed had been, reopened. Rumours spread about suspects being questioned, even arrested. Passports were supposed to have been taken from individuals and a whole host of other bizarre claims appeared. I was certain that nothing official would happen until after the appeal – if at all.

At his first press conference, Stephen took to the TV cameras immediately. When asked what he would like most now he was free he replied, 'A wife and a family. I'm a bit old to start having children, but I would be prepared to marry a single mother and help raise her children.'

He showed he had retained his cheeky sense of humour. When

describing his first pint of beer for twenty-seven years, he was jokingly warned not to get too much of a taste for it. 'Don't worry,' he said, 'not at the price it is nowadays.'

He was asked what he had been doing in the days since his release, and explained he had been looping the loop over Bakewell. A local hotelier had given him a ride in his two-seater plane. It was something Stephen thought he might like to take up as a hobby.

The questions came thick and fast: 'What event did you most regret missing, during your twenty-seven years in prison?'

'The fall of the Berlin Wall,' he replied without any hesitation. 'That meant freedom for millions – not just one individual.'

Despite a marathon effort to secure his release on bail, Stephen had to wait twelve months for the appeal. Just before Christmas 2001, Stephen's legal team e-mailed me the dates they had been given. Two days, 15 and 16 January had been set aside.

2002

32

IT WAS AT 9.30a.m. on the 15 January 2002 when Kath and I arrived outside the Court of Appeal in the Strand in London. There were at least a hundred reporters, photographers and camera crews from media organisations throughout the world waiting to greet us. The sky was grey but the atmosphere was one of excited optimism.

Stephen's appeal was due to start at 10.30a.m. but there were the usual number of interviews to be gone through before we entered the court. It was all a blur but the sense that things were finally coming to an end was overwhelming. The Fleet Street pack was braying, but for once in a very positive way. They were obviously 100 per cent behind the cause.

My heart was racing and I was fighting for breath in the crush. 'Good luck, Don,' I heard twenty or thirty times as we made our way through the crowd to the court. It's just a pity they hadn't been so supportive in the early days, but there had always been bigger stories. A backward boy from Bakewell didn't make great copy – especially when the police told everybody it was an open and shut case.

The appeal was to be heard in court 6, on the first floor of the hugely impressive building which houses one of the biggest collections of courts in Britain. As Kath and I climbed the stairs we could see there was already a large crowd outside, including Stephen, his parents and his sister. Stephen came across and greeted me warmly. As always he looked calm and totally in charge of the situation. God knows what he was really thinking behind his cool exterior.

Just before ten the doors opened and we all filed in. There were two entrances and people scrambled through them to get the best seats. We were ushered into a set of seats below the bench where the three law lords would sit. Right in front of me was Matt Barlow, the reporter the *Mercury* had sent to London to cover the appeal. He wasn't even born when Stephen was sent to jail. To our right the QCs for the defence and the Crown took up their positions, with their legal back-up teams in the row of seats behind them.

The row further back, in the main body of seats which directly faced the bench, was occupied by Ray, Nita and Christine, sandwiched between journalists on either side. In the rows behind them sat Stephen's MP Patrick McLoughlin, and his former MP, Matthew Parris, Bakewell's vicar, the Revd Edmund Urquhart, and reporters from broadcasting and newspaper groups from all over the world. Derbyshire police were also represented.

Appeal court 6 is a small court that looks for all the world like a church with its hard wooden pews, ancient oak panelling and a bench for the judges, which gave the impression that an organist might appear at any minute and start to play the first hymn. The side walls were entirely covered with bookshelves filled with volumes of dusty law books.

Just before the starting time the court, built to accommodate about sixty people, was filled to overflowing. For as well as journalists, police, family, friends and supporters, there were several law students and others who were simply downright curious.

It was a momentous occasion in the history of the British courts, but even after twenty-eight years there was no sense of urgency as tapes, dictaphones and computers were set up by the clerks, the microphones were tested and the huge bundles of legal documents were carried in.

Beside the bench was the dock and just before 10.30 Stephen appeared, escorted by a female warder, because, of course, if the appeal were to fail it would be her job to take him back down to the cells to continue his sentence. He was still a convicted murderer out on bail. When they sat down, Stephen stared straight ahead, showing no emotion. He briefly nodded in the direction of his family. He was so small you could only see the top half of his head above the dock.

At precisely 10.31 the three law lords, Lord Justice Pill, sitting with Mrs Justice Hallett and Mr Justice Davis, entered from a door behind the bench and the court rose. The proceedings commenced. The British Justice system which had crucified the man before it with its archaic rulings would not give up easily. It would have to have its pound of flesh – and we were obliged to sit and listen.

The scenario had to be played out in its entirety by the hugely paid bewigged men and women who sit in judgement over us mere mortals. Although they knew they would have to admit defeat, they also knew the great British public would have to yawn and bear it while they played out the bizarre ritual which had only one conclusion.

The lawyer for the Defence, Ed Fitzgerald QC, addressed the court. The two pillars of the Defence case were the manner in which the confession was obtained and how the forensic evidence had not originally been presented properly. Fitzgerald took us, at great length, over ground which I had presented in my submissions years previously, and which had been heard at the bail hearing. The police conduct over a nine-hour period was in breach of Judges Rules. Stephen should have been told that he was under arrest, and cautioned. He should also have been told that he had the right to a solictor. A forensic expert, who had proved the blood-stains on Stephen were consistent with *his* version of events, was inexplicably not called, Fitzgerald told the expectant court.

He pointed out that Stephen was not offered access to a solicitor or his parents, and that he had been questioned for several hours before finally being cautioned at 10.30p.m. He maintained that the confession was unreliable and should have been excluded, and that the conviction was unsafe. He talked of alternative suspects, but said he did not intend to name any names, and mentioned a witness who had seen Wendy in the arms of another man in the cemetery at eight minutes past one. This witness, Jayne Atkins, still refused to talk to the Defence to this day because she was afraid of harassment, but had reaffirmed her original evidence to the CCRC. The whole tragic episode in the cemetery was gone over in the minutest detail with the law lords making copious notes and occasionally asking points of clarification. But unless the Crown decided to challenge the basic breaches and inconsistencies, it had already become obvious to those who understood the complexities of the case that the appeal would have to be granted.

Fitzgerald had been on his feet for more than two hours. Now it was the turn of Anthony Bevan QC for the Crown. And within the first few seconds of his speech it was obvious there was to be no challenge.

Bevan came directly to the point. 'The Crown accepts there were substantial and significant procedural breaches,' he said. 'Downing should have been cautioned hours before he actually was. He should have been offered access to a solicitor or relative. And there may have been deliberate breaches of the Judges Rules by the police.'

After his opening remarks the court adjourned for lunch from one o'clock until 2.15. It seemed to be all over bar the shouting. But it wouldn't be over till summing-up – surely that couldn't take too much longer.

Kath and I tried to grab some lunch at the nearest pub but there just wasn't time. After a quick drink we called at a sandwich shop before we returned to court. I was glad to get back to the relative calm of the courtroom. I took off my jacket before proceedings recommenced as I had started to find the atmosphere stifling.

On his return Bevan continued to catalogue a series of damning procedural errors, which had prompted even the judge at the original trial to highlight his concerns that the confession may have been obtained, in the legal phrase, 'by oppression'. He had then asked the Defence if they were alleging impropriety on the part of the police.

'No sir,' the Defence had replied at the time. The confession was allowed to stand, the police got away with breaching Judges Rules, and Stephen was found guilty by the jury after one hour's deliberation. Mr Bevan said he did not want to accuse Stephen's original Defence counsel of ineptitude but reiterated that he would find it difficult to argue that the conviction was safe. Bevan sat down at 3.15.

Lord Justice Pill then said it would be in everybody's best interests if the judgment were made that afternoon. He ordered a thirty-minute adjournment.

The three judges filed back in at 3.49. The decision Stephen had waited twenty-eight years for was about to be made. The court was hushed. Stephen sat in the dock, staring straight ahead, but I noticed that his blink rate was up. I could feel that Kath was very tense beside me. Across the court Ray sat hunched forward, his hands clasped together as if he were praying – maybe he was. Nita sat next to him, tiny and bird-like, clutching a handkerchief. Sister Christine, who had broken down in the corridor outside the court during the final adjournment, had regained her composure and looked towards the bench with an imploring expression.

Lord Justice Pill began his summing up. He spoke for seventy minutes. (Later Stephen was to say that those seventy minutes seemed longer than his twenty-seven years in jail.) Lord Justice Pill made four main points.

1 The forensic evidence of the blood-staining could not be relied upon.
2 The appellant's confession was not reliable. It was difficult to understand why it was not challenged at trial.
3 There seemed to be nothing unusual about the appellant's appearance or demeanour at the time of the murder.
4 The appellant denied making the statements which the police produced.

Lord Justice Pill then took us through the fateful day in detail pointing out all the inconsistencies and breaches of judges rules. The tension in court was reaching boiling point. Surely he had to come to his decision soon. At 4.55 he finally got to it.

I rule that Mr Downing's initial confessions to the police were unreliable and it follows the conviction is unsafe. We do not address ourselves to the question of whether or not Mr Downing was guilty.

The Crown does not seek to uphold the conviction. The conviction is quashed.

There was not a flicker of emotion, not a hint of sympathy, for twenty-seven wasted years. Nor was there any apology for an appalling miscarriage of justice on behalf of the system the appeal court judges represented.

Immediately after the verdict was delivered the judges stood up, drew aside and almost ran past the thick curtains which covered the door behind the bench. The door opened and they disappeared, never to be seen again. It was almost as if they did not want to be present to witness the celebrations when this innocent man at last walked free.

I glanced across to the dock. Stephen's face lit up. An almost beatific smile engulfed his features. The moment he had awaited, for almost three decades had finally arrived.

Then, just like a football crowd's reaction to a last-minute winning goal, the court erupted. Ray, Nita and Christine hugged each other, and the tears began to flow.

The final verdict had been delivered with such seemingly indecent haste that Christine hadn't heard the last barely audible words of Lord Justice Pill. 'Conviction quashed – he's free,' Nita repeated to her before the emotion of the moment overwhelmed her.

MPs, friends, supporters, journalists and passers-by who had just happened to drop in leapt to their feet as one – smiling, back-slapping and unashamedly crying. I hugged Kath. I could feel the relief flowing from her. But there was also a sense of anti-climax. What was to happen now? Would the case be reopened?

One man in court was not celebrating – the representative of the Derbyshire police who gathered up his notes and left quietly.

Stephen was then led from the dock for the last time.

I fought my way through the crowds and eventually reached the main entrance to the court. As I walked towards the television lights and flashbulbs I was temporarily blinded. Over the barrage of questions that threatened to engulf me I managed to blurt out, 'I would have liked the judges to go a step further and say Stephen is innocent. They could have been more positive. I think Stephen will be a little disappointed. We want the case reopened – the real killer is still out there. I call upon the government to launch an enquiry into what went wrong all those years ago. I also think the law lords should have made some reference to the fact that Stephen has served ten years beyond his recommended tariff, simply because he continued to protest his innocence.'

The media wanted me to find Stephen and I went back into the court building to discover him talking with his legal team. When his family saw me we all hugged and shook hands before I reminded him that there were several hundred people outside wanting to hear what he had to say. He walked from the court a free man to face the world's press with the statesmanlike dignity we have all come to expect. Not for him the traditional punching the air, the whoops of delight. Only an ear-to-ear beam as he walked slowly – as always – down the steps towards the pavement and the waiting journalists.

No matter how much they tried to draw him, Stephen still showed no bitterness – no words of recrimination or hatred would come from his mouth. When asked about his feelings towards the police he simply said, 'I hold no bitterness towards the Derbyshire police. They are now a different force altogether. It's all in the past. Let's forget it.' He continued, 'I'd just like to say thank you to my family for all their support and care, and also to my legal team and all my supporters.'

Bob Wood, Deputy Chief Constable of Derbyshire police, said later, 'The police respect the judgment of the court in this case. There was a trial in 1974 before a high court judge and later that year the matter was referred to the Court of Appeal. It was open to the Defence on either occasion to raise any issues of irregularity in the police procedures then in force. Police procedures have improved considerably since 1973. The Police and Criminal Evidence Act 1984 became law in 1986 and marked a drastic change in how police dealt with prisoners. PACE ensures that people have access to solicitors or legal advice soon after they are arrested. Prisoners who have learning difficulties are supported by specially trained advisers or social workers who help them understand what is happening to them. These advisers can also take an active part during police interviews if they think it is appropriate.

'The Derbyshire Constabulary has fully co-operated with the CCRC throughout their inquiry and handed over all the existing files relating to this case.'

Mr Wood said that the force would carefully consider the appeal judges' comments in full before making any decisions about reopening the case. He added, 'In July 1997 the Criminal Case Review Commission received an application to review the case of Stephen Downing. In November 2000 the CCRC referred the case back to the Court of Appeal after completing a lengthy investigation.

The commission considered all the evidence put before them. They decided that despite many assertions by Mr Downing's supporters that there may have been other possible suspects none of their enquiries have given rise to sufficient new evidence to justify an investigation by another force.'

Two days later the Commons debated the case. Stephen's MP, Patrick McLoughlin, called for an inquiry, saying that the Downing and Sewell families had both suffered. 'Enquiries need to take place not only for the sake of Stephen Downing's family but also for the family of Wendy Sewell. This is a very sad and moving case,' he said.

Leader of the House of Commons Robin Cook replied that there could be 'no more appalling injustice' than for Stephen to have been imprisoned for as long as he had. He went on, 'There has obviously been a serious miscarriage in this case and I'm sure my colleagues at the Home Office will want to consider what lessons can be learned from this.'

This case has already raised a number of key issues within British law. It has helped change our perception of human rights reviews and registered a legal landmark ruling within European law. It has also highlighted the need for constant vigilance to help prevent other similar claims of injustice.

I am proud of my own small contribution to society. I took the trouble to stop and listen to a small voice in the dark. I have won many a major battle on behalf of Stephen Downing. I just hope we can finally win the war and fully persuade the authorities to agree to an unconditional surrender.

After almost 10,000 days of wrongful imprisonment the rest of Stephen's life is now his own. I wish him well.